OXFORD WORLD'S CLASSICS

WHO BETRAYS
ELIZABETH BENNET?

JOHN SUTHERLAND is Lord Northcliffe Professor of Modern English Literature at University College London, and is the author of a number of books, including *Thackeray at Work*, *Victorian Novelists and Publishers*, and *Mrs Humphry Ward*. He has also edited *Vanity Fair*, *Pendennis*, *The Woman in White*, Trollope's *Early Short Stories*, *Late Short Stories*, and *The Way We Live Now* and has written *Is Heathcliff a Murderer?* and *Can Jane Eyre Be Happy?* in Oxford World's Classics.

OXFORD WORLD'S CLASSICS

For almost 100 years Oxford World's Classics have brought readers closer to the world's great literature. Now with over 700 titles—from the 4,000-year-old myths of Mesopotamia to the twentieth century's greatest novels—the series makes available lesser-known as well as celebrated writing.

The pocket-sized hardbacks of the early years contained introductions by Virginia Woolf, T. S. Eliot, Graham Greene, and other literary figures which enriched the experience of reading. Today the series is recognized for its fine scholarship and reliability in texts that span world literature, drama and poetry, religion, philosophy and politics. Each edition includes perceptive commentary and essential background information to meet the changing needs of readers.

OXFORD WORLD'S CLASSICS

JOHN SUTHERLAND

Who Betrays Elizabeth Bennet?

Further Puzzles in Classic Fiction

OXFORD
UNIVERSITY PRESS

Oxford University Press, Great Clarendon Street, Oxford OX2 6DP

Oxford New York

Athens Auckland Bangkok Bogotá Buenos Aires Calcutta
Cape Town Chennai Dar es Salaam Delhi Florence Hong Kong Istanbul
Karachi Kuala Lumpur Madrid Melbourne Mexico City Mumbai
Nairobi Paris São Paulo Singapore Taipei Tokyo Toronto Warsaw

and associated companies in Berlin Ibadan

Oxford is a registered trade mark of Oxford University Press

British Library Cataloguing in Publication Data

Data available

Library of Congress Cataloging in Publication Data

Data available

ISBN 0-19-283884-9

1 3 5 7 9 10 8 6 4 2

Typeset by John Sutherland
Printed in Great Britain by
Cox & Wyman Ltd.,
Reading, Berkshire

Contents

Contents

Introduction and Acknowledgements

> If there is anything pleasant in life, it is doing what we aren't meant to do. If there is anything pleasant in criticism, it is finding out what we aren't meant to find out. It is the method by which we treat as significant what the author did not mean to be significant, by which we single out as essential what the author regarded as incidental.
>
> (Ronald Knox)[1]

This is the third in a series of investigations into classic fiction which began with *Is Heathcliff a Murderer?* The last volume (*Can Jane Eyre Be Happy?*) was, like its predecessor, kindly received by the critics. I was gratified by N. John Hall, writing in the *Washington Post*, who saluted me as a leader among 'the younger school of Victorianists' (I am 60). Ours is a venerable specialism. Also gratifying was a 1997 conference seminar at Bologna University devoted to my 'line', and entitled 'Is Ophelia a Virgin?' Bologna, I am pleased to note, is the academic home of Umberto Eco and, as lovers of delicatessen will know, baloney.

In a thoughtful piece in *Essays in Criticism* ('Sutherland's Puzzles') Kenneth Newton—himself a distinguished puzzle-poser—wondered whether the appeal of my two small collections might not be pernicious: 'Have his "puzzle" books been so successful because they appeal to the ingrained anti-theoretical prejudices of non-academic readers?' Generously, Professor Newton concluded: 'Even if one rejects Sutherland's general approach, one can sympathise with the position that academic criticism should seek to communicate with a wider audience, and there could ultimately be serious cultural consequences if it fails to do so.'[2] I would agree, adding only that the 'serious cultural consequences' may have already happened.

As before I am grateful for letters from Oxford World's Classics readers. 'Non-academic readers', many of them; and some of the 'academic' readers still in primary school (see 'How do the Cratchits cook Scrooge's turkey?'). Typically, these readers are sharper, more accurate, more knowledgeable, and, not infrequently, more owlish than even I like to be. I have gladly made use of their suggestions, or taken issue with them, in a number of the following chapters. I acknowledge these correspondents there and thank them here.

Kathleen Glancy began her letter:

Though some may take issue with the title piece of *Can Jane Eyre be Happy?*—even now you may be in hiding from the Mr Rochester Revenge Squad—I entirely agree with your premise. Have you ever considered how odd it is that no one in England *is* aware of Rochester's marriage? After all, when a second son of noble birth marries a lower class heiress her family would normally look to publicize the event as much as possible. So far as I am aware the London papers would be perfectly willing to publish notices of marriages which had taken place abroad.

Miss Glancy went on to disagree with some points I made about *Mansfield Park*, and offered a puzzle on *Pride and Prejudice* which I have tried to solve (see 'Who betrays Elizabeth Bennet?'). Felicity Luke raised another neatly observed conundrum in the novel, which I cannot answer:

Why does Charles Bingley need to rent an estate? We have to assume that his money does not come from trade, since, if so, Mr Darcy would be too proud to be his friend, and his sisters would not be so snobbish. There is no mention of a living father or an elder brother . . . At the end of the book, we are told that Charles buys an estate near Pemberley, so clearly he did not expect to inherit any family seat. Is there some mystery of Georgian inheritance law which provides the answer?

Is there?[3]

Though hardly a member of the Rochester Revenge Squad, Brian Haylett did begin his letter: 'I am sure I cannot be the only one to be *un*happy with the title essay of *Can Jane Eyre be Happy?* Mrs Fairfax an informer? Rochester a regressive seducer? Can this be the book I taught for four years at A-level?' On the basis of the close exposition of Brontë's novel that followed, I have to say that the pupils taught by Mr Haylett were very lucky in their teacher. Welcome support on the Rochester issue came from M. M. Gilchrist ('his treatment of Bertha is dreadful, and I agree that Jane should be worried'). Dr Gilchrist adds: 'I would extend this judgement to his twentieth century incarnation, the murderous Max de Winter; yet another case of "let's blame the victim; she can't defend herself".'[4]

Brian Nicholas wrote a learned and wide-ranging letter, beginning with the rousing slogan: 'down with diegesis, up with mimesis!' Among Professor Nicholas's many points (which ranged from the chaste impenetrability of Victorian underwear to the temperature on the day of the Donwell Abbey outing in *Emma*), I was particularly taken with an observation on *Madame Bovary* (apropos my essay on Fanny Hill's contraceptive devices):

I've often wondered why Emma Bovary didn't become pregnant again, even if the somnolent Charles had ceased his attentions (or, more likely, had them rebuffed). Rodolphe, the cad, would I suspect, not have been too particular about withdrawing. Léon was perhaps temperamentally more considerate; but Flaubert's use of the word *ébahissements*, to describe the early days of their love-making, suggests that caution was thrown to the winds. The answer seems to be that Emma doesn't become pregnant because Flaubert decides that she shan't. If it suits their plot and theme, even the 'realists' are happy to avail themselves of conventional literary omissions and silences: the author himself as ultimate and infallible contraceptive.

The epigram is wise, witty, and—I suspect—true. Still on sex and the Victorian novelist, Professor Nicholas and Peter Merchant both pointed out a passage I had missed in George Moore's *Esther Waters* in claiming that the only reference to menstruation in Victorian fiction is in *Adam Bede*.[5]

Deirdre Le Faye, the learned editor of the most recent collection of Jane Austen's letters, agreed and disagreed with me on a number of points. We disagree, for instance, on the issue of whether Fagin's sausages are innocent mutton or guilty pork. I extend my discussion with Miss Le Faye in the following chapter on *Emma* ('Apple-blossom in June—again').

Miss Le Faye offered a number of incidental corrections in her long and detailed letter. I was grateful, for instance, to learn that there *was* a Goswell Street during Mr Pickwick's residence in London. The Pickwick Bicycle Club, in a collective submission, made the same observation, with other pleasing pedantries worthy of the great Samuel. 'In the desperate hope of being named in your next collection', John Carthew wrote to offer the persuasive suggestion that Pickwick's 'odd ignorance' (as I called it) of 'nearby Stroud' may 'not be an error if Stroud Glos. is intended'. I am very glad to name Mr Carthew and put on record his well-taken query.

Professor M. Hammerton noted that, in spite of my assertions to the contrary (in 'How Good an Oarswoman is Maggie Tulliver?'), 'wooden machinery' was very common throughout the nineteenth century. 'If you want ocular proof,' Professor Hammerton went on to add, 'I recommend that, the next time you are in Sheffield, you drop into the

Abbeydale Industrial Hamlet to see the splendid wooden machinery of the forge there.' I shall do so. He also pointed out that the apparatus Shelley is described as experimenting with as an undergraduate 'is not a dynamo, which was invented in 1831. From the description it must have been some kind of electrostatic generator, like a Wimshurst machine. I recall as a schoolboy, using one to charge the brass door handle of a classroom with a harmless 50,000 volts for the benefit of a much disliked teacher.' Professor Hammerton is evidently not a man to cross. To my relief, he concludes: 'Having picked all these nits, I must say that I vastly enjoyed your books. They are the sort of thing to which more *littérateurs* should aspire, instead of nauseating us with phoney philosophy and psychobabble.'

Michael Grosvenor Myer wittily corrected me on the issue of Long John Silver: 'he does *not* have a "peg leg" but a crutch: his leg is amputated too near the hip to make a peg leg possible.' Mr Myer, who I suspect may be an old boy, was also informative on the question of Daniel Deronda's Eton experiences:

He would only necessarily have experienced 'the school's communal sleeping and bathing facilities' (*CJEBH?*, p. 173) if he had been a Colleger. If, however, like the majority of Etonians, he was an Oppidan, his experience would have depended on the facilities provided by his 'm'dame', who could well have afforded her charges individual sleeping quarters and baths.

Mr Myer, who obviously follows the civilized practice of reading the same books as his wife, adds:

Re. Elfride's underwear [in *A Pair of Blue Eyes*]: my wife Valerie Grosvenor Myer, while convinced by your main drift, notes that stories about knotting ropes of bedsheets etc. to make lifesaving ropes must be apocryphal since, unless the material is rotten, it cannot be torn with bare hands. A sharp knife or pair of scissors would be needed to make the initial incision.

Elfride may have had a small pair of scissors in her reticule, perhaps?

Mrs Rosemary Owen took exception to my surmise that in naming Emma's great adversary 'Augusta Hawkins', Jane Austen may have been making a point about the origins of her family's wealth in slave-trading. Mrs Owen informed me that 'My grandfather Thomas Hawkins was a direct descendant of Sir John Hawkins and I do not wish to number Augusta Elton and Selina Suckling among my relations. If Jane Austen indicated a connection she was, I'm afraid to say, at fault.'

Slavery and Jane Austen continues to fascinate. Roy S. Robinson writes that 'one thing that has always puzzled me is the source of the wealth of men such as Bingley and Darcy'. Since both these rich men hail from the north of England, *ergo* their wealth may originate in Liverpool's lucrative 'trade in human flesh' (as Jane Fairfax feelingly puts it).

Norma Postin wrote to say that she had:

long felt sorry for the furmity woman. Her court appearance in Chapter 28 of *The Mayor of Casterbridge* gives details of her offence. Quite late at night—at 11.25 to be exact—she needs to have a pee so she crouches in the gutter at the side of the road near the church. Along comes the constable who shines a light in her direction as she 'committed the nuisance'. A very private moment. It is no wonder that she swears at him. I mean, any woman would.

I have followed up Ms Postin's womanly indignation in the chapter, 'Why are there no public conveniences in Casterbridge?'

Frances Twinn pointed out a number of mysteries in the novels of Elizabeth Gaskell. Those on *Ruth* and *North and South* I have taken the liberty of pursuing. I have left uninvestigated a question she raises about *Wives and Daughters*, namely, 'the extent to which there may have been an affair between Mrs Kirkpatrick (later Mrs Gibson) and Mr Preston'. The evidence is convincing. Mrs Twinn is writing a doctoral dissertation on Gaskell, which I look forward to reading.

Derek Miller, on the question of Daniel Deronda's circumcision, pertinently pointed to the significance of the hero's 'musing about the possibility that he is illegitimate at thirteen, his barmitzvah year'. This, I am sure, was intentional on George Eliot's part and Mr Miller's observation enriches our appreciation of the novel.

Noting (as did others) a problem with the single footprint in *Robinson Crusoe*, as depicted by Cruikshank, being the wrong way round, Paul McQuail had an interesting recollection about the subject of another essay in *Can Jane Eyre Be Happy?*:

'The Yellow Wallpaper' may have been nearly unavailable in the UK for many years. I first came upon it as one of the stories dramatized on radio in 1946 or 1947, introduced by Valentine Dyall as the 'Man in Black'. I was disconcerted by its difference from all the other stories in the series as a boy of 12 or 13; but it is the only one of the many 'Man in Black' stories that stayed in my mind.

I have often thought it would be worth collecting readers' earliest experiences of classic fiction. I suspect I must have heard the programme Professor McQuail mentions (I was addicted to the 'Man in Black', and Valentine Dyall's spine-chilling baritone), but it has left no trace in my memory. I *can* remember, vividly, Poe's 'The Tell-Tale Heart', and its unbearably throbbing climax.

Dr Frank Formby wrote from Australia to tell me that 'I read with great interest and enjoyment your book *Can Jane Eyre Be Happy?* lent to me by my father.' Dr Formby offered an expert opinion on Heathcliff's cause of death, about which I posed a puzzle in that book:

It certainly sounds as if Heathcliff's death was most unusual. As a palliative care physician, I can offer the following comments: 1. In seriously unwell patients the desire to drink fluids is often absent but it is such a powerful drive that it seems improbable that it could be absent in a healthy person merely through distraction. Abstinence from fluid might lead to death from dehydration and renal failure in four days. The person would most likely be incoherent and semi-conscious in the last day or two. (Don't try this at home!). 2. Abstinence from food would not lead to death in a healthy person in four days. It would take more like 30–60 days as long as the fluid intake was maintained. (In the absence of eating, as little as 300 ml per day would suffice.) This is borne out by the experience of a colleague of mine in Perth, WA, who looked after some shipwreck survivors. They were relatively healthy after surviving on 300 ml of water per day with a small amount of glucose for about 35 days. 3. It is definitely possible that an otherwise healthy person under great psychological stress could die 'of a broken heart' or however you care to term it. I have witnessed this myself. The experience of Australian Aborigines is relevant here. If a traditional aborigine has a bone pointed at him by a sorcerer, he is likely to die despite all medical intervention unless the 'spell' is reversed or he can be convinced that it has been reversed.

I have drawn on the expertise of many colleagues in this present volume: Alison Winter and Ken Fielding on a number of matters relevant to nineteenth-century science; Charles Mitchell and Andrew Lewis on questions of law; Jonathan Grossman, Charlotte Mitchell, Andrew Sanders, Fred Schwarzbach, Rosemary Ashton, Margaret Harris, John Mullan, Rachel Bowlby, and Phil Horne as critics of fiction; and on Mac Pigman for literary and technical advice. Guilland Sutherland and Jane Dietrich read the typescript and offered a number of welcome corrections. As before, I am immensely grateful to my editor at OUP, Judith Luna, for encouragement and judicious improvements at every stage.

Daniel Defoe · *Moll Flanders*

Why is Moll's younger brother older than she is?

As Ian Watt notes in *The Rise of the Novel*, the attentive reader will find an 'inordinate number of cracks' in the plot of *Moll Flanders*. Some, in fact, are less cracks than gaping fissures. There are, Watt goes on to observe, two possible lines on the inconsistencies in Moll's account of her life. We can read her narrative 'ironically'. In this mode of reading 'errors' are assumed to have been cunningly planted by Defoe to be picked up by the wideawake reader.[1] Defoe *designed* such glaring anomalies as Moll's remembering to the farthing the value of gold watches she stole twenty years ago, but forgetting the names (and even, apparently, the number) of her children. These are to be taken 'ironically' as signs of her incorrigible callousness. Similarly ironic are such jarring pieties as her reflection, after stealing a little girl's gold necklace, that by her theft she had 'given the parents a just reproof for their negligence, in leaving the poor lamb to come home by itself, and it would teach them to take more care next time' (p. 194). Like the sadistic Victorian flogger telling his victim that 'this hurts me more than it hurts you', Moll is—if we follow this line of explanation—a double-dyed hypocrite.

Ian Watt eschews this super-subtlety. He prefers a reading of *Moll Flanders* which sees Daniel Defoe as a hurried writer, catering for readers who were not trained—as modern 'sleuthing' readers are trained—in the intricacies of detective fiction. The novel had not fully risen, nor had the skills of the novel's consumers. 'We take

novels much more seriously today,' Watt claims. Defoe,
in his day, was a hasty writer for unserious readers; an
artist who worked 'piecemeal, very rapidly, and without
any subsequent revision'.[2] Watt calculates that Defoe put
out 'over three thousand pages of print in the year that
saw *Moll Flanders*' and, we may assume, blotted very few
of those pages.

There are, to the modern eye, some astonishing anomalies in the novel. Moll, for example, signs off on the last
page in 1683, with the information that she is 'almost
seventy Years of Age'. This means that during the 1640s—
while Moll is swanning around Virginia—there is a civil
war going on in Britain. The conflict was particularly
savage in Colchester, where the heroine has deposited two
of her (nameless) children. That momentous upheaval is
never mentioned, any more than is the execution of King
Charles (worth a parenthesis, one would have thought)
or the Restoration. The 'Great Fire of London' ravages
the capital without Moll, apparently, noticing. She does,
however, tell us in some detail about a household fire in
which she is bruised by a mattress thrown out of a top
window by a desperate occupant.

One can, of course, rationalize these oversights in terms
of Moll's class origins. The great waves of history wash over
the working classes without their noticing. When Winston
Smith (in *Nineteen Eighty-Four*) tries to extract from the
old man in the pub what life before the Revolution was
like, he is absolutely frustrated by the old prole's inability
to *know* what he remembers or remember what he knows:

A sense of helplessness took hold of Winston. The old man's
memory was nothing but a rubbish heap of details . . . They
remembered a million useless things, a quarrel with a workmate,
a hunt for a lost bicycle pump, the expression on a long-dead
sister's face, the swirls of dust on a windy morning seventy years
ago; but all the relevant facts were outside the range of their

vision. They were like the ant, which can see small objects but not large ones.[3]

So too with Moll. She remembers the mattress, but forgets all the great historical events of what Dryden called the 'Annus Mirabilis', 1666. The Great Fire of London, the Dutch invasion of the Thames, the Wren rebuilding of the capital all pass unobserved. Dryden is the laureate's history. Moll's is 'prole' history. Bicycle pumps and mattresses. Like the 'ironic' approach, it's another flattering way of reading Defoe's fiction—flattering both to him and to us. But Watt's analysis is more convincing, in my view, than subtle readings which cast Moll as an 'unreliable narrator' and her omissions as 'symptomatically' self-revealing. Even Kurt Waldheim's amnesia did not extend to forgetting there was a war going on in 1939–1945.[4]

Ian Watt concludes that *Moll Flanders* is not a 'work of irony' but it is an 'ironic object' (p. 135). By which he means we can read it more sophisticatedly than Defoe wrote it but should be careful about reading our sophistication *into* the novel. None the less, one of the striking things about Defoe is how, in some important aspects, his narratives hold together well. Moll's age, for instance, is accurately recorded throughout all the complex vicissitudes of her life and emblazoned on the 1721 title-page (see overleaf).

If, as Watt suspects, Defoe wrote at reckless speed he must surely have had a 'Memorandum' to hand to remind him of Moll's current age as he wrote. The narrative offers a chronologically coherent account of Moll's childhood until, at 'between seventeen and eighteen' (p. 18), she leaves the household where she has been seduced by one brother to marry the other. 'Betty' (as she is then called) is married five years, before Robin dies (p. 58). She promptly disposes of her two children to the care of their

THE
FORTUNES
AND
MISFORTUNES
Of the FAMOUS
Moll Flanders, &c.

Who was Born in NEWGATE, and during a
Life of continu'd Variety for Threescore Years,
besides her Childhood, was Twelve Year a
Whore, five times a *Wife* (whereof once to her
own Brother) Twelve Year a *Thief,* Eight Year a
Transported *Felon* in *Virginia,* at last grew *Rich,*
liv'd *Honest,* and died a *Penitent.*

Written from her own MEMORANDUMS.

LONDON: Printed for, and Sold by W.
CHETWOOD, at *Cato's-Head,* in *Russel-
street, Covent-Garden*; and T. EDLING, at
the *Prince's-Arms,* over-against *Exerter-Change*
in the *Strand.* MDDCXXI.

grandparents and, as a 23-year-old widow, marries (after
a few months' courtship) her gentleman draper. Their
marriage lasts 'about two years and a quarter' (p. 62)
before they part company (rendering Moll's subsequent
'marriages' bigamous—something that she conveniently
forgets in her 'penitent' phase of life).

At this point, Betty becomes 'Mrs Mary Flanders'—
a handsome 25- or 26-year-old young woman of (apparent) means and respectability. After 'half-a-year's' interval
(p. 66) in this character, Mary marries her American sea-
captain. He takes her back as his new bride to his home
in old Virginia, where they have three children; at which
point, to her horror, she discovers that her husband is her
half-brother.

After eight years in America, Mary returns to Britain
(p. 104), leaving her 'brother-husband' free to claim that
she has died. He may thus marry again, if he wishes (she
will, if she can). Moll is, she says, 'far from old' (p. 106) and
must be, we calculate, around 34 when she migrates back
to England. Although the years abroad have been hard on
her, she is still a viable, if hardly nubile, commodity in the
sex market. She now takes up residence in Bath, picking
up (after a couple of seasons) with a wealthy man whose
wife is insane. This arrangement lasts 'near two years', at
which point, Mary must be 36 or 37.

As her sexual charms wane she declines from 'friend'
to 'whore'. 'Thief' is still to come, with menopause. Over
the next 'six years' she bears three children (that we know
about) to her 'protector' (p. 120). As she now assesses her
life, Moll ruefully notes:

I had the World to begin again; but you are to consider, that I
was not now the same Woman as when I liv'd at *Redriff* [i.e.
Rotherhithe]; for first of all I was near 20 Years older, and did not
look the better for my Age, nor for my Rambles to *Virginia* and
back again; and tho' I omitted nothing that might set me out to

Advantage, except Painting, for that I never stoop'd to . . . yet
there would always be some difference seen between Five and
Twenty, and Two and Forty. (p. 127)

By Moll's own several accounts, we can confirm that she
was indeed around 26 when she married her Virginian
captain. He, we know, was born in the colony. As her
'mother-in-law' ('mother') tells Moll, when she (the older
woman) arrived in Virginia, 'she very luckily fell into a
good Family, where behaving herself well, and her Mistress dying, her Master married her, by whom she had my
Husband and his Sister' (p. 88). We are told that this lady's
son, Moll's husband, 'was above thirty' at the time of their
arrival in Virginia—when Moll is, as calculated, 26–7. He
is, therefore, some five years older than she (as a 'captain',
he could scarcely be in his early twenties).

There is a major problem here, created by Defoe's punc-
tiliousness about his heroine's dates and chronology. If
they were born to the same mother Moll must have entered
the world in England at least five years before her mother
can: (1) have emigrated to Virginia; (2) have worked as a
servant until her mistress died; (3) have married her master; (4) have borne a son. That son (subsequently Moll's
'husband') must be significantly *younger*, not significantly
older than his English sister.

It could be one of the many 'cracks' in Defoe's narrative.
But the anomaly usefully directs us back to Moll's brief,
superficially clear, but actually very perplexing account
of her origins. Her mother, as she says, was convicted of
'borrowing three pieces of fine *Holland*'. Of this crime, Moll
says, 'the Circumstances are too long to repeat, and I have
heard them related so many Ways, that I can scarce be
certain which is the right Account' (p. 8). In the weeks
while awaiting trial at Newgate, Moll's mother took the
precaution of getting herself pregnant (by the gaoler, we

assume). Hence the private joke in her later assumed name, 'Flanders'—three pieces of Holland procreated her.

Moll's mother 'pleaded her belly' to escape, got herself a seven-month reprieve (she must have just made it), and subsequently had her sentence commuted to transportation. At six months, young Moll was consigned to the 'bad Hands' of 'some Relation of my Mothers' (p. 8). Her first conscious recollection is as a 3-year-old child among a nomadic company of *Gypsies*, to whom she was sold—evidently to be used as a child beggar or whore. Luckily, she somehow got away from this gypsy band, and found herself in Colchester—where her next fifteen years were to be spent.

There are a number of oddities in this account. Clearly Moll knows her true name—although we never do. It is by this name that she identifies her mother, a quarter of a century later in Virginia. How *does* she know her name? The gypsies would surely have renamed her, to protect themselves. She can hardly have been baptized. Who was it who told her the circumstances of her mother's arrest and trial, 'so many Ways' that she cannot be sure 'which is the right Account'?

If her unnamed maternal relatives told her, a 2-year-old girl at the time, the account would surely have fallen on uncomprehending ears. Who were these relatives of her mother, anyway? How did the gypsies come by her? And why—if the gypsies bought or abducted her—did they simply let her go? As a 3-year-old child, Moll can, by her own account, have known nothing of her origins—certainly not enough to fill in, as she does, missing parts of her mother's recollections many years later. It is difficult, on the narrative evidence, to see how she could even have known her own name.

'Gypsy abduction' is a favourite childish fantasy. In order to make sense of the gross disparity of age between

the heroine and her Virginian husband (more so given
Defoe's accuracy elsewhere about this aspect of his plot),
one is driven to assume that Moll is lying. She was
more than 3 when she arrived in Colchester, and there
is some prehistory which we do not know about. Moll,
we deduce, is some years older than she claims and is
clumsily masking what she knows of her birth and that
disreputable 'Relation of my Mothers'. Whores' peniten-
tial confessions are, by their nature, suspect documents.
By opening with a precise, but so easily exploded (and
arguably romantic), account of her origins, Moll brands
herself as untrustworthy, but not for that reason entirely
unsympathetic. Who, with Moll's past, would not tell a few
fibs about her childhood?

The Oxford World's Classics *Moll Flanders* is edited by G. A.
Starr.

Henry Fielding · *Tom Jones*

Who has Susan been talking to?

According to Coleridge, the three best-constructed plots in world literature are *Oedipus Rex*, *The Alchemist*, and *Tom Jones*.[1] In Fielding's novel the chapters in the inn at Upton show the plot-wright's art at its most virtuosic. Few now read his plays, but the novelist's long apprenticeship on the stage must have prepared him in handling the intricate plot machinery of Books 9 and 10—a section of the narrative which, as Tony Richardson's 1963 film showed, adapts wonderfully to the conventions of high-speed theatrical farce.

To summarize: the Upton sequence begins with Tom taking a leisurely farewell from the Man of Hill at dawn, before starting on his way. The two gentlemen enjoy a philosophic view of the early morning landscape from a neighbouring eminence, Mazard Hill. (Partridge, who is not philosophical, has elected to stay in bed.) The idyll is disturbed when Tom spies a lady being murdered (or worse than murdered) in a thicket. The would-be murderer turns out to be none other than the hero's old foe, Northerton (who escapes to do more bad things). The voluptuous victim is—although Tom does not know it—Mrs Waters, alias our old friend Jenny Jones.

Rather oddly, Mrs Waters does not now or later tumble to Tom's identity (there are so many Tom Joneses in the world, presumably), although tumbling is much on her mind. Manfully, the young man resists her delicate invitation to take his rescuer's reward, and conducts the lady to a convenient inn at 'the famous town of Upton'

(p. 430). The sleepy Partridge is directed to follow in his own time.

A near-naked woman, accompanied by a dishevelled young buck, are not the custom the landlord and his wife think appropriate to their genteel establishment. A brawl ('the Battle of Upton') ensues, elaborately described in Fielding's mock-heroic style. Tom is saved from mortal injury at the hands of the broom-wielding landlady by the nick-of-time arrival of Partridge, who is promptly belaboured by the inn's 'robust and manlike' maid-of-all-work, Susan. Enter a sergeant of musketeers, who recognizes Tom's companion as 'Mrs Waters'—his commander's 'wife'. As an officer's lady she is, of course, now made welcome at the inn and peace breaks out.

While the debris of the fracas is being cleared up, a mysterious lady and her attendant have arrived in a coach and four. Tom is bent over the distraught (and still interestingly undressed) Mrs Waters, and Partridge is washing blood from his nose at the courtyard pump. Neither takes any notice of these newcomers. The alert reader suspects that they may be Sophia and Honour. But they are, as later emerges, Mrs Fitzpatrick—a lady in flight from her violent husband—and her attendant. It is their intention only to rest an hour or two, and travel on post-haste, overnight.

It is now teatime, and a number of strands of the plot run concurrently. In her private apartments, Mrs Waters takes some refreshment with Tom who finally surrenders to her charms (incestuously?). This is an afternoon engagement, to be followed up by further nocturnal action(s). Meanwhile, downstairs in the kitchen, a relaxed Partridge, the ladies' coachman, the sergeant, and (between their duties) the landlord and landlady chat and drink the evening away.

The sergeant tactfully describes Mrs Waters's fondness

for errant young officers like Northerton (with whom she was eloping, before he decided to kill her for her diamond ring and ninety guineas). Partridge, who like Cassio has very poor brains for drinking, boasts about his 'friend' Mr Jones and what great expectations 'the heir of Squire Allworthy' has. As the drink flows, quarrels break out, a thoroughly drunk sergeant and coachman come to blows— but so overcome are they with the landlady's dubious 'perry', that they can do each other no harm.

The coachman is now far too drunk to take Mrs Fitzpatrick away from the inn and she reluctantly decides to stay the night. By midnight, only Susan is up—'she being obliged to wash the kitchen, before she retired to the arms of the fond, expecting ostler'. Enter, furiously, an Irish gentleman looking for his escaped wife. Susan assumes Mrs Waters must be the runaway, and directs Mr Fitzpatrick (as it turns out to be) to the lady's bedroom. It may, of course, be that Susan's motives are mischievous— she knows full well that something untoward is going on in Mrs Waters's room.

Misdirected by Susan, the irate husband bursts in to be confronted by a naked Jones. On seeing the woman's clothes around the bed, and a form therein, Fitzpatrick naturally assumes that he is being cuckolded in front of his very eyes. A furious fight ensues. The uproar brings in another Irishman who is sleeping in an adjoining bedroom (the narrator has been too busy to tell us about *his* arrival at the inn).

'Mr Maclachlan' is, it turns out, known to Fitzpatrick and—candles now being brought—he points out to his friend that the lady in the bed is not Mrs Fitzpatrick caught *in flagrante delicto* but some other lady. Quick-wittedly, Mrs Waters further protests that Mr Jones, in an adjoining room, was himself drawn in by the noise of Fitzpatrick's irruption. To proclaim her innocence before the world, she begins to shout out hysterically 'Help! Rape! Murder! Rape!'

The landlady finally arrives and all is more or less set straight. Fitzpatrick, not thinking to search other rooms in the inn, retires to share Mr Maclachlan's bed ('errant scrubs', the landlady disgustedly comments; she has been cheated out of a fee). Partridge now comes down to the kitchen. He too has been wakened by the noise and terrified, as he says, by a 'screech owl' outside his window. He persuades Fitzpatrick's two manservants to keep him company, and takes to drinking again.

Susan now admits two women travellers into the inn. They turn out to be Sophia and her maid, Mrs Honour. Partridge, however, does not recognize them, muffled up as they are at this time of night. Moreover, it has been many years since he resided in their village. Sophia retires to a bedroom to rest; Honour comes down to the kitchen and— despite the hour—peremptorily demands cooked food. Susan and Partridge are vexed and the schoolmaster-barber lets slip, talking to the landlady, that his sleeping friend is 'Jones . . . Squire Allworthy's son'. Mrs Honour 'pricks up her ears', returns to tell Sophia what seems like good news, then returns to the kitchen.

A thoroughly confused Partridge, under the imperious maid's interrogation as to where Jones is, informs her 'plainly that Jones was in bed with a wench, and made use of an expression too indelicate to be here inserted'. Exit Mrs Honour again, to pass on this awful intelligence to Sophia. Distraught, Sophia summons Susan to her bedroom. She and Mrs Honour cross-examine the maid, and by a mixture of bullying and bribery (Susan's price is an exorbitant two guineas) persuade the wench to test the truth of what Partridge has said by going to Jones's bedroom. It is empty, Susan reports. Mr Jones must be with Mrs Waters. On being told, Sophia 'turns pale':

Mrs Honour begged her to be comforted, and not to think any more of so worthless a fellow. 'Why there,' says Susan, 'I hope, madam, your ladyship won't be offended; but pray, madam, is not your ladyship's name Madam Sophia Western?' 'How is it possible you should know me?' answered Sophia. 'Why, that man that the gentlewoman [Mrs Honour] spoke of, who is in the kitchen, told about you last night.' (p. 471)

Susan goes on to say that Partridge further said that Sophia was 'dying for love of the young squire, and that he was going to the wars to get rid of you'.

Sophia now sees that Tom Jones has played her false. He is not her true love. She gives Susan a third guinea and instructs the serving-woman to place the muff Jones gave her in the unfaithful young man's room, with her name attached on a piece of paper. This will lead to further complications after she has left (which she and Mrs Honour do forthwith), shortly before Squire Western arrives.

The Upton chapters are done in masterly fashion, and there is a touch of justified bravado in Fielding's challenge to the 'reptile critics' to find fault with his design, if they can. The narrator succeeds, against all the odds, in keeping Partridge and Mrs Waters (Tom's two putative parents), apart while keeping Tom and Partridge together. The schoolmaster-barber might plausibly fail to recognize Sophia and Honour. He would certainly remember the fascinating Jenny Jones.

There is, however, a puzzle embedded in this virtuosic stretch of narrative. How does Susan know Sophia's name, and how has she come by the remarkably untrue allegation that Mr Jones was running away to the wars to be rid of Sophia? If we look back at what Partridge actually said in the kitchen (Susan, incidentally, is not recorded as being present at the time), it is very different. After he has boasted that he is Mr Jones's friend, *not* his servant, and that Mr Jones is the 'heir of Squire Allworthy' (a magnate known, even at this distance, to the inn's hosts), Partridge is asked by the landlord: 'how comes it . . . that such a great gentleman walks about the country afoot?' It is a shrewd question. 'I don't know', Partridge lamely retorts, then gets into his stride:

' . . . great gentlemen have humours sometimes. He hath now a dozen horses and servants at Gloucester; and nothing would serve him, but last night, it being very hot weather, he must cool himself with a walk to yon high hill, whither I likewise walked with him to bear him company.' (p. 446)

Hereafter, the discussion disintegrates into drunken quarrelling and even more drunken fisticuffs.

How, one may ask, did Susan get hold of her (nearly accurate) version of things? There are a number of possibilities. In his cups, Partridge may have drivelled out a whole string of indiscretions, at a time when Susan was moving in and out of the kitchen about her business. This might have taken place during some un-narrated portion of the story, while the reader's attention was directed elsewhere. It is, however, very hard to find an occasion when Partridge's public indiscretions could have occurred. All the chinks are filled. And no one but Susan seems to be privy to them.

Alternatively, one might think that Susan—who is mischievous (*vide* the business with Mr Fitzpatrick)—is making it all up. But there is a garbled version of the truth here, and she knows Sophia's identity (she is, in fact, the only person in the inn to penetrate the disguise). There is a strong kernel of truth in what she knows, or thinks she knows. She must have had it from someone in the know.

What seems most likely is the following. After their epic battle at the beginning of the Upton episode, Partridge and Susan make up, as we are told. He forgives his scratches, she forgives the black eye he has given her: 'between these two, therefore, a league was struck, and those hands became now the mediators of peace.' Flirtation, we deduce, may have followed amity—with the promise of even closer intimacies, when Susan should have time for them.

Susan, we infer, must be a paragon of chambermaids. She is manifestly on duty at crack of dawn on the two days covered by the Upton business (see pp. 473, 480). Thus it is, for instance, that she can participate in the morning 'Battle of Upton'. As is made clear, the day's business at the inn in this summer-time of year begins two hours before dawn, at five o'clock. This estimable servant is still, as we are told, working at midnight. First up, she is last to go to bed. Nor can she expect sleep even when she does get to bed. The ostler will doubtless want to keep her from slumber for a little while, at least.

What seems plausible is the following. Susan cemented her 'league' with Partridge by retiring with him, or visiting his bedroom, shortly after he retired—an arrangement made earlier in the day, after the 'battle'. Before leaving Partridge's embrace for that of the ostler (in the straw, with his horses) she indulged in some pillow talk. Partridge, indiscreet as ever, told her things he should not have done. On her part, she cunningly milked him for anything she could learn about who his master was, and any details of his amours. It was while she was on her way from one bed to another (the business about 'being obliged to wash the kitchen' was a lie) that Susan chanced to be up at midnight when Fitzpatrick arrived.

There is some warrant for this line of speculation. In her inquest after the Fitzpatrick imbroglio we are told that 'the landlady, remembering that Susan had been the only person out of bed when the door was burst open', goes on to ask some searching questions. She clearly is suspicious about the maid being up at midnight. Susan, we are told, 'related the whole story which the reader knows already, varying the truth only in some circumstances, and totally concealing the money she had received'. Among those 'varied circumstances', we may suppose, is the true account of what she happened to be doing out of bed (or between beds) at that ungodly hour.

The Oxford World's Classics *Tom Jones* is edited by John Bender and Simon Stern, with an introduction by John Bender.

Who betrays Elizabeth Bennet?

Elizabeth Bennet's final put-down of Lady Catherine de Bourgh in Volume III, Chapter 14 of *Pride and Prejudice* ranks with Lady Bracknell and the handbag as one of the most memorable scenes in literature. As Jane Austen tells it, it is a conflict of battleaxe versus rapier with the old battleaxe comprehensively vanquished. Lady Catherine flies the field with her magnificently hollow rebuke: 'I take no leave of you, Miss Bennet. I send no compliments to your mother. You deserve no such attention. I am most seriously displeased' (p. 318).

What has so seriously displeased Lady Catherine is the report that Elizabeth is about to become engaged to Darcy—a marital prize she has reserved for her own daughter Anne. The couple are 'tacitly' engaged—she loftily tells Miss Bennet. But, as she is obliged to add: 'The engagement between them is of a peculiar kind' (p. 315). The de Bourghs have not troubled, that is, to secure the young man's compliance in the matter.

Elizabeth holds her ground, parrying all the older woman's attempts to coerce her into an 'undertaking'—a surrender, that is, of any claim to Darcy. By sheer dialectical skill, Elizabeth neither admits any intention of marrying the gentleman nor offers any guarantee that she will not. Her sub-zero *politesse* drives de Bourgh to paroxysms of fury and what even she, imperceptive as she is, dimly perceives to be foolishness: 'Obstinate, headstrong girl! I am ashamed of you! Is this your gratitude to me for my attentions to you last spring?

Is nothing due to me on that score?' (p. 316). After her
antagonist bustles away in a rage, Elizabeth wonders:

from what the report of their engagement could originate,
Elizabeth was at a loss to imagine; till she recollected that
his [Darcy's] being the intimate friend of Bingley, and *her*
[Elizabeth's] being the sister of Jane, was enough, at a time
when the expectation of one wedding, made every body eager
for another, to supply the idea. (p. 319)

It's a weak supposition—unworthy of the sharp-witted
Miss Bennet. And it is exploded immediately by her father.
He has received a perplexing letter from Mr Collins: 'He
begins with congratulations on the approaching nuptials
of my eldest daughter [Jane and Bingley], of which it
seems he has been told, by some of the good-natured,
gossiping Lucases' (p. 321). Jane Austen laid this train
of gossip at the end of Volume III, Chapter 13, when
Mrs Bennet goes to her sister, the lawyer's wife, and
'was privileged to whisper it to Mrs Philips, and *she*
ventured, without any permission, to do the same by all
her neighbours in Meryton' (p. 311). Among whom, we
deduce, are the Philips family's close neighbours at Lucas
Lodge. As we follow the line of clues, Lady Lucas has
written to her daughter Charlotte, now Mrs Collins, and
she has passed the news of Jane and Bingley's engagement
on to her husband and his patroness over dinner at
Rosings.

All this is transparent enough, and fits in with the
gossipy world of Longbourn and Meryton (separated, as
we are told, by only a mile's 'short walk', p. 14). But Mr
Collins's letter contains something else. He goes on to
felicitate Mr Bennet on the impending marriage of his
daughter Elizabeth to 'one of the illustrious personages
in the land' (p. 321). Who can this 'illustrious personage'
be, Mr Bennet wonders? It must be Darcy. But, to a
commonsensical man like him, it *cannot* be 'Mr Darcy,

who never looks at any woman but to see a blemish, and who probably never looked at *you* in his life! It is admirable' (p. 322). And preposterous. The effect of this double-fronted attack is—of course—to put any possible union between Mr Pride and Miss Prejudice entirely out of the question. Wheels are being spoked (particularly if, as we suspect, similar rumours are being cast to embarrass Darcy).

There is a puzzle underlying this interesting tangle, pointed out to me by Kathleen Glancy:

How could there be a report in Meryton about *anyone*, much less one of Mrs Bennet's daughters, getting married, which has *not* reached the ears of Mrs Bennet herself? It can't have done or her attitude to Darcy would have undergone its dramatic metamorphosis far sooner than it does. Her sister Mrs Philips can't have heard it either, for she would have passed it on to Mrs Bennet at once. It is all the more amazing because it is known to Sir William and Lady Lucas.

Does such a report exist? Is Mr Collins, for heaven knows what reason, *lying* when he informs Lady Catherine in conversation and Mr Bennet by letter about Elizabeth's impending marriage to one of the most illustrious persons in the land? Or, even more horrible, has Jane Austen blundered. Can the puzzle be made sense of, Miss Glancy asks?

It is indeed puzzling. The Philips' house, Lucas Lodge, and Longbourn are all at a convenient walking distance from each other, and gossip flashes between them as fast as ladies can move between the establishments on their daily round of 'calls'. Why then are Mr and Mrs Bennet in the dark, and Mr Collins and Lady Catherine—the two most obtuse and imperceptive characters in the novel—all-knowing on this confidential matter? Mrs Bennet, of course, is obtuse and imperceptive on all subjects save one—her daughters' marriage prospects. If there were so much as a whisper about the possibility of a match for Elizabeth with Darcy, she would have been on fire with the intelligence.

There is, I think, a plausible explanation to Miss Glancy's puzzle. The most interesting character in the novel, who Jane Austen clearly does not have room to develop fully, is Charlotte Collins (née Lucas). Formerly Elizabeth Bennet's particular friend, Charlotte delivers her opinions with impressive authority. Early in Chapter 6, on the subject of the relation of the sexes, Charlotte utters what I think is the longest speech (the irrepressible Miss Bates excepted) of any woman in all the six novels. Laden with Johnsonian epigram ('if a woman conceals her affection with the same skill from the object of it, she may lose the opportunity of fixing him; and it will then be but poor consolation to believe the world equally in the dark', p. 17) it eloquently expresses Charlotte's pragmatic philosophy of sex:

'There is so much of gratitude or vanity in almost every attachment, that it is not safe to leave any to itself. We can all *begin* freely—a slight preference is natural enough; but there are very few of us who have heart enough to be really in love without encouragement. In nine cases out of ten, a woman had better shew *more* affection than she feels.' (p. 17)

Charlotte evidently believes that women are so socially disadvantaged that they must strike, like bandits, when opportunity offers—and if necessary dissimulate to get their prize. This is theory. It is put in practice when Charlotte takes Mr Collins on the rebound, only hours after Elizabeth has rejected his proposal of marriage. No woman with a scintilla of 'pride' would do such a thing. A 27-year-old woman driven by cold reason might—if the calculation were to her advantage. Such a woman would weather out the scorn of being thought second-best. Words will never hurt her. Charlotte's acceptance of Mr Collins leads to a painful rupture between the former friends. Elizabeth is surprised by the intelligence into a wounding tactlessness:

'Engaged to Mr. Collins! my dear Charlotte,—impossible!'

The steady countenance which Miss Lucas had commanded in telling her story, gave way to a momentary confusion here on receiving so direct a reproach; though, as it was no more than she expected, she soon regained her composure, and calmly replied,

'Why should you be surprised, my dear Eliza?—Do you think it incredible that Mr. Collins should be able to procure any woman's good opinion, because he was not so happy as to succeed with you?' (p. 113)

Charlotte was quick to perceive subliminal attraction between Elizabeth and Darcy: 'I daresay you will find him very agreeable' (p. 81) she tells her friend, as early as Chapter 18. Over the years Charlotte has had to put up with many slights from the Bennets. In Chapter 5 Mrs Bennet, recalling the glories of the ball, complacently tells her:

'*You* began the evening well, Charlotte,' said Mrs. Bennet with civil self-command to Miss Lucas. '*You* were Mr. Bingley's first choice.'

'Yes;—but he seemed to like his second better.'

'Oh!—you mean Jane, I suppose—because he danced with her twice. To be sure that *did* seem as if he admired her—indeed I rather believe he *did* . . . ' (pp. 14–15)

Women as clever as Miss Lucas do not forget these things.

Charlotte is off-stage for the second half of the novel—disposed of in the great marriage auction. But simply because she is not seen, we should not imagine that she is getting less clever or less sharp. Having to dine every evening with the Revd Mr William Collins and the Rt. Hon. Lady Catherine de Bourgh would turn a saint's milk of human kindness to vinegar. What we may assume is that an embittered Charlotte is determined to settle accounts with Elizabeth. She will poison Elizabeth's prospects, with a pre-emptive strike that she knows will provoke an outburst of the young woman's incorrigible 'prejudice'. It is a stroke of well-conceived malice. It fails—but only just.[1]

The Oxford World's Classics *Pride and Prejudice* is edited by James Kinsley and Frank W. Bradbrook, with an introduction by Isobel Armstrong.

What do we know about Frances Price (the first)?

In a short note in the Jane Austen Society *Report* for 1982 Deirdre Le Faye points out a problem in the sketched background to *Mansfield Park*. It relates to the three Ward sisters, each of whom plays a significant, if supporting, role in the novel's plot.[1] The problem is laid out in Jane Austen's typically crisp *mise en scène* in the first two pages of the narrative. 'About thirty years ago,' the novel opens, 'Miss Maria Ward of Huntingdon, with only seven thousand pounds, had the good luck to captivate Sir Thomas Bertram, of Mansfield Park, in the county of Northampton' (p. 1).

Given its date of publication, 1814, the 'thirty years ago' reference would set Maria's happy catch in the 'season' of 1784 or thereabouts. Huntingdon and Northampton are neighbouring counties and the same social set attends the same events. We get a momentary glimpse of the family behind the bride, but no more than a glimpse: 'All Huntingdon exclaimed on the greatness of the match, and her uncle, the lawyer himself, allowed her to be at least three thousand pounds short of any equitable claim to it.'

The lawyer uncle and the dowry (albeit three thousand short) indicate professional respectability and a middle rather than upper station in life (the younger sons of the nobility go into the church or the army, not the law; noble wives bring with them property, not money). We know absolutely nothing of the Ward parents. But

Maria, we are told, 'had two sisters to be benefited by her
elevation . . . Miss Ward and Miss Frances'. The honorific
'Miss Ward' (without the Christian name, which we never
know) indicates that she is the oldest of the trio. 'Half-
a-dozen' years later (1790-ish) Miss Ward, having now
been somewhat long in the shop window, is obliged to
lower her sights and accept 'the Rev. Mr Norris, a friend
of her brother-in-law, with scarcely any private fortune'.
Why Miss Ward, unlike her younger sister, has little or no
dowry we are not told.

Sir Thomas's patronage gives Mr Norris a living in
the environs of Mansfield Park in Northamptonshire and
with it a comfortable income of 'a very little less than a
thousand a year'. The Norrises have no children (and are
careful not to adopt one, in the shape of young Fanny), and
we may suppose that Mrs Norris takes wise precautions
against any expensive little strangers. The 'less than a
thousand pounds' does not admit of such extravagances.
The less constrained Lady Bertram has four children: two
boys and two girls. It is, as Deirdre Le Faye plausibly
surmises, at some point shortly after Mrs Norris's wedding
that the third sister, Frances Ward, makes her disastrous
choice of partner. She 'married, in the common phrase,
to disoblige her family, and by fixing on a Lieutenant of
Marines, without education, fortune, or connections, did
it very thoroughly'. He was evidently wholly unknown
to the Ward family. Sir Thomas can do nothing in this
unfortunate case. Lieutenant Price's line of profession
'was such as no interest could reach'. And, to seal the
rupture, there is a sharp exchange of letters in which
Frances makes 'disrespectful reflections on the pride of
Sir Thomas'.

Over the next eleven years, in their series of married
quarters in Portsmouth, Mrs Price goes on an orgy of
childbearing, with nine lying-ins. A contrite letter gets

a helpful response from Mansfield Park—leading to the launching of the two oldest Price children, William and Fanny, into more respectable courses of life than their parents. Frances's husband has not risen in his branch of the service. He is still only a lieutenant—indeed is no further forward ten years later, in 1808–11, the date at which the novel proper begins.[2]

The questions which Deirdre Le Faye asks are the following:

1. How did Miss Frances Ward—of Huntingdon—fall into the way of a lieutenant of marines in faraway Portsmouth? Unlike Northampton, this is not neighbouring territory.

2. Did Frances Ward elope with Lieutenant Price, prefiguring Maria Bertram's conduct? That she did is hinted by the tart comment: 'to save herself from useless remonstrance, Mrs Price never wrote to her family on the subject, till actually married' (p. 1).

3. Why cannot Sir Thomas's 'interest' help Lieutenant Price?

Le Faye surmises, plausibly, that Frances cannot have been working as a governess in Portsmouth—that being the only line of away-from-home work which someone of Miss Ward's class might take up. As we see her in later life, Mrs Price is incompetent to have filled such a role. She might, conceivably, have been visiting relatives in the south-west. But, as Le Faye sees it, elopement is the most likely scenario. It is a case of 'family history repeating itself'.

Le Faye's speculations are as convincing as any speculation can be. We assume, if only from the evidence of the sexual activity, that there was a kind of Mellors-the-gamekeeper masculinity about Lieutenant Price which made him irresistibly attractive to the lawyer's genteel niece. Those manly attractions had probably worn rather

thin by the time of her ninth pregnancy—but by then
Frances's lot was fixed.

There are some other deductions to be drawn from the
parental Price plot, once it is brought to the reader's
attention. The marines were responsible for discipline in
the shipyards and ports. The navy—manned as it was in
large part by press-ganged crews, with discipline enforced
by the cat—was in a constant state of seething discontent
and mutiny. Major garrisons of marines were kept in the
principal ports such as Chatham and Portsmouth.

An oddity of the marines was that commissions were
not by purchase after 1755 (they remained so in the
regular army until the 1870s). This explains why it is that
Sir Thomas cannot instantly help Lieutenant Price. As a
branch of the services, the marines had earned great credit
for their part in putting down the 1796 mutinies at the
Nore and Spithead. It is more than likely that Lieutenant
Price played a part in this operation. As a mark of favour,
they were renamed the 'Royal Marines' in 1802, although
Jane Austen does not use that title.

It is clear from Fanny's experiences when she is given
her punishment posting to Portsmouth that Lieutenant
Price is not a pleasant paterfamilias. He drinks in his
mess, is coarsely sarcastic at home, neglects his worn-
down wife, and evidently rules his wayward children
harshly. But, as Fanny notes in her father's conversations
with Henry Crawford, on duty he is not unprepossessing
in public. He would seem to be a good marine.

We have, I think, to leave the courtship of Frances Ward
and Lieutenant Price in the dark in which Austen chose
to keep it. But an authorial motive can be discerned in
Austen's having made her heroine's father a marine. The
marines were famous throughout their long history, but
particularly after 1796 (and particularly at Portsmouth),
as the embodiment of martial discipline of a ruthless kind.

It is as just such an act of discipline that mutinous Fanny is sent back to Portsmouth, to bring her to her senses with— metaphorically—a touch of the lash (it is not inconceivable that she might get the odd physical cuff from her drunken lieutenant father).

Meanwhile—ironically—discipline at Mansfield Park falls to pieces with the elopements. I think Jane Austen chose a lieutenant of marines not because she had, stored away in the back of her mind, some 'pre-plot' in which she saw the courtship of Miss Ward and her unsuitable suitor in any detail. She chose him because he fitted into the thematic pattern of her novel: *Mansfield Park: or Discipline*.[3]

The Oxford World's Classics *Mansfield Park* is edited by James Kinsley with an introduction by Marilyn Butler.

Jane Austen · *Emma*

Apple-blossom in June—again

In *Is Heathcliff a Murderer?* I defended what is thought to be Jane Austen's most egregious 'error' in her fiction, arguing that it was no error at all if one read it aright. The company go for a picnic to the grounds of Donwell Abbey.[1] It is 'the middle of June', 'almost Midsummer', as we are precisely informed (the actual day can be calculated as the 22nd of the month). Strawberries are in prospect: 'the best fruit in England—every body's favourite'. They are in plentiful supply, we understand. It has been a good crop—and on time. During a quiet moment on the expedition, standing on a hill, Emma gazes at the Surrey landscape spread out before her. It is 'a sweet view—sweet to the eye and the mind. English verdure, English culture, English comfort, seen under a sun bright, without being oppressive.'

Emma is content, not to say downright pleased with herself. She has successfully removed Harriet from the 'degrading' connection with her former suitor, Robert Martin of Abbey-Mill Farm. She is at this moment looking down on the farm. Her protégée (who is also looking down at the farm) is now destined for much better things than Mr Martin:

There had been a time . . . when Emma would have been sorry to see Harriet in a spot so favourable for the Abbey-Mill Farm; but now she feared it not. It might be safely viewed with all its appendages of prosperity and beauty, its rich pastures, spreading flocks, orchard in blossom, and light column of smoke ascending. (p. 326)

As the notes to the Oxford World's Classics edition comment: 'the anomaly of an orchard blossoming in the strawberry season' was noticed by some of the novel's first readers, notably Jane's brother Edward who archly requested: 'Jane, I wish you would tell me where you get those apple-trees of yours that come into bloom in July.' None the less, the novelist did not correct 'the mistake' because, the family surmised, 'it was not thought of sufficient consequence'.

It is, of course, late June, not July. None the less, the anomaly is singular—Miss Austen, as R. W. Chapman notes, seldom makes such mistakes. But it is not, I suggested, 'a mistake'. Not, that is, if one takes into consideration that there are three 'anomalies' in the offending sentence: (1) the late blossom; (2) a fire burning at Abbey-Mill Farm on a scorching day in late June; (3) that '"spreading flocks" would more plausibly refer to the lambing season, in early spring, when flocks enlarge dramatically'.

We should, I suggested, read the passage not as a snapshot of what is before Emma as she stands on the hill, but as a montage—a sequence of the turning seasons. I directed the reader to a passage which performs the same kind of trick in a poem by one of Austen's favourite poets, William Cowper, in which the poet, looking on a winter landscape, simultaneously sees features of spring and summer. What Austen implies by the 'spreading flocks, orchard in blossom, and light column of smoke ascending' sentence, I suggest, is: 'now Harriet, so effectively separated from Mr Robert Martin, the occupant of Abbey-Mill Farm, is immune to its varying attractions over the course of the year—whether in spring, early summer, midsummer, or autumn.'

I received a number of polite objections to this admittedly ingenious line of argument—on the score of all three 'anomalies'. As to the sheep, Claire Lamont commented: 'I query whether the reference to "spreading flocks" is seasonal. Sheep spread out in the field when they are content, and huddle together when they are frightened. Shepherds take pleasure in seeing their flocks well spread out and it is just the sort of reference the passage needs to imply prosperity and calm.' It's a nice point, although not entirely clinchingly so, I think.

Dr Lamont also has some misgivings about the June kitchen fire:

I don't know what happened to summer fires in Surrey; if the passage were set further north I would not hesitate to believe that a fire would be burning all the year round, and that the summeriness of the scene is indicated by 'light column' as a description of its smoke. I am haunted by references to domestic fires which are never let out until the goodwife dies—but they are probably all Scottish references.

Deirdre Le Faye (as the editor of the most recent edition of Austen's letters) also took exception to the 'anomaly' of summer smoke—claiming that it was a perfectly normal feature of the rural landscape:

There would have to be a fire all the year round in the kitchen for cooking and hot water. Kitchens *were* notoriously hot and awful; that's why cooks had a free beer issue as well as wages, and are always portrayed as red-faced and sweaty. Abbey-Mill Farm would have been big enough, and the Martins rich and socially rising enough (they are quite literate, and Mrs Martin's daughters go to the respectable boarding school in Highbury), to have a separate dining room.

The question is, I think, open. I have looked, for example, at John Constable's numerous studies of home-county farms and mills in summer, over the period 1810–20, and see no smoke whatever from chimneys.[2] This is not, of course, conclusive evidence. But, at midday, in midsummer, on a scorching hot day, there was, I suspect, little likelihood of a kitchen fire at Abbey-Mill Farm.

There is, however, one other piece of evidence, pointed out to me by Brian Nicholas. As Professor Nicholas observes:

In spite of the weather, a fire had been kept going 'all the morning' at the Abbey, in preparation for Mr Woodhouse's arrival, and its 'slight remains' were still hot enough for Frank Churchill to sit as far away from them as possible when he arrived in the late afternoon. Emma is on Mr Knightley's ground [Abbey-Mill Farm is clearly close to Donwell Abbey], able to look both down to the farm and up to the Abbey. Perhaps the two are conflated in her idyllic vision (or maybe there was another damp-fearing hypochondriac living at the farm).

Professor Nicholas's acute observation is, I think, slightly favourable to my reading (although the 'conflated vision' hypothesis is beguiling). Clearly, fires are exceptional.

Another assault on my suggested reading came from an unexpected source—namely, an article in the scientific journal *Nature*. It was brought to my attention by Professor Judah, of the Department of Physiology at University College London. The article in question is by Euan Nisbet, a member of the Geology Department, Royal Holloway College, London. In his article Dr Nisbet correlates weather references in the text of *Emma* with data from an early nineteenth-century survey of the British weather, *The Climate of London* (1833), by Luke Howard. Howard's book is 'one of the founding texts of British meteorology'. On her part, Jane Austen, as Dr Nisbet notes, was 'an acute observer of the weather'—an amateur meteorologist, one might go so far as to say. *Emma* was written over 1814–15, and can plausibly be seen as accurately reflecting the weather conditions of that period, specifically those of summer 1814. As Dr Nisbet notes:

The crisis in the book occurs just before midsummer's day. Austen makes the fascinating observation of an 'orchard in blossom', her famous 'error'. What are apple trees doing in flower in mid-June? But is this error—or clue? The weather was unusual in 1814. The annual mean temperature was one of the coldest in Howard's record, and in May and June the means were colder than 1816, 'the year without a summer' after the eruption of the Tambora volcano in what is now Indonesia. In the cool spring of 1996, mild in comparison to 1814, apple trees flowered as late as early June . . . Is it presumptuous to attempt to match the weather to the novel? Possibly—an author has the light of imagination. But Austen is accurate. If she says the orchard was in bloom, then it surely was in bloom.[3]

This is very elegant research and, on the face of it, convincing. There are, however, some niggling objections to the hypothesis that Jane Austen is mirroring 1814's anomalous weather patterns in *Emma*. If it had been an unusually cold spring, one would expect some clue in the text such as 'orchards *still, even at this late time of year*, blossoming'. If Jane Austen were an acute meteorologist, she would surely offer some other incidental comment on the huge abnormality of the seasons. One also has to take into account that, internally, there are no references to a wintry spring elsewhere in Jane Austen's narrative, which covers a period of many months (in 1814, as Dr Nisbet would have us believe). There is snow at the Westons' Christmas party, which throws poor Mr Woodhouse into panic—but snow in December is not unexpected. In fact, as spring draws on the weather around Highbury seems generally clement. When Mr Weston reports that young Churchill is coming (it must be around March) he says:

'Frank comes to-morrow—I had a letter this morning—we see him to-morrow by dinner time to a certainty—he is at Oxford to-day, and he comes for a whole fortnight; I knew it would be so. If he had come at Christmas he could not have stayed three days; I was always glad he did not come at Christmas; now we are going to have just the right weather for him, fine, dry, settled weather. We shall enjoy him completely . . . ' (p. 168)

A couple of paragraphs later, we are informed:

Emma's spirits were mounted quite up to happiness. Every thing wore a different air; James [the coachman] and his horses seemed not half so sluggish as before. When she looked at the hedges, she thought the elder at least must soon be coming out; and when she turned round to Harriet, she saw something like a look of spring, a tender smile even there. (p. 169)

Elder is the most forward of the common English trees. Normally elder would come into leaf in late February or March, and into blossom in late April or May. There is nothing here to suggest retardation of this normal sequence of events. Indeed, if 'come out' means 'blossom', spring would seem to be early this year. And, of course, there are the strawberries. If the year were so behind as for blossom to be on the apple trees, the picnickers would have no strawberries to picnic on. Unless, that is, Frank Churchill did one of his mysterious trips to France.

Beguiling as the 'freezing 1814' thesis is, it is—on inspection—less than overwhelmingly persuasive. The balance of evidence seems to me still to warrant reading the 'orchards in blossom' sentence as a montage of the turning year rather than a snapshot. But, clearly, not everyone will be convinced.

The Oxford World's Classics *Emma* is edited by James Kinsley, with an introduction by Terry Castle.

Walter Scott · *Rob Roy*

How old is Frank?

Middle-aged readers will take heart from the fact that Walter Scott did not publish his first novel until the age of 43, with *Waverley* (1814). Once started, the Wizard of the North made up for lost time, writing eighteen novels in ten years. Churning out three- and four-deckers at his factory rate of production (and he did much else than write novels) meant that Scott was occasionally obliged to be rough and ready in the finer points of construction. His fiction is speckled with piddling errors for his pedantic editor ('Dr Dryasdust', as Scott called the genus) to clear up. On his part, Scott did not fret about his slips, seeing them as a small tax to be paid for his speed of composition.

Rob Roy (1817) has a lot of narrative errors: the hero crosses over an historically yet-to-be-built bridge to reach the inn at Aberfoil where so many exciting events occur; he attends an historically yet-to-be-built church in Glasgow; and reads yet-to-be-published books. One possible explanation is that the narrator's memory may not be all it once was. Old men forget, and they embellish what they dimly remember. This explanation would be more convincing, however, if we knew exactly what was going on in Frank's life as he tells his story, and how old he actually is. In fact, we have only the sketchiest portrait of the narrator in old age (if it is old age). We apprehend that he is telling the adventures of his early youth by letter to his friend Will Tresham, and that all ends happily with his marriage to Die Vernon. But since then, we gather, great sadness has supervened:

How I sped in my wooing, Will Tresham, I need not tell you. You know, too, how long and happily I lived with Diana. You know how I lamented her. But you do not—cannot know, how much she deserved her husband's sorrow. (p. 452)

This is tantalizing. Has Diana died? Has she run away? Fallen into madness? Why, after a long and happy marriage, should Frank feel such 'sorrow' for his departed wife—if she is indeed departed and was his wife. Are there children? The novel breaks off before offering any explanation, with the terse editorial statement: 'Here the original manuscript ends somewhat abruptly. I have reason to think that what followed related to private affairs' (p. 452).

It is all very baffling. Nor is it easy to work out exactly how ancient a man is talking to us, because the evidence points in a number of irreconcilable directions. In his opening comments Frank implies that he is very far gone in years. He is, he avers, in 'the decline of my life'; the narrative is offered to those 'who love to hear an old man's stories of a past age' (p. 65). The 'past age' is we may assume 1714–15, at which point Frank is 'some twenty years old'—born in 1694 or 1695, we can calculate.

But how old is the 'old man' now talking to us? Here again one encounters perplexing anachronism. On one side, a string of references date the narrator's 'now' as the 1770s, which would put Frank in his mid-eighties. On page 72, for example, he refers to Postlethwayte's *Universal Dictionary of Trade and Commerce* (1766) with a comment that indicates he knows the date of its publication. On page 89, Frank quotes from Adam Smith's *Wealth of Nations* (1776). Most precisely, on page 96 he observes, apropos of irresponsible politicians: 'We have seen recently the breath of a demagogue blow these sparks into a temporary flame, which I sincerely hope is now extinguished in its own ashes.' A footnote explains: 'This seems to have been written about the time of Wilkes and Liberty' (p. 461). Modern readers probably need to have it explained that the allusion is to the period 1762–8, when John Wilkes was most aggressive in his political provocations. The remark about 'now extinguished' must refer to Wilkes's expulsion from the House of Commons in 1769. All this points one way: Frank is narrating probably around 1770–5.

How, then, do we account for another footnoted passage, in Chapter 32 (p. 370), referring to the surprise attack by Rob Roy's caterans on the English horsemen under Captain Thornton? Scott observes: 'It was not indeed expected at that time, that Highlanders would attack cavalry in an open plain, though late events have shown that they may do so with success.' A footnote clarifies the allusion: 'The affairs of Prestonpans and Falkirk are probably alluded to, which marks the time of writing the Memoirs as subsequent to 1745' (p. 464). But it cannot be *long* after. The phrase 'late events' suggests that the 1745 battles (chronicled by Scott in *Waverley*) are recent, not more than a year or so since, one would guess. Certainly one would never say 'late events have shown' about something that happened thirty years ago.

Is Frank a quavering 80-year-old, writing in the 1770s? Or is he in his full-throated early fifties, writing around 1748? If we are to respond intelligently to the novel, we must 'hear' the narrator's voice, its timbre, tone, and strength. Age is a factor. Perhaps there are two layers of composition, one belonging to the 1740s, the other to the 1770s. But why, then, talk about 'the time of writing the Memoirs' as one time? Why, as in the other cases mentioned, highlight this awkward anomaly with a footnote which only serves to plunge the reader into gratuitous quandaries?

It would be plausible to argue, as an older school of commentators liked to, that *Rob Roy* is a hopelessly ramshackle piece of fiction with some wonderful moments and memorable characters. Or one might argue, as some modern critics have, that the flawed surface of *Rob Roy* is artful in the highest degree. Scott, that is, carefully inserted the errors into his novel as some Victorian geologists believed God put the fossils into the rocks.[1]

The explanation, in my view, lies between these extremes. Scott, as has been noted, wrote *Rob Roy* hurriedly. There was nothing exceptional about that; he wrote everything *currente calamo*. But *Rob Roy* faced other difficulties than the routine tight schedule. In March, a couple of months before signing the contract for his new novel, Scott had been taken ill with stomach cramps at a dinner party. He rose from the table with a scream of agony which electrified his guests, and for a few days seemed to be at death's door.

Over the next few months, as he embarked on *Rob Roy*, he remained ill and 'weak as water'. R. P. Gillies, who saw him in Edinburgh that summer, describes a living corpse, 'worn almost to a skeleton'. Scott told Gillies: 'the physicians tell me that mere pain cannot kill; but I am very sure that no man would, for another three months, encounter the same pain and live.'[2] The cramps (which turned out to be gallstones) continued into the autumn. Against the recurrent agony, Scott took dangerously large amounts of opium. But despite the devastating pain, and the dulling narcotics, he raced ahead with his novel in hand. The first volume of *Rob Roy* was finished in August, and the whole thing wrapped up by December. It was, as Scott told his friend and printer James Ballantyne with characteristic understatement, 'a tough job'.

What I suspect happened was that Scott, attacked as he was by pain and dulled by painkillers, slipped without noticing between his own age (47 in 1817) and Frank's putative four-score and more. Listening to *Rob Roy* we should school ourselves to hear an aged narrator but, every so often, allow the rich mellow tones of middle-aged Walter Scott (with their Lowland burr) to break through. How old is Frank? It's hard to say.

The Oxford World's Classics *Rob Roy* is edited by Ian Duncan.

Clachan of Aberfoyle[3]

Mary Shelley · *Frankenstein*

Why is the monster yellow?

Simon Levene writes wittily in response to *Is Heathcliff a Murderer?*, correcting an error and pointing out an unobserved other puzzle in *Frankenstein*:

without seeming ragingly pedantic, may I mention p. 27, where you refer to a 'metallic bolt' attaching [the monster's] head to its body? In fact, it is not a bolt but the ends of the electrodes through which the electricity flows into the monster. More to the point, why should Victor Frankenstein ever *construct* a body? Why wouldn't *one* body have done quite as well?

Mr Levene's 'one body' question sticks in the mind. After wrestling with it, I would offer two possible lines of explanation. The first is to be found in the epigraph from Milton's *Paradise Lost* (x. 743–5) on the novel's title-page:

> Did I request thee, Maker, from my clay
> To mould Me man? Did I solicit thee
> From darkness to promote me?—

As commentators have often noted, Mary Shelley's novel conforms closely to Milton's epic as source text. We are not shown how God creates Adam from his constituent clay. But it is quite clear how he creates that lesser order of creation, Eve. He takes a body-part—Adam's rib—and out of that *membrum* makes woman. This notion of making the whole new person out of the part(s) of another person is clearly alluded to in Mary Shelley's description of the scientist-hero's midnight raids: 'I collected bones from charnel houses; and disturbed, with profane fingers, the tremendous secrets of the human frame . . . The

dissecting room and the slaughter-house furnished many
of my materials' (pp. 36–7). Victor seems to be doing two
things here: investigating the anatomy of the 'human
frame' and assembling the wherewithal—the 'Adam's
ribs'—with which to compose such a frame.

The other objection to Victor's using an intact body
for his monster is theological. There are any number of
accounts of hanged criminals being taken down too soon,
and crossing back from death to life. Much fiction has built
itself around the conceit.[1] As Marilyn Butler notes in her
Oxford World's Classics edition of the 1818 text:

a number of well-known attempts had been made to induce life,
whether by animating single-cell creatures, such as body para-
sites, or by reviving dead bodies, including executed criminals.
Some of the best-known were associated with Luigi Galvani.
(p. 255)

The problem (for Mary Shelley) was that such back-
from-the-dead survivors—prisoners taken down prema-
turely from the gallows, for example—come back not as
newborn babes, but as their former selves. So too, if
Galvani had succeeded in reviving a dead body it would
have returned as its former self. Shelley wanted 'creation',
not 'resurrection'. It was necessary to dissolve the pre-
existing personalities (and by implication the multiple
'souls') of the bodies from whom the miscellaneous parts
were gathered.

Significantly, this is an area in which the archetypal
film version, that by James Whale in 1931, goes directly
against Mary Shelley's portrayal. The deformed servant,
Fritz, is shown breaking into the anatomy laboratory
to steal a brain, and—having accidentally dropped the
brain of a genius—takes instead that of a psychopathic
criminal (without telling his master). We are to assume
that traces of the criminal's previous criminality infect

the monster, although Whale does not follow up this line in the melodramatic middle and late sections of the film narrative.

It would be interesting to know how Mary Shelley imagined that a brain could be transplanted, without trailing clouds of the previous owner's character. She sidesteps the problem by artfully hazing over the description of how the monster is actually made. And she goes on to imply (without ever clearly asserting) that the monster is less a kind of physiological jigsaw man—assembled from bits and pieces gathered from hither and yon—than a culture *grown* from a soup, or distillate, extracted from all the *membra disjecta* Victor has assembled from his midnight raids. Wisely, perhaps, Mary Shelley does not go into detail about what goes on in Victor's 'filthy workshop' as, to their detriment, all film versions of *Frankenstein* have done.

Shelley does, however, go into some detail about the physical appearance of the newborn (newly assembled) monster:

It was already one in the morning; the rain pattered dismally against the panes, and my candle was nearly burnt out, when, by the glimmer of the half-extinguished light, I saw the *dull yellow eye* of the creature open; it breathed hard, and a convulsive motion agitated its limbs.

How can I describe my emotions at this catastrophe, or how delineate the wretch whom with such infinite pains and care I had endeavoured to form? His limbs were in proportion, and I had selected his features as beautiful. Beautiful!—Great God! *His yellow skin* scarcely covered the work of muscles and arteries beneath; his hair was of a lustrous black, and flowing; his teeth of a pearly whiteness; but these luxuriances only formed a more horrid contrast with his watery eyes, that seemed almost of the same colour as the *dun white sockets* in which they were set, his shrivelled complexion, and straight black lips. (pp. 38–9; my emphasis)

Jonathan Grossman raises an interesting query about this. 'Last semester' (i.e. winter 1997), he writes:

I heard Professor Anne Mellor (whose work I very much like) give an interesting talk about Frankenstein's monster as an 'Oriental' menace. The problem with the argument was that it rested wholly on the thinnest of evidence: the creature's infamous yellow eyes and yellow skin. It seems to me a long way from these yellow eyes and yellow skin to the 'Yellow Peril'. How does one build an Asian body out of the corpses of Europeans?

I tend to agree with Professor Grossman—thought-provoking as Professor Mellor's thesis is. But, as Grossman says, the yellow eyes are perplexing. He pursues the problem, arguing that we should not assume 'that the irises themselves are a cat-like yellow'. As he confesses, Victor has raided slaughterhouses in his midnight expeditions. But it is extremely unlikely (unless he ventured as far afield as Korea, which would give substance to the Yellow Peril hypothesis) that he found cats' heads in the local shambles or butcher-shop. We assume, therefore, that it is the 'whites' of the monster's eyes which are yellow—or 'dun white'.

Grossman concludes that 'the poor creature is born with jaundice.' He called up a doctor friend, who confirmed that 'the whites of the eyes as well as the skin do turn yellow and that it is one of the main signs of jaundice. Diagnosis: a liver condition? Bad liver transplant?'

There is a persuasive biographical explanation for the yellow monster being jaundiced. As commentators (particularly feminist commentators) have noted, the creation scene in *Frankenstein*, and the concomitant disgust of Victor for his creation, can be read as an allegory of post-natal shock and depression. In February 1815 Mary Wollstonecraft, aged 17, gave premature birth to a daughter—Clara—who died a few days later; of what, we do not know. In January 1816 she gave birth to a son, William. Mary and Percy Shelley did not marry until December 1816. While she was completing *Frankenstein* in May 1817 Mary was pregnant with her third child. She knew about natal depression and was familiar with the physical appearance of newborn children.

Jaundice is a very common and (to the mother's eye) alarming condition in newborn babies. One (or both) of Mary's children may well, one assumes, have been born with it, possibly fatally in Clara's case. Interestingly, no later references seem to be made to the monster's having a yellow skin or eyes. He is 'ugly' and 'loathsome', but not—as far as we know—'yellow'.

The Oxford World's Classics *Frankenstein* is edited by Marilyn Butler.

===

Does Dickens lynch Fagin?

===

The above title might be rephrased: 'Does Dickens *lynch* Fagin? or is "the Jew" executed fairly, after due process of law?' In *Can Jane Eyre Be Happy?* I pointed to what struck me as a number of oddities in the trial which climaxes *Oliver Twist*. Specifically:

(1) We are never distinctly told what offence (let alone what capital crime) Fagin has committed.

(2) Dickens gives no direct description of the court proceedings, focusing instead (with great literary effect) on Fagin's distracted reactions.

(3) By the best judgement we can make, Fagin is convicted on 'conspiracy' to murder Nancy, or 'complicity' in that murder (which is in fact committed, without Fagin's knowledge, by Bill Sikes). Fagin himself had nothing to do with the deed, told no lies to Bill Sikes who *did*, most brutally, commit the murder, and is—apparently—sent to the gallows on the perjurious evidence of Noah Claypole.

(4) As a petty criminal, bent on saving his own skin, Claypole's testimony would seem self-evidently tainted. 'A good defence counsel', I wrote, 'could discredit him very easily.'

(5) The trial takes place on Friday. As soon as the verdict is announced, before sentence is passed, the crowd outside the courtroom utter 'a peal of joy . . . greeting the news that he would die on Monday'. This is disquieting: 'Two weekend days would hardly seem to give the remotest chance of the appeal to which Fagin surely has a right. And how does the crowd outside *know* that Fagin will be hanged on Monday, before the judge has put on his black cap and pronounced sentence? Are they deciding the matter? Is the bigwig judge dancing to the mob's savage tune?'[1]

The whole process was, I suggested, a legal lynching; Fagin ('the Jew') is railroaded to the gallows because the mob—infuriated by accounts of the inquest in the press—has been denied revenge on Sikes and wants a scapegoat to satiate its appetite for blood: 'Jewish blood?—so much the better!'. Injustice was done. Fagin should certainly have been transported, or imprisoned: he is a criminal.[2] But hanging seems vindictive and racially motivated.

A number of readers wrote to point out that there is, in fact, a clear premonition of the charge Fagin will be brought up on and its inevitable outcome. Donald Hawes directed my attention to Kags's forecast in Chapter 50: 'if they get the inquest over, and Bolter [i.e. Claypole] turns King's evidence: as of course he will, for what he's said already: they can prove Fagin an accessory before the fact, and get the trial on Friday, and he'll swing in six days from this, by G—!' (p. 322). Professor Hawes adds: 'George Saintsbury (in his chapter on Dickens in the *Cambridge History of English Literature*) quotes G. S. Venables: Dickens hanged Fagin for being the villain of a novel.'

Missing Kags's prediction is a culpable oversight but does not, I think, invalidate the main points about the unfairness of the legal process which Dickens describes. A letter from Andrew Lewis, Senior Lecturer in Laws at University College London, did, however, hole my arguments below the waterline. His letter is so interesting (and informative) that I will quote it at length. 'Dear Professor Sutherland,' Mr Lewis began:

I hope you will forgive the following mixture of comment, query and sheer impudence from a colleague. I have just been reading, as holiday pleasure, your latest Puzzles in Literary Fiction and cannot forbear to add to the perils of the terrible meshes of the law!

In your chapter on Fagin you seem to me to fall into

error regarding the management of criminal trials in the mid-nineteenth century. You are surely right that it is for the murder of Nancy that we are to suppose that Fagin is tried, though for inciting rather than conspiracy, and so as a principal. You are wrong to think that he could not be an accomplice, legally-speaking. The penalty for this was death by hanging and was, as now with life imprisonment, fixed by law, giving the judge no option but to pass sentence of death. It is for this reason that the crowd outside can anticipate the sentence on hearing of the verdict.

The judge had no option to sentence to death for murder and no control over the timing of the execution unless he ordered a respite. There were no appeals from criminal convictions before 1907—though a judge could refer a case to higher authority if he were troubled by a result. Fagin therefore has no prospect of such a hearing. He could seek a royal pardon, but again these requests were normally channelled through the judge. The judge shares our prejudices against Fagin and has no cause to postpone giving sentence and no reason to order a respite of execution. Execution will therefore proceed as normal at the conclusion of the current court sittings: we are to suppose therefore that Fagin's is the last trial in the current session which will end on Friday or Saturday—courts sat on Saturdays in the nineteenth century. Execution of sentences will commence on the next weekday, the date of which will have been known well in advance, not least to those in the crowd intending to view the scene.

There are two other incidental problems with your account. You suppose that Fagin could argue 'in his defence' that he never expressly mentioned Nancy's informing on Bill. As noted above, even if demonstrated this seems irrelevant on a charge that he incited Bill to kill her. But in any case prisoners were barred from giving evidence in their own behalf before 1898. They were allowed to make unsworn statements from the dock but it can be assumed that these carried little weight. Moreover before 1836 those accused of felony were not allowed counsel except to argue legal points. There is plenty of evidence that this provision was frequently ignored in practice, even in the Old Bailey, but barristers had to be paid and we cannot discount the possibility that Dickens intends us to understand that the wicked old Jew is being deprived, quite lawfully, of even such protection as a 'good defence counsel'.

This comprehensively contradicts the case I was making. More importantly, however, it vindicates Dickens's accuracy. The novel is, I think, much stronger for Mr Lewis's expert commentary. There was, however, a related puzzle which seemed to complicate Lewis's explanation. Dickens's *A Tale of Two Cities* has in its early chapters a vividly described criminal trial, again at the Old Bailey. It is a 'Treason Case', prosecuted by the Attorney-General, for which the penalty at this period (the late eighteenth century) is 'quartering'. As one of the vulturous spectators tells Jerry Cruncher:

'he'll be drawn on a hurdle to be half hanged, and then he'll be taken down and sliced before his own face, and then his inside will be taken out and burnt while he looks on, and then his head will be chopped off, and he'll be cut into quarters. That's the sentence.'

'If he's found Guilty, you mean to say?' Jerry added, by way of proviso.

'Oh! they'll find him guilty,' said the other. 'Don't you be afraid of that.' (p. 70)

But Charles Darnay is not found guilty of being a French spy. He is saved by his resourceful defence team, Messrs Carton and Stryver. By cross-examination of the (suborned) witness, Stryver gets him to admit he could not tell the difference between Darnay and Stryver's learned friend, Mr Carton. Therefore the identification of Darnay as the man who committed the alleged act of espionage is invalid. 'The upshot . . . was, to smash this witness like a crockery vessel, and shiver his part of the case to useless lumber' (p. 86). Darnay is duly acquitted. Now it is quite clear that in this case at the Old Bailey, the same court where Fagin will be tried in fifty or so years time, the prisoner most certainly *does* have a defence counsel. And that counsel can demonstrably cross-examine witnesses aggressively and to great effect. If Darnay can be saved from quartering by his resourceful defence counsel, why can't Fagin be saved from hanging?

I put this apparent anomaly to Andrew Lewis. Again, however, I had underestimated the meshes of the law. 'Dear Professor Sutherland,' he replied:

I am currently down in Cornwall so do not have a *Tale of Two Cities* with me. However from what you say about the charge against Carton it is probably Treason. For this (more serious) category of crime counsel seemed always to have been allowed (as they were in cases of misdemeanour). No one seems to have a satisfactory explanation for this apparent anomaly.

What one deduces from this is that, where the law was concerned, Dickens was more historically accurate than a modern reader may appreciate. And where the law itself was not consistent, or even 'an ass' (as in the anomaly about prisoners not being able to testify in their own defence), Dickens faithfully followed its idiocies.

The Oxford World's Classics *Oliver Twist* is edited by Kathleen Tillotson. The Oxford World's Classics *A Tale of Two Cities* is edited by Andrew Sanders.

===

How do the Cratchits cook Scrooge's turkey?

===

At Christmas 1997 I set ten puzzles from Dickens's *Christmas Carol* for the readers of *The Sunday Telegraph*, offering a small prize (a 'shiny half-crown') for the best answers. The puzzles were:

1. In what sense is it a 'carol'? (even with the *sotto voce* addition 'in prose').

2. We are told that Scrooge is 'an excellent man of business'; what business?

3. How can Scrooge run his 'firm' (as it is called in the fifth stave) with just one, 15s. a week, clerk?

4. When Scrooge goes to his 'empty house' on Christmas Eve, there is 'a small fire in the grate; spoon and basin ready; and the little saucepan (Scrooge had a cold in his head) upon the hob'. Who has lit his fire and prepared his supper? The house is clearly deserted when the ghost of Marley appears—otherwise Scrooge's first act would be to ring for his servant.

5. What happens to the destitute woman and child collapsed opposite Scrooge's house in the small hours of the morning. The 1951 Alistair Sim-starring film gets round the problem by having her expire during the night. Which means that we should visualize a regenerate Scrooge blithely ordering his turkey from the 'clever boy' across two corpses. Dickens says nothing more of her. Has she, like Jo in *Bleak House*, been 'moved on'? Or was she, like the 'wandering spirits', visionary?

6. At the end of 'Stave One' and his interview with Marley's ghost, we are told that Scrooge 'went straight to bed, without undressing, and fell asleep upon the instant'. But when he awakes in 'Stave Two' he is 'clad but slightly in his slippers,

dressing-gown, and nightcap'. When did he undress?

7. It is 'past two' (on Christmas morning, presumably) when Scrooge falls asleep. He wakes up on the stroke of twelve, for his encounter with the Spirit of Christmas Past. Is it Boxing Day, or has the interview with Jacob Marley (which took place between midnight and two) never happened?

8. The Spirit of Christmas Past takes Scrooge back to critical moments in his former life. Why cannot he 'do a Marley' and tell his younger self to mend his ways. If he did so would he, Scrooge as we know him, be erased?

9. The Spirit of Christmas Present allows Ebenezer to eavesdrop on the Christmas parties—those of the Cratchits, and of his nephew Fred and his wife. But, after his regeneration, these parties will be very different (Scrooge will physically attend Fred's, and Bob's will be dominated by the mysterious turkey). The vision of 'Christmas Present' is, in the event, not that. Nor is it Christmas Past, nor Christmas future. Is it then, Christmas Might-Have-Been? Where in time is it?

10. In 'Christmas yet to Come' we foresee two deaths the following Christmas: Tiny Tim's (who is dead and about to be buried) and Scrooge's (who dies and is laid out on Christmas Eve). The postscript tells us specifically, that 'Tiny Tim did NOT die'— presumably thanks to Scrooge's providing expensive medical treatment. Will Scrooge die next Christmas, at the 'appointed' date?

I received a number of ingenious solutions to these puzzles. Many more than I had half-crowns. It was generally agreed that Scrooge must be a moneylender. The principle evidence is the exchange between husband and wife in 'Stave Four', when they anxiously enquire between themselves to whom their debt will be transferred, and the husband says: 'I don't know. But before that time we shall be ready with the money and even though we were not it would be bad fortune indeed to find so merciless a creditor in his successor' (p. 78). The 'time puzzles' were explained in terms of Scrooge's observation 'The Spirits have done it all in one night. They can do anything they like'—so, therefore, can Dickens the narrator do anything he likes with chronology. As for the midnight change of dress, it was suggested that, as old men with grumbling prostates do, Scrooge got up during the night. The preparation of Scrooge's gruel was probably the work of the slatternly laundress who is described gloating over the old miser's death in the last stave. She evidently comes in for a few hours each day and leaves before her employer returns from work. Tiny Tim will not die, it was agreed. Nor would Scrooge die next Christmas, on the basis of the remark in the last paragraph: 'it was *always* said of him, that he knew how to keep Christmas well' (my emphasis). That 'always' prophesies that Scrooge will be around for many years to come.

The most delightful and comprehensive set of answers came from Class 7E (aged 10 to 11) of St Christopher's School, Isa Town, in the State of Bahrain. Their English teacher, Mrs G. M. G. Stevenson, set the puzzles as a class assignment on her pupils' return from the Christmas Holiday. I would have disbursed a sack of half-crowns, if I'd had them, for Class 7E. I was particularly taken by a 'puzzle for you', from Anna Jordan, Jessica Salah, and Lily Constantine (see overleaf; the relevant pages in the Oxford World's Classics edition are 85–7).

Children often read adult novels in very rational ways. There is, I think, a thought-provoking puzzle here. Scrooge awakes at the beginning of Stave Five in his own bed. The sun is pouring into his bedroom and the church bells ('Clash, clang, hammer; ding, dong, bell. Bell, dong, ding; hammer, clang, clash!') are calling the London faithful to prayer. It is, presumably, eleven o'clock in the morning. Scrooge calls out from his window to the 'remarkable boy', and sends him off for the huge prize turkey ('it's twice the size of Tiny Tim').

Now we have a question for you!

On page 82-84 New Windmill Edition
Scrooge sends the prize turkey to Bob Cratchit's
house. However the turkey was unplucked &
uncooked, so how on earth did they manage to
cook it in time for Christmas lunch?

By our estimation, to prepare a turkey it
takes at least 1 hour to pluck, 1 hour to clean and
stuff and in the case of a very large turkey, 8
hours to cook - a total of 10 hours. In any case,
would they have a big enough oven to cook it in?

SIGNED,

Anna Jordan
Jessica Salah
Lily Constantine
and
the sleuths of 7E
ST.CHRISTOPHER'S SCHOOL
BAHRAIN

We may wonder that a butcher's will be open at this hour on Christmas Day—and that the turkey should still be unsold. But open the shop is, and unsold the bird is. Scrooge sends the turkey off, by cab, to Camden Town. The poulterer's man is not, apparently, instructed to say that the bird comes from an anonymous donor. And he must know who is paying for it, or at least where the purchaser lives. But it is quite clear from Bob's demeanour the next day that he does not know that the turkey came from Scrooge. Another mystery. Did the Cratchits not think to ask about their mysterious benefactor? Do vast turkeys arrive at their door every holiday?

The turkey will not arrive much before noon. Scrooge does not go to the Cratchits for dinner—but to his nephew Fred's. Fred and his wife have their Christmas dinner at a 'civilized' hour, 'in the afternoon'. Unless they have a taste for raw poultry the Cratchits, as the sleuths of Class 7E point out, have many hours' preparation ahead of them. It is hard to think that they will be able to sit down at table until the small hours of the morning.

But, if we read carefully, this seems to be Scrooge's plan. As we are told:

But he was early at the office next morning. Oh, he was early there. If he could only be there first, and catch Bob Cratchit coming late! That was the thing he had set his heart upon.

And he did it: yes, he did! The clock struck nine. No Bob. A quarter past. No Bob. He was full eighteen minutes and a half behind his time. (p. 89)

Scrooge remembers that, in return for getting Christmas Day off, Bob undertook to be at work 'all the earlier next morning' (Boxing Day). And here he is fully eighteen-and-a-half minutes late. How did Scrooge know that Bob, as presumably he never is (otherwise he would be out of a job), would be late on this day of all days? Because Scrooge knew that the Cratchits would be up till all hours of the morning cooking that monstrous turkey. Scrooge, that is to say, may have undergone a dramatic change of heart. He may even have become the most un-Scrooge-like philanthropist. But he has not become a fool, nor has he lost all his malice—even though it now takes the form of malicious gamesomeness. Bob Cratchit's life in the office will not necessarily be a bed of roses henceforth.

The Oxford World's Classics volume of Dickens's *Christmas Books* is edited by Ruth Glancy.

===

How many siblings has Dobbin?

===

In a late 'Roundabout Paper' Thackeray makes a charming *mea culpa* on the subject of his propensity to small narrative error:

I pray gentle readers to deal kindly with their humble servant's manifold shortcomings, blunders, and slips of memory. As sure as I read a page of my own composition, I find a fault or two, half-a-dozen. Jones is called Brown. Brown, who is dead, is brought to life. Aghast, and months after the number was printed, I saw that I had called Philip Firmin, Clive Newcome. Now Clive Newcome is the hero of another story by the reader's most obedient writer. The two men are as different in my mind's eye, as—as Lord Palmerston and Mr Disraeli let us say. But there is that blunder at page 990, line 76, volume 84 of the *Cornhill Magazine*, and it is past mending; and I wish in my life I had made no worse blunders or errors than that which is hereby acknowledged.[1]

It is uncivil of the reader to dwell upon these little slips. George Saintsbury, noting Thackeray's tendency to misquote from memory, is even in two minds as to whether the conscientious editor should correct such errors. Saintsbury, in his authoritative 'Oxford' edition of the collected works, decided not to for the good reason that, as he says, Thackeray's misquotations are usually improvements—improvements, that is, on such sources as Horace, Shakespeare, or the Bible (Saintsbury had a high opinion of his author).

Thackeray's slips of name or detail cannot be said to be improvements of this kind, but they often witness to the suppleness of his narrative and his serialist's quick wits.

It is to catch in motion this agility in Thackeray that I want to follow the inconsistent line indicated in the above title. Put another way, what happens to Dobbin's siblings, and why?

Of the five principal characters in *Vanity Fair*, we know a lot about the family backgrounds of the Sedleys, the Osbornes, and the Crawleys. We know tantalizingly little about Becky's (unrespectable) and Dobbin's (respectable) families. It is with the Dobbins that I shall be concerned here. One can assemble a patchy family history, but it needs putting together from clues, hints, and circumstantial evidence. And there remain, after all the evidence is assembled, some teasing holes.

William Dobbin is introduced in Chapter 5 of *Vanity Fair* in a showcase chapter, 'Dobbin of Ours' ('Ours' being military slang for his regiment).[2] We know, from manuscript evidence, that the idea of Dobbin, as George Osborne's *fidus Achates*, came late during Thackeray's five-year-long meditation of his 'novel without a hero'. In a flashback to William's and George's schooldays at 'Dr Swishtail's Academy' we learn about the respective backgrounds of these two 'not heroes'—one the embodiment of snobbishness, the other of good-hearted clumsiness. It is the early years of the nineteenth century (1801–2, as we can deduce). Osborne, the younger boy by a year or two, is a merchant's son. Dobbin is horribly bullied by his schoolfellows at Dr Swishtail's when it is discovered (after young Osborne 'sneaks' on him) that his father is a grocer. His 'nobler' schoolfellows tease the tradesman's son—whom they nickname 'Figs'—mercilessly. Not only is Mr Dobbin a grocer, he is—we deduce—a penurious grocer:

it was bruited abroad that [Dobbin] was admitted into Dr. Swishtail's academy upon what are called 'mutual principles'—that is to say, the expenses of his board and schooling were defrayed by his father in goods, not money; and he stood there—

almost at the bottom of the school—in his scraggy corduroys
and jacket, through the seams of which his great big bones
were bursting—as the representative of so many pounds of
teas, candles, sugar, mottled-soap, plums (of which a very mild
proportion was supplied for the puddings of the establishment),
and other commodities. A dreadful day it was for young Dobbin
when one of the youngsters of the school [Osborne], having
run into the town upon a poaching excursion for hardbake and
polonies, espied the cart of Dobbin & Rudge, Grocers and Oilmen,
Thames Street, London, at the doctor's door, discharging a cargo
of the wares in which the firm dealt. (p. 48)

A crisis comes in Dobbin's schoolboy life when he is writing
a letter to his mother, 'who was fond of him, although she
was a grocer's wife, and lived in a back parlour in Thames
Street'. Cuff, the school 'cock', insults 'old mother Figs',
provoking the great fight in which, to everyone's surprise,
'Figs' licks his opponent and his fortunes rise.

We jump forward to 1813. It seems that William Dobbin
Sr.'s fortunes have risen even more precipitately than
those of his son. George is now a lieutenant, and the
slightly older Dobbin a captain, in a regiment of the line
('Ours'). George visits the house of his sweetheart, Amelia
Sedley, and the subject of his inseparable comrade (and
slavish admirer) Dobbin comes up. As usual, the company
jeers. Dobbin has a lisp, big feet, and awkward manners.
They recall an event, seven years ago, when he 'broke the
punch-bowl at the child's party'. 'What a gawky it was!',
Mrs Sedley recalls, 'good naturedly':

'and his sisters are not much more graceful. Lady Dobbin was at
Highbury last night with three of them. Such figures, my dears.'
'The Alderman's very rich, isn't he?' Osborne said archly. 'Don't
you think one of the daughters would be a good spec for me,
ma'am?'
'You foolish creature! Who would take *you*, I should like to
know, with your yellow face? [He is just back from service in

the malarial West Indies.] And what can Alderman Dobbin leave
among fourteen?' (p. 57; see also note, p. 892)

The 'fourteen children' reference was published in the
first serial version of *Vanity Fair*. Subsequent editions
remove it.[3] Mrs Sedley's 'three daughters' reference (with
the implication that there are many more than 'three of
them') was let stand, although it does not fit with what
follows later in the narrative.

We may note in passing that the 'fourteen children'
reference identifies the Dobbins as a lower-class kind of
people. Genteel middle-class families like the Osbornes
(who have three children) and the Sedleys (who have two)
practised decent restraint—possibly even some primitive
form of birth control. It was only the socially undisciplined
lower classes who bred like rabbits.

None the less, it would seem that the Dobbins have in
a very short time risen meteorically in the world since
those black days when 'Figs' was the butt of schoolboy
humour at Swishtail's. Even with fourteen children to
look after, 'Sir William Dobbin' still has enough to buy
his son a commission in 'Ours'. Army commissions were
expensive commodities in the early nineteenth century—
it could have cost the Alderman up to £5,000 to make his
son a captain.

From the coincidence of names we assume that William
is the oldest son and, in the nature of things, favoured.
English primogeniture will assure him the lion's share of
his father's fortune eventually—and clearly Dobbin *père*
will cut up extremely well. But one recalls that the grocer,
partner of the mysterious Rudge, could not even afford
Dr Swishtail's modest school fees. A parenthetic history of
Dobbin Sr.'s rise is given on page 59:

Dobbin, the despised grocer, was Alderman Dobbin—Alderman
Dobbin was Colonel of the City Light Horse, then burning with

military ardour to resist the French Invasion. Colonel Dobbin's corps, in which old Mr. Osborne himself was but an indifferent corporal, had been reviewed by the Sovereign and the Duke of York; and the colonel and alderman had been knighted.

He is a 'Colonel', not on the basis of any military prowess, but because he is paying for all the men's uniforms, steeds, and equipment.

Where has the Dobbin money come from? And how has 'Sir William' enriched himself so quickly? Not, surely, from rice, dried figs, and sugar. Fortunes were made in provisions—but not rapid fortunes. The key, I suspect, is that Dobbin and Rudge, as we are informed, dealt in 'oil'; and their premises in Thames Street were conveniently close to where the freighters carrying it would unload. In his description of the London background to George and Amelia's wedding, the narrator mentions the revolutionary changes in street-lighting which were taking place in the early years of the century (see p. 262). The first, and temporary, breakthrough was whale-oil street-lamps. In 1807 the 'New Patriotic Imperial and National Light and Heat Company' demonstrated the glories of coal-gas lighting in Pall Mall. This inspired a huge boom (although gas, as a source of lighting, was not introduced into homes for many years). We may assume that Dobbin & Rudge got in on the street-lighting boom early—initially as suppliers of whale oil.

Whatever the source of their sudden wealth, the Dobbin family is now middle class—if rather uneasily so. Thackeray duly subjects them to a little behind-the-scenes *embourgeoisement* himself. From subsequent passing references we deduce that Dobbin now has two (not three or more) unmarried sisters. On page 218 (Chapter 18) we learn their names: Miss Ann (the elder, apparently) and Miss Jane. There are, apparently, no married Dobbin sisters or brothers.

What happened to the other eleven children? Has some
awful plague swept through Thames Street? One assumes
that they have gone the same way as Dobbin's lisp and his
big feet. Thackeray, as he penned the early chapters, saw
a rather more dignified narrative future for William. As
part of this 'dignifying' process, the rabbit-sized brood of
Dobbins was thinned down to a genteel three offspring.

The Misses Dobbin are spiteful about the long-suffering
Amelia (currently being neglected by George), and Dobbin
jumps down their throats: 'You're the wit of the family,'
he bitterly tells Ann (who has archly suggested that he
should offer for Miss Sedley), 'and the others like to hear
it.' That phrase, 'the others', suggests that some of those
fourteen Dobbins have survived Thackeray's slaughter of
the innocents. Who are they? Apart from Jane (whose
name Thackeray seems to forget—he never mentions it
again) we never know.

In Chapter 35 Sir William Dobbin makes his only direct
appearance in the action when, at his son's request,
he calls on Mr Osborne to try and soften the brutish
merchant's attitude towards the just-widowed Amelia, his
daughter-in-law. There are no physical details given—but
we assume, from the act itself, that he is a considerate
man. During his long years in India, Major Dobbin (the
promotion must have been another expensive purchase)
keeps in touch by letter with his 'two' sisters—both
still unmarried. Ann—the 'clever' one—is his principal
correspondent.

At Dobbin's instruction the Misses Dobbin (now forty-
something genteel old-maids) call on Amelia in their
splendid 'family carriage' and take young Georgy off to
their 'fine garden-house at Denmark Hill, where they
lived, and where there were such fine grapes in the hot-
houses and peaches on the walls'. Later this establishment
is called 'Sir William's suburban estate' (p. 762). It is

evidently very grand—much grander than the Osborne town-house in Russell Square. Denmark Hill, south of the Thames, was very much in the country at this point. It was a favourite residential area for tradesmen who had struck it very rich. Ruskin's family (John Ruskin Sr. had made *his* money in sherry) resided there, and the author gives a vivid description of the bucolic beauties of the place in the early chapters of his autobiography, *Praeterita*. It is pleasant to think of Sir William Dobbin raising his hat to Mr and Mrs John Ruskin when their carriages crossed paths at Camberwell Green.

The grown-up Dobbin does not, apparently, write to his mother. We assume that Lady Dobbin—who was fond of her boy at Dr Swishtail's when nobody else was—is a poor penwoman. Possibly she worked in the Dobbin & Rudge establishment as a servant, or perhaps she was Rudge's daughter. A later reference to the plural 'parents' (whom he does not immediately visit on his return from India, in his haste to get to Amelia, see p. 748) indicates that Mrs Dobbin is still alive in the early 1820s. The Misses Dobbin remain as spiteful in middle age as they were in youth. Ann (p. 550) maliciously informs Amelia that Dobbin is going to marry the irresistible Glorvina. Ann also maliciously writes to Dobbin to tell him that Amelia is about to marry the Revd Mr Binney. This bombshell it is which brings Dobbin back post-haste from India to England.

Apart from one interesting reference (which I shall come to later), the Dobbin family fades into the background over the next ten years of Thackeray's panoramic narrative. When he returns to England, as has been noted, Dobbin on his first visit to Amelia, 'did not like to own [to Amelia] that he had not as yet been to his parents' and his dear sister Anne'. 'Ann' has become 'Anne' (Thackeray's gremlin strikes again)—but what has become of Jane? Surely she is too far gone in age to have found a husband? And only a few months earlier, the 'Misses Dobbin' were visiting Amelia. Has Jane Dobbin suddenly died? Was it this that William gave as his excuse to Colonel O'Dowd for rushing back to England?

In his will Osborne leaves Dobbin, in recognition of his many years of support of Amelia and her son, 'such a sum as may be sufficient to purchase his commission as a lieutenant-colonel'. Dobbin, however, is obliged to wait until a vacant colonelcy comes up. He is still a major during the Pumpernickel episode, a few months later. Finally, on page 862, he gets the promotion after he has given up his allegiance to Amelia and returned to active service: 'I'll go into harness again,' he thinks, 'and do my duty in that state of life in which it has pleased Heaven to place me . . . When I am old and broke, I will go on half-pay, and my old sisters shall scold me' (p. 863). One notes that Colonel Dobbin has *sisters* (not just Ann) again.

Why, one wonders in passing, cannot Sir William buy Major William his promotion to lieutenant-colonel? Too much is happening, however, for the reader to dwell on such tangential questions. There is the tremendous reconciliation between Dobbin and Amelia ('God bless you, honest William!—Farewell, dear Amelia—Grow green again, tender little parasite, round the rugged old oak to which you cling!', p. 871). Amelia is now rich with her Osborne bequest.

Dobbin duly retires and has his half-pay pension. He is—as we deduce—the oldest son and principal heir of a very rich London merchant. Between them, Colonel and Mrs Amelia Dobbin should be very 'warm' indeed. But Colonel and Mrs Dobbin do not live like excessively wealthy people. 'When Colonel Dobbin quitted the service,' we are told:

which he did immediately after his marriage, he rented a pretty little country place in Hampshire, not far from Queen's Crawley . . . Lady Jane and Mrs. Dobbin became great friends—there was a perpetual crossing of pony-chaises between the Hall and the Evergreens, the colonel's place (rented of his friend Major Ponto, who was abroad with his family). (p. 872)

The Dobbins seem well off, but not excessively so. They rent, but do not buy a house. If he were Croesus-rich, Dobbin would surely go into politics. Instead of which, he buries himself in the country, in a house which is not his own, writing a history of the Punjab.

What, one may idly wonder, has happened to all Sir William's wealth? A possible, if hypothetical, explanation may be found in the narrative's most tantalizing reference to the Dobbin family. It occurs in Chapter 46, ('Struggles and Trials'), during the period of Dobbin's long Indian exile—around 1825 in historical time. Amelia is still living in poverty at Fulham, but has not yet surrendered Georgy to his grandfather. The Dobbin ladies, at William's instruction, are being kind to the impoverished widow. They particularly want little George to visit them at Denmark Hill. Amelia suspects (correctly) that the Misses Dobbin have been conspiring with Miss Osborne and George's grandfather:

Of late, the Miss Dobbins more than once repeated their entreaties to Amelia, to allow George to visit them . . . Surely, Amelia could not refuse such advantageous chances for the boy. Nor could she: but she acceded to their overtures with a very heavy and suspicious heart, was always uneasy during the child's absence from her, and welcomed him back as if he was rescued out of some danger. He brought back money and toys, at which the widow looked with alarm and jealousy: she asked him always if he had seen any gentlemen—'Only old Sir William, who drove him about in the four-wheeled chaise, and Mr. Dobbin, who arrived on the beautiful bay horse in the afternoon—in the green coat

and pink neckcloth, with the gold-headed whip, who promised to
show him the Tower of London, and take him out with the Surrey
Hounds.' (p. 583)

Mr Osborne ('an old gentleman, with thick eyebrows,
and a broad hat, and large chain and seals') is also
lurking around, Amelia discovers—scheming to abduct
Amelia's boy. But it is the Dobbins who attract the reader's
attention. Sir William, of course, is the former alderman,
Dobbin's father. He is still *nouveau riche* enough to be
delighted with his four-wheeled chaise. But who—one
wonders—is this dashing 'Mr Dobbin' with the colourful
clothes, the bay horse, and the gold-headed whip?

It is, one has to assume, one of Sir William's offspring
and—by the look of things—a prodigal son. William
Dobbin (as Thackeray's illustrations make clear) is no
model of fashion:

A fine Summer Evening

This newly introduced 'Mr Dobbin' is, we assume a scapegrace younger brother: one who dresses like a 'swell', adorns himself with expensive jewellery, and rides to hounds in neighbouring Surrey. He presumably works in his father's firm ('Dobbin and Son'). Why did Thackeray insert a passing reference to this dandy brother so late in the narrative? He could, of course, be a ghostly survivor from the horde of fourteen which has been so ruthlessly culled. But 'Mr Dobbin' is so sharply etched here that one feels Thackeray must have had a role—or a potential role—for him to play. This is late in the narrative; Thackeray had lived with his 'people' for more than a year. Why add at this stage to his dramatis personae?

One knows that Thackeray was in some doubt as to how to wind up his story; whether, for example, to conclude in eighteen or expand to twenty numbers. In fact, he and his publishers decided on twenty instalments, and Thackeray devised the Pumpernickel interlude to create the necessary extension. One is very glad he did so; it is a delightful excursion. What Thackeray also held in reserve, I suspect, was a never-written (but there if needed) subplot in which Sir William Dobbin's business was to be ruined (as, in the event, Jos Sedley is ruined in the last pages, as was his father before him).

In this unwritten turn of plot, The 'dandy Mr Dobbin', scapegrace that he was, would take over the family firm, on the death or retirement of Sir William and ruin it. Amelia would take Colonel Dobbin not as a rich, but as a poor man—thus atoning for her 'selfishness' over the years, and repaying his kindness when *she* was penniless.

If he intended to follow this line, Thackeray in the event decided differently. The dandy Mr Dobbin never reappears after his one dashing entrance. Georgy never gets his visit to the Tower of London, nor his gallop with the Surrey hounds. It tingles, rather like a phantom narrative limb.

One would like to have seen more of the dashing Dobbin younger brother, cutting a swathe through the family fortune so virtuously acquired by his father.

The Oxford World's Classics *Vanity Fair* is edited by John Sutherland.

Georgy a Gentleman

Emily Brontë · *Wuthering Heights*

═══

Heathcliff's toothbrush

═══

Judged purely by his actions Heathcliff is a villain: a wife-beater, a child-abuser, a white-collar thief, and—as I would maintain—a murderer. The murder, moreover, is a peculiarly sordid and cold-blooded crime. None the less readers, even those who accept that he probably killed his foster-brother Hindley, persist in seeing Heathcliff as a heroic and tragic figure. There is no obvious clash when glamorous matinée idols like Laurence Olivier and Timothy Dalton, or paragons of showbiz Christianity like Cliff Richard, play him on film, television, or stage.

An explanation for this 'sympathy for the devil' paradox is to be found in a muttered ejaculation of Heathcliff's, overheard by Nelly in the intensity of his grief and sexual frustration after Cathy's death: 'I have no pity! I have no pity! The [more the] worms writhe, the more I yearn to crush out their entrails! It is *a moral teething*, and I grind with greater energy, in proportion to the increase of pain' (p. 152; my italics). The key to our sympathy for Heathcliff, I have suggested, is to be found in that arresting phrase, 'moral teething', and what it implies— particularly to parents:

When a baby savagely bites its teething ring, it is because it (the baby) is experiencing excruciating pain from the teeth tearing their way through its gums. So Heathcliff may be seen to inflict pain on others (hurling knives at his wife, taunting Edgar, striking young Catherine, lashing his horse) only because he feels greater pain himself.[1]

Middle-class Victorian parents popularized the so-called

'teething ring' as a home remedy for the baby suffering the pangs of first dentition. The term is first recorded as a dictionary item in 1872 (Mark Twain, interestingly, is the first writer cited as using it). It is clear, however, that as objects of everyday nursery use teething rings had been around for many years before the 1870s. The rings—fashioned out of ivory, bone, or other semi-precious materials—were popular christening gifts throughout the nineteenth century. Since dentition can start as early as the fourth month of life they were, like silver spoons, matinée coats, or 'christening cups', articles of immediate practical use to the mother. In the early twentieth century vulcanized rubber was favoured, and latterly hard plastic.

For the Victorians, coral teething-rings had a particular vogue: hence Browning's little rhyme (a jeweller is speaking, trying to push his wares on an unwilling customer):

> 'Which lies within your power of purse?
> This ruby that would tip aright
> Solomon's sceptre? Oh, your nurse
> Wants simply coral, the delight
> Of teething baby, the stuff to bite!'

The teething ring, as standardized by Victorian mass production, combines a number of sensible design features. It is larger than a baby's mouth, so as not to be swallowed; it is circular, so little users should not poke themselves in the eye. It is hard, so that it should not be broken, dented, or abraded and become a harbour for germs. Ideally it is shiny (but not coated), so it can be rinsed in boiling water between use.

In *Wuthering Heights* this sudden snapshot of Heathcliff as a baby munching angrily on his little teething ring takes us back to his first appearance, a waif abused by his foster-siblings (including the young Nelly—who hates him as a usurper of *her* adoptive privileges). It evokes a reflexive pang of parental solicitude in the reader. This brute was once a helpless infant, we apprehend. The effect is to soften our feelings: the kind of 'goo-goo! diddums!' response which even the starchiest adults indulge in when presented with a babe in arms.

There are, in fact, two images embedded in Heathcliff's outburst—the merciless stamping and the baby's ferocious chomping of its toothless gums. One may digress for a moment on the worms, whose entrails Heathcliff imagines grinding into the dust. In the first place, it might be objected that earthworms don't have entrails as such ('intestines', 'bowels', 'internal organs') but a kind of digestive fluid. The digestive processes of *lumbricus terrestris* are strikingly simple. As M. S. Laverack puts it in *The Physiology of Earthworms* (New York, 1963): 'the alimentary canal is virtually a straight tube with little specialism in its structure, save for the muscular triturating gizzard.' C. A. Edwards and J. R. Lofty are even terser in *The Biology of Earthworms* (London, 1972): 'The alimentary canal or gut of earthworms is basically a tube extending from the mouth to the anus.' Nutrition-rich dirt goes in one end, pure dirt comes out the other.

I have never stamped on worms, although I have accidentally trodden on them. It wasn't entrails that came out, so much as squish and dirt. This objection to 'entrails' is pedantic, but I guarantee that if Ms Brontë submitted her novel to an American publisher in the 1990s, some bright-eyed young editor, hot out of Radcliffe or Yale, would insist on a change to bring Heathcliff into line with zoological fact.

On one level, Heathcliff's 'writhing' allusion is clearly to the proverbial truth that, given sufficient provocation, 'even a worm will turn'. One may also catch a faint Shakespearian echo of Lear's despairing cry: 'as flies to wanton boys are we to the gods, they kill us for their sport.'

Stamping on worms is, similarly, not an adult form of rage. Nor is it 'babyish'—their aim isn't good enough, and one wouldn't want to do it without shoes. Lear's 'wantonly schoolboyish' fits the action rather well.

There are other literary antecedents which may well have been consciously or unconsciously in Brontë's mind. The notes to the Oxford World's Classics edition of *Wuthering Heights* draw attention to a premonitory passage in Scott's *The Black Dwarf*, a gothic effusion, more popular with the nineteenth century than with us (p. 354). I suspect that Heathcliff's graphic and unpleasant worm-stomping image may also owe something to another famous hero-villain of nineteenth-century fiction. In 1832 Bulwer-Lytton wrote a novel about a glamorous 'scholar' murderer, Eugene Aram. Sensationally, the novelist implied in his text and declared outright in his preface that Aram was justified in his homicide, because he was intellectually superior to his victim and could make good scholarly use of the money he stole. The novel caused a terrific furore.[2] *Eugene Aram* was duly reissued, with a new apologetic foreword and a 'morally' revised text, in 1840.

Aram was a historical character (1704–59). One of the paradoxical features in his personality was that— although a proven murderer and misanthropic in a fashionably Byronic way—he was, in his everyday life, so 'benevolent' that he would even avoid stepping on worms. As the narrator puts it in the novel:

A resistless energy, an unbroken perseverance, a profound, and scheming, and subtle thought, a genius fertile in resources, a tongue clothed with eloquence—all, had his ambition so chosen, might have given him the same empire over the physical, that he had now attained over the intellectual world. It could not be said that Aram wanted benevolence, but it was dashed, and mixed with a certain scorn: the benevolence was the offspring of his nature: the scorn seemed the result of his pursuits. He would feed the birds from his window; he would *tread aside to avoid the worm on his path*.[3]

Bulwer-Lytton's preface confirms that this business about worms was a matter of historical record. 'That a man ... so benevolent that *he would turn aside from the worm in his path* should have been guilty of the foulest of human crimes, viz.—murder ... presents an anomaly in human conduct so rare and surprising, that it would be difficult to find any subject more adapted for metaphysical speculation and analysis.'[4]

The *Eugene Aram* controversy continued throughout the early 1840s—and was picked up, I suspect, even in remote Haworth, to be echoed in Emily Brontë's enigmatic murderer. Heathcliff, however, is—while similarly 'Byronic'—a more complex and callous conception than Aram. Unlike Bulwer-Lytton's murderer, he harbours no benevolent feelings towards earthworms. None the less, the oddly tentative '*yearn* to crush out their entrails' suggests that he may not actually do it. He merely *wants* to, when he sees them writhing. 'Is Heathcliff a worm-murderer?' Perhaps not.

The Aram and *Black Dwarf* allusions are speculative. But I felt I was on rock-firm ground with the 'moral teething' analysis. It was cut from under my feet (and arguably Emily Brontë's as well) by a letter from Dr Graham Turner. After some courtesies about how much he had enjoyed *Is Heathcliff a Murderer?*, Dr Turner launched the following torpedo:

I am afraid I must differ regarding the contents of the second paragraph on page 57. I should explain that before I retired I was a part-time consultant in paediatric dentistry at the Leeds Dental School. I fear you are repeating what is now widely regarded as an old wives' tale! The primary dentition in general will erupt from the age of four months to perhaps 30 months in late

erupting mouths. Very often the initial eruption is accompanied
by fever, malaise and what appear to be sore gums. Many mothers
are familiar with the grizzling unhappy child, who may have a
temperature of 38 or 39 degrees. An aspirin brings relief and, hey
presto, the mother believes that the drug has relieved the pain. I
believe this is nothing to do with the teeth.

Dr Turner, who has spent a lifetime learning about
such things, declares that proverbial 'teething pains' are
an 'old wives' tale', despite young mothers' beliefs to the
contrary. The industry which turned out those thousands
of Victorian teething rings was as redundant as the
charlatans who sell 'Pixie's charms' to gullible magazine
readers. Instead of 'the more the worms writhe . . .
entrails . . . it is a moral teething', Heathcliff should have
ejaculated something along the lines of:

The more the earthworms writhe, the more I yearn to squeeze out
with my foot the complex liquid enzymes which serve to break
down the nutritious proteins which they absorb through their
body sacs. It is a feverish infection of the gums which frequently
accompanies first dentition and which is frequently mistaken for
'teething pains', which of course it is not, although typically it
coincides with the eruption of the infant's milk teeth.

One might go on from Dr Turner's 'Old Wives' fallacy to
note as significant the fact that Emily Brontë was a spinster and that Haworth Parsonage was that rarity among
Victorian households, a populous home without babies:
neither Elizabeth, Anne, nor Emily bore a child; Branwell
never married and Charlotte died in pregnancy before
giving birth. What did the Misses Brontë—compared
to, say, Mrs Gaskell—know, at first hand, about little
strangers?[5]

But the 'old wives' tale' about teething is, I think,
obstinately adhered to as folk-wisdom by a majority of
young mothers, even those of the present day. My own
wife, for instance, is convinced that our child underwent

agonizing 'teething pains', and got relief from biting down
on his teething ring (she contorts her face into a mime of
his furious 'chomping' while telling me this). The guides
to baby care to be found in today's high street bookshops
confidently assert that babies undergo pain when cutting
their teeth. They get relief from vigorous—even violent—
chewing during this phase, the mother is instructed.
Many baby-care manuals continue to recommend teething
rings—scrupulously cleaned and chilled—but not frozen
(just like James Bond's martinis).

These are not matters on which literary criticism can
adjudicate. But Dr Turner's letter demonstrates what I
have always believed—namely, that dentists read novels
differently from academics. So do clergymen, deep-sea
divers, and ballet-dancers. That is to say, we each of us
as readers bring our life experiences to novels and find
aspects of that life experience reflected in them. It is
extremely valuable, and sometimes a salutary lesson, to
see novels as others, with different backgrounds, see them.

Alerted by Dr Turner, one may think more about
the subject. I cannot recall dental care featuring promi-
nently in English fiction until Graham Greene, who is
obsessed with teeth to an almost pathological degree. The
Victorians, I think, were generally philosophical about
dental decay—although the middle and upper classes
(particularly the upper) were not entirely negligent of oral
hygiene. As the German historian Treitschke scathingly
noted, 'the English think Soap is Civilization'.[6] Doubtless
the Victorians had the same illusion about toothpaste
(or 'powder') and they were probably more careful than
their continental neighbours. There is, for example, a
telling moment in *Anna Karenina*, where Levin looks in
the mirror and subjects himself to an honest physical
inventory: 'Yes! There were grey hairs on his temples.
He opened his mouth: his double teeth were beginning

to decay. He bared his muscular arms. Yes, he was very strong' (p. 348).

Levin is an aristocrat, and, at 32, still a young man. None the less, he clearly regards tooth decay in the same fatalistic spirit that Vronsky (another, and more dashing young man) regards his baldness. These are less marks of premature decay than of physical maturity. For the Russians, what mattered was not the man's outer physiological casing, but his 'soul'. We see things in a less philosophically Russian way. No Hollywood director, contemplating a big-budget production of *Anna Karenina*, would cast a bald actor for Vronsky, or a black-toothed actor with halitosis for Levin.

Dr Turner's letter, in its wider context, makes one curious about Heathcliff's teeth. They are, manifestly, in extraordinarily good shape for someone of his age (39, going on 40), in his age (the early nineteenth century), and—most importantly—his class of society (a 'slovenly squire' is how Lockwood first describes him). Heathcliff is routinely described during the course of the narrative as grinding, clenching, and gnashing his teeth. That he has a perfect set (as well as an ungrizzled and still-thick head of hair) in middle age is revealed in Nelly's recollection to Lockwood of finding his emaciated corpse at the window, where he has starved to death waiting for his spectral love, Cathy:

'I hasped the window; I combed his black long hair from his forehead; I tried to close his eyes—to extinguish, if possible, that frightful, life-like gaze of exultation, before any one else beheld it. They would not shut—they seemed to sneer at my attempts, and his parted lips and sharp, white teeth sneered too!' (p. 335)

How, one may wonder, has Heathcliff managed to keep his 'sharp, white teeth' in such good condition? As a young man at Wuthering Heights, reduced to the condition of a serf by the malevolent Hindley, bodily cleanliness was the least of young Heathcliff's concerns. As Nelly recalls:

Nobody but I even did him the kindness to call him a dirty boy, and bid him wash himself, once a week; and children of his age seldom have a natural pleasure in soap and water. Therefore, not to mention his clothes, which had seen three months' service in mire and dust, and his thick uncombed hair, the surface of his face and hands was dismally beclouded. (p. 52)

It is hard to imagine his teeth gleaming, with Tom Cruise-like brilliance, through these dingy clouds. It is, in fact, a point of honour with young Heathcliff to be uncleanly. When Cathy seems to look down on him, he blurts out, 'I shall be as dirty as I please, and I like to be dirty, and I will be dirty' (p. 53). All the signs are that Heathcliff's teeth will go the same way as Joseph's. From his 'mumbling', his dyspepsia, and his invariable diet of porridge, we gather that the old servant, 'hale and sinewy' though he may be, is as toothless as a hen.

After his mysterious three years' absence, Heathcliff returns 'transformed', as Nelly wonderingly observes. He is well dressed, neatly barbered, and 'athletic'. Above all, Heathcliff is 'clean'. We may plausibly infer that he has also acquired habits of dental hygiene in the great world. What would they be? There were, at the turn of the nineteenth century, three favoured modes of teeth-cleaning, described by J. Menzies Campbell in *Dentistry Then and Now* (Glasgow, 1963). The commonest utensils were toothpicks—a means of oral hygiene raised to a high level in ancient Rome, and in many ways still the most efficient technique. Shakespeare makes several references to toothpicks and, as Menzies Campbell notes, characteristically does so in such a way as to suggest that they were 'a symbol of gentility and not in general use in England'.

As Jaques's 'sans teeth' suggests in *As You Like It*, ordinary working-class folk who were lucky enough to survive to old age did not expect to bring their teeth with them. In the 1790s, when Heathcliff was on his travels, toothpicks would still have been associated with a gentleman's toiletry—like personal razors. As Menzies Campbell notes, 'In a 1791 newspaper advertisement, Sharp of 131 Fleet Street, London, was offering for sale an extensive choice of elegant tooth-pick cases'. The second approved method was a kind of primitive 'brushing', using the index finger covered with cloth. Sponges, with dentifrice lotions or powders to whiten the teeth, were a further refinement. It was Lord Chesterfield's habit, in the 1750s, to clean his teeth daily with a sponge dipped in tepid water with a few drops of arquebasade (an aromatic liquor). Brushes of the kind we are familiar with were available in the late eighteenth century, but again only to the upper classes. As Menzies Campbell points out:

In the late eighteenth century, exquisite silver tooth-brush sets were manufactured and sold by certain leading silversmiths, located in both London and the Provinces. These consisted of: (a) a tooth-brush with bristles inserted in a wooden or ivory base; (b) a tooth-powder box with two compartments and closely adjusted lids, and (c) a tongue scraper resembling a very thin spatula. They fitted into straight grained red goatskin (usually) covered cases of an exterior design similar to one holding razors.[7]

The point is made that, on his return, Heathcliff has learned the gentlemanly use of the razor during his absence. On first seeing his face, Nelly notes that his cheeks are '*half* covered with black whiskers'. Other male denizens of Wuthering Heights, we gather from Lockwood's appalled description, have shaggy beards. Hareton's whiskers, for example, 'encroach bearishly over his cheeks'. We may assume that Heathcliff has brought back in his portmanteau with his razors a set of toothbrushes. The whiteness of his teeth—which Nelly observes on his corpse—is evidently helped by the fact that, unlike Joseph and Hareton (who are described sitting by the fire of an evening, pulling on their clay pipes 'like automatons', p. 312), he does not smoke.

It would be quite in character for Heathcliff's care of his teeth to be kept decently off-stage. Unlike continentals and Americans, who promiscuously picked their teeth in public (something that infuriated Dickens on his first visit to the USA almost as much as their public spitting), the British have always regarded cleaning teeth as a private act. As private, that is, as bathing; if not quite as private as defecation.

Heathcliff, for all his savagery, maintains a certain decorum, even *in extremis*. Like other 'slovenly squires', he almost certainly sleeps in his shirt of a night. But when Lockwood cries out during his nightmare in Cathy's room, and Heathcliff bursts in, he is described as standing 'near the entrance, in his shirt *and trousers*; with a candle dripping over his fingers, and his face as white as the wall behind him' (p. 24, my emphasis). Heathcliff is quite indifferent to the searing pain of the boiling wax seeping over his fingers, is at his wits' end with shock, but has none the less taken time to put on his unmentionables before rushing out of his bedroom. This may be Yorkshire, but he is no bare-legged savage.

The Oxford World's Classics *Wuthering Heights* is edited by Ian Jack, with an introduction by Patsy Stoneman. The Oxford World's Classics *Anna Karenina* is translated by Louise and Aylmer Maude, with an introduction and notes by Gareth Jones.

Charles Dickens · *Dombey and Son*

═══

Does Carker have false teeth?

═══

Dentists, as I observed in the previous chapter, read novels differently. Under their specialist gaze, nineteenth-century fiction, particularly, reveals itself as even coyer about teeth—particularly artificial dentures—than about sex. The point is made by John Woodforde in his delightful chronicle, *The Strange Story of False Teeth*:

Embarrassment dates from the nineteenth century. By about 1840 laboured attempts at a natural appearance had brought false teeth into the category of the modern male toupée: however blatantly artificial and loose, they had to be passed off as the work of nature . . . The trials of wearers were made the more embarrassing by post-Regency puritanism which decreed it a vanity, like dyeing one's sidewhiskers, to resort to artificial teeth at all . . . The extreme reticence enforced by propriety inhibited the Victorian novelists, despite their liking for lengthy descriptions of the person. Just as one might read all the works of Dickens or Thackeray without learning of the existence of prostitutes, so one might read a whole library of Victorian novels without learning that anyone's teeth were artificial. An occasional reference to fierceness was as much as convention would allow.[1]

Woodforde's peer into the mouth of nineteenth-century fiction is extraordinarily stimulating. The remark about 'an occasional reference to fierceness' means, I take it, that anyone who makes a 'show' of their gnashers should be suspected of falsity. It usefully directs us back to Thackeray's famous portrait of the Marquis of Steyne in *Vanity Fair* and the 'suppressed woodcut' which accompanies it:

The candles lighted up Lord Steyne's shining bald head, which was fringed with red hair. He had thick bushy eyebrows, with little twinkling bloodshot eyes, surrounded by a thousand wrinkles. His jaw was underhung, and when he laughed, two white buck-teeth protruded themselves and glistened savagely in the midst of the grin. (pp. 473–4)[2]

This is the early 1820s. It is not preposterous to suppose that Steyne has ornamented himself with what were called 'Waterloo teeth'. As Woodforde notes, there was at this period a healthy market

for human teeth plundered from the corpses of [the] battlefield by characters known as resurrectionists. These could sometimes deceive the eye provided they were kept steady on the gums and slightly covered by the lips. Even when a corpse was badly decomposed, its front teeth remained saleable . . . Many people unknowingly wore teeth extracted from young men on the field of Waterloo . . . Gruesome and downright unhygienic as the use of such objects now seems, it may be surmised that in the twenty-first century it will be thought equally unpleasant that the best wigs and toupées of the 1960s were made of human hair.[3]

It would surely cross the mind of an alert reader of 1847 that those prominent, half-covered 'buck [i.e. front] teeth' of the balding (his 'red' hair must be the result of dye), physically decayed, morally degenerate Steyne were not *his* teeth. They might even—to pursue the thought to a macabre conclusion—be George Osborne's, yanked from his stiffening jaws at Quatre Bras by some corpse-robbing resurrectionist.

Astute as Woodforde's comments are, he is wrong to imply that Thackeray and Dickens, to take the two eminent names he mentions, *never* mention false teeth in their fiction. They do. In Thackeray's *Pendennis*, for instance, old Major Pendennis (known irreverently as 'Wigsby' behind his back) has teeth as false as his magnificent head of hair. 'Chatter your old hivories at me, do you . . . ?' his rebellious servant, Morgan, has the gall to ask him in their great showdown with each other (p. 878). The Major has a 'Wellington nose' and slavishly models his haughty manner on that of the Iron Duke. It is not far-fetched to imagine that he too has Waterloo teeth, to complete his Wellingtonian toilette.

In *The Virginians* (a sequel to *Esmond*) Thackeray actually builds a whole comic sub-plot around a false-teeth joke. The young American, Harry Esmond Warrington, comes to England and, in his innocence, is entrapped by the wiles of the not-so-young Lady Maria. Harry's aunt, Baroness Bernstein (formerly Beatrix Castlewood, the belle of *Esmond*, now a terrifying dowager), schemes to free her young relative from his unwise infatuation. The old lady is too cunning to attempt a frontal attack. As they play picquet one evening (Maria having retired, indisposed), the Baroness sets to work on the young man.

'That absurd Maria!' says Madam Bernstein, drinking from a great glass of negus, 'she takes liberties with herself. She never had a good constitution. She is forty-one years old. All her upper teeth are false, and she can't eat with them. Thank Heaven, I have still got every tooth in my head. How clumsily you deal, child!'

Deal clumsily, indeed! Had a dentist been extracting Harry's own grinders at that moment, would he have been expected to mind his cards, and deal them neatly . . . Maria is forty-one years old, Maria has false—oh, horrible, horrible! Has she a false eye? Has she a wooden leg? I envy not that boy's dreams that night.[4]

In fact, Maria's teeth are her own, the narrator ('who knows everything') later informs us. But the damage is done. Harry can never love a woman with 'false—oh, horrible'.

Dickens also introduces false teeth into his fiction, notably *Dombey and Son*. Our first introduction to Mrs Skewton, via Major Bagstock, highlights the many artificial aids to the lady's superannuated beauties. 'How long have you been here, bad man?', she archly quizzes Bagstock from her wheelchair, when they meet (his friend Mr Dombey and her daughter Edith in attendance) in the street at Leamington:

'One day,' replied the Major.

'And can you be a day, or even a minute,' returned the lady, slightly settling her false curls and false eyebrows with her fan, and showing her false teeth, set off by her false complexion, 'in the Garden of what's-its-name—'

'Eden, I suppose, Mama,' interrupted the younger lady, scornfully. (p. 241)

There are at least three subsequent references to Mrs Skewton's false teeth—all barbed with Dickensian satire at her preposterous attempts at 'juvenility', even after the stroke which totally paralyses her. She dies, false teeth in frozen jaw. 'Cleopatra' Skewton's flashing dentures are, like Yorick's 'chapfallen grin' in *Hamlet*, a *memento mori*.

More enigmatic are Carker's teeth, to whose gleaming and suspicious perfection we are directed, time and again, in *Dombey and Son*. They are prominent in the first description we are given of the 'general manager' in Chapter 13:

Mr Carker was a gentleman thirty-eight or forty years old, of a florid complexion, and with two unbroken rows of glistening teeth, whose regularity and whiteness were quite distressing. It was impossible to escape the observation of them, for he showed them whenever he spoke; and bore so wide a smile upon his countenance (a smile, however, very rarely, indeed, extending beyond his mouth), that there was something in it like the snarl of a cat. (p. 144)

As Woodforde notes, 'in even lighthearted Victorian photographs people smile with closed lips'. Carker's promiscuously displaying every perfect tooth in his head (something which is commented on repeatedly in the novel) would be as shocking as flaunting a wantonly unzipped fly. Dickens evidently gave instructions to his illustrator, Phiz, to draw attention to the general manager's toothsome smile and a set of snappers that would do the Cheshire Cat proud:

Mr Carker introduces Himself to Florence and the
Skettles Family

Carker's 'glistening' teeth, in the mouth of a 40-year-old man, and their astonishing 'regularity and whiteness', are surely too good to be true. They must be porcelain, we suspect. One of the problems with ivory, animal, or human bone false teeth was that they discoloured and became unpleasantly smelly, generating awful bad breath. Porcelain-based or 'mineral-paste' false teeth did not yellow or rot, and preserved the wearer from this added embarrassment of halitosis. Porcelain snappers had a vogue in Britain in the early to mid-nineteenth century. But, as Woodforde records, 'so-called mineral or porcelain teeth . . . had a very artificial appearance in the mouth and made a grating sound when brought together. They were over-white, opaque and brittle.' John Gray, in *Preservation of the Teeth* (1838), was dismissive: 'The things called mineral, or Jews' teeth, are now plentifully manufactured of porcelain; but they always look like what they are, and can never be mistaken for teeth.'[5]

Are Carker's magnificent white teeth his own? Most middle-aged Victorian readers (Dickens was 36 years old at the time of writing *Dombey and Son*) would have been very suspicious. We never know for certain. It would be revealing to examine the bodily remains of Carker that only the dogs seem interested in on the railway line. And it may be significant how often the word 'false' enters the final explosive quarrel between him and Edith. In the two pages recording their last, melodramatic exchange, 'false' comes up six times, and direct allusion is made to Carker's 'shining' teeth. Subliminally, the echo thrown back from this exchange is 'denture'. Myself, I think all that glistens in Carker's mouth is not tooth—human tooth, that is.

As the century progressed, dentistry professionalized itself, legislation against quacks was introduced, and standards of dental hygiene improved—led by America with its (to Dickens) obnoxious toothpicks. Toothbrushes became common articles of bathroom furniture. Initially there would be only one toothbrush for the whole Victorian family, as there were common hair- and boot-brushes for everyone to use. With the suction plate, and more reliable spring mechanisms and better equipped workshops, false teeth and bridges for the masses became an affordable 'cheap luxury'; so much so that in the early twentieth century, among the self-improving working classes, it was common as a dowry for a young bride to have all her teeth pulled so that she might go to the altar with a perfect (if artificial) dazzling smile.

The first 'unembarrassed' reference to false teeth in Victorian fiction is, I believe, in *King Solomon's Mines* (1885). Captain Good, Alan Quatermain, and his friends, are confronted by a savage African tribe:

'What does the beggar say?' asked Good.

'He says we are going to be scragged,' I answered grimly.

'Oh, Lord!' groaned Good; and, as was his way when perplexed, he put his hand to his false teeth, dragging the top set down and allowing them to fly back to his jaw with a snap. It was a most fortunate move, for the next second the dignified crowd of Kukuanas gave a simultaneous yell of horror, and bolted back some yards.

'What's up?' said I.

'It's his teeth,' whispered Sir Henry excitedly. 'He moved them. Take them out, Good, take them out!'

He obeyed, slipping the set into the sleeve of his flannel shirt.

In another second curiosity had overcome fear, and the men advanced slowly. Apparently they had now forgotten their amiable intention of doing for us. (pp. 112–13)

False teeth are not a matter of private shame here, but of imperial pride—'white man's magic'—one of the 'wonders of civilization' with which to dazzle the backward peoples of the earth. Perhaps if Carker had slipped his dentures out from time to time as a party trick we might like him

more. Or possibly, like the Kukuanas, we might merely
find him even more terrifying than he already is.

The Oxford World's Classics *Dombey and Son* is edited by Alan
Horsman. The Oxford World's Classics *King Solomon's Mines* is
edited by Dennis Butts. The Oxford World's Classics *Pendennis*
is edited by John Sutherland.

Charlotte Brontë · *Villette*

===

Lucy Snowe, cement-mixer

===

One of the most emotionally charged scenes in *Villette* is that in Chapter 26 ('A Burial'). Lucy Snowe discovers that Madame Beck has invaded her bureau and has read her 'triply-enclosed packet of five letters' from Dr John. Not quite love letters, they are none the less dear to Lucy. And she is apprehensive that her ruthless enemy will again steal her letters and show them to M. Emmanuel. Rather than destroy them (to do so would be to destroy part of herself), Lucy determines to secrete the letters where the prying eyes of Madame Beck can never find them.

The act is highly ritualistic. First she makes a 'little roll' of her precious letters, wraps them in 'oiled silk', and binds them with twine. In one of the town's pawnshops she discovers what she next needs, 'a thick glass jar or bottle'. She inserts her little roll, then gets 'the old Jew broker to stopper, seal, and make it air-tight'. He looks at her suspiciously while doing so, as well he might.

All this takes place during 'a fine frosty afternoon'. At seven-thirty the same night, Madame Beck being occupied with the boarders, Lucy shawls herself (it is bitterly cold) and goes through the garden into the '*allée defendue*'. This was earlier described in Chapter 12. It is a lane at the back of the house, 'forbidden to be entered by the pupils' (p. 132). At the end of the walk is a relic from the long-distant days when the pensionnat was a convent—an ancient, largely dead, pear-tree, nicknamed (for its age) Methuselah. At its root, as we are told in Chapter 12

you saw, in scraping away the mossy earth between the half-bared roots, a glimpse of slab, smooth, hard, and black. The legend went, unconfirmed and unaccredited, but still propagated, that this was the portal of a vault, emprisoning deep beneath that ground, on whose surface grass grew and flowers bloomed, the bones of a girl whom a monkish conclave of the drear middle ages had here buried alive, for some sin against her vow. (pp. 130–1)

It would seem that curious passers-by are in the habit of inspecting the slab—may even dare to lift it one day. None the less it is here, alongside the putative remains of this rebel, her predecessor, that Lucy will bury her precious cargo:

Methuselah, though so very old, was of sound timber still; only there was a hole, or rather a deep hollow, near his root. I knew there was such a hollow, hidden partly by ivy and creepers . . . I cleared away the ivy, and found the hole; it was large enough to receive the jar, and I thrust it deep in. In a tool-shed at the bottom of the garden, lay the relics of building-materials, left by masons lately employed to repair a part of the premises. I fetched thence a slate and some mortar, put the slate on the hollow, secured it with cement, covered the whole with black mould, and, finally, replaced the ivy. This done, I rested, leaning against the tree; lingering, like any other mourner, beside a newly-sodded grave. (p. 369)

This is an important scene in the novel—a climax of renunciation and self-denial—symbolized by the act of 'burying', in a sealed cylinder, the emotional part of herself. But a number of questions protrude. The earlier references to 'scraping' away at the base of Methuselah, with all its grisly associations, suggest that it is something which the horrified girls (braving Madame Beck's punishments) do— to give themselves the delicious *frisson* of contemplating the murdered nun's grave. This is not, one would have thought, a sensible place to hide one's intimate letters. Sooner or later, someone will go beyond 'scraping' and dig.

And what has happened, between Chapters 12 and 26,

to the 'vault' and the smooth, hard, black slab? In the later chapter it is just a hole in the ground. And then, coming down to practical matters, there is the business with the 'mortar'. One thing any bricklayer would have told Miss Snowe is, 'don't mix cement during a frost'—it won't hold. If cement freezes while still 'setting', it will simply crumble.

But what, exactly, is the mortar for? To create a cover over the 'slate', over the bottle with its edges against the dirt sides of the hole? The cement simply would not hold—there is no adhesive surface for it to bond against. You would just lift the slate out. And has Charlotte Brontë realized that you have to mix mortar—the substance is a precisely measured mixture of sand, water, and cement? I suspect that here she is confusing it with ready-to-use putty.

It creates an odd and distracting image—distracting because it works against the solemnity with which Brontë clearly wants to invest this episode. We have to imagine this gentlewoman mixing cement (since the temperature is below freezing, a fruitless task), getting the water from we know not where (the garden pump?). There are the other distractions of the disappeared slab. Where it either was, or was not, Lucy Snowe has laid another slab, or slate. This, even if her cement holds (which it will not), will be easily lifted, since it adjoins loose earth. Lucy should really have done what any other young Victorian maiden would have done in the circumstances: thrown the letters in the fire.

The Oxford World's Classics *Villette* is edited by Herbert Rosengarten with an introduction by Margaret Smith.

==

Is Betsey Trotwood a spinster?

==

In *Can Jane Eyre Be Happy?* I referred in passing to Miss Trotwood, in *David Copperfield*, as a 'spinster'. Donald Hawes writes to correct the error: 'Of course she uses her maiden name and lives as a single woman (as we're told in Chapter 1). But she was a married woman, in fact, who separated from her husband.' Professor Hawes adds:

> what I find slightly puzzling is her telling David that she believes that her husband 'married another woman' (Chapter 47). No explanation is given of the legality or illegality of this marriage as far as I know. I also find it strange that John Forster in his *Life of Dickens* refers to her as 'Mrs Trotwood'.

The second wife is indeed puzzling, as is the mis-titling of Miss ('Mrs') Trotwood by someone as close to Dickens in the planning of his fiction as Forster. Once pointed out, it is tempting to follow up the 'Mrs Trotwood' puzzle for what it reveals about Dickens's use of peripheral detail, and his habit of keeping latent plots 'in reserve' (as I will argue).

Dickens, writing serially to the month as he did, clearly left much to his powers of extemporization. His working notes indicate that, even in the privacy of his own study, he did not hazard long-term projections about the future directions of his story (hence our frustrations with the tantalizingly incomplete *Edwin Drood*). But in order to extemporize effectively he had at every stage to keep a range of possibilities open—any of which might lead up to alternative plot-lines, if required. If never used, these untaken narrative options (roads not taken) might well remain as small motes to trouble the pedantic reader's eye.

David Copperfield opens with a teasing uncertainty as to what will follow: 'Whether I shall turn out to be the hero of my own life, or whether that station will be held by anybody else, these pages must show.' The details of Miss Betsey Trotwood's early life seem, however, certain enough:

An aunt of my father's, and consequently a great-aunt of mine, of whom I shall have more to relate by-and-by, was the principal magnate of our family. [She] . . . had been married to a husband younger than herself, who was very handsome, except in the sense of the homely adage, 'handsome is, that handsome does'— for he was strongly suspected of having beaten Miss Betsey, and even of having once, on a disputed question of supplies, made some hasty but determined arrangements to throw her out of a two pair of stairs' window. These evidences of an incompatibility of temper induced Miss Betsey to pay him off, and effect a separation by mutual consent. He went to India with his capital, and there, according to a wild legend in our family, he was once seen riding on an elephant, in company with a Baboon; but I think it must have been a Baboo—or a Begum. Anyhow, from India tidings of his death reached home, within ten years. How they affected my aunt, nobody knew; for immediately after the separation, she took her maiden name again, bought a cottage in a hamlet on the sea-coast a long way off, established herself there as a single woman with one servant, and was understood to live secluded ever afterwards, in an inflexible retirement. (pp. 2–3)

The time reference 'within ten years' is significant. And it is clear, from subsequent events, that all this happened— including her widowing—before the marriage of Mr and Mrs Copperfield, and the birth of David.

We never know what Miss Trotwood's married name was, nor her errant husband's Christian name. He was born in Hornsey, as we discover much later (although the manuscript shows that this was not Dickens's first intention). 'Born in Hornsey' is the sum total of his given biography—apart from the elephant, the Begum, and the mysterious other wife. On David's birth, Miss Betsey cut off all communication with the Copperfields, on grounds of their having perversely brought a boy, not a girl (a little Betsey), into the world.

When, aged 10, David runs away to Dover and is adopted by Miss Trotwood (who promptly changes his name to 'Trotwood Copperfield'), he learns something about Mr Dick, his aunt's inseparable companion. The amiable lunatic had been sent away 'to some private asylum-place' by an unsympathetic brother. He was, however, ill treated at the asylum, 'So I [Miss Betsey] stepped in . . . and made him [the brother] an offer . . . after a good deal of squabbling . . . I got him' (p. 199).[1] As with David, she promptly changed her ward's name: Richard Babley (her 'babbling baby') became 'Mr Dick'. Miss Trotwood has an odd passion for changing names, we note (before 1837 there was no obligation to enter them with the Registrar of Births, Marriages, and Deaths). Mr Dick is not, however, a penniless waif like David. He has, we later learn, an income of £100 a year. On her part, Miss Trotwood, as we later learn, has £5,000 in the consols, which at their standard yield of 3 per cent would give her an annual income of £150. We may assume, if he too has his funds in the consols, that Mr Dick has some £3,000 invested.

Unless Miss Trotwood settled this sum on him (which is doubtful, given her own slender resources) she must have had some claim other than innate benevolence to ownership, and—as one guesses, power of attorney. Mr Dick is a valuable commodity—adventurers would marry 'heiresses' with that kind of dowry. It is unlikely that Mr Dick—a man of property—would be *given away* for adoption to an eccentric old woman who felt sorry for him in his asylum, and who had no near connection with him. What was she doing inspecting the inmates of asylums anyway? Was she perhaps locked up in one herself for a while, after the catastrophe of her marriage?

It emerges, about a third of the way through the narrative, that Miss Trotwood's husband is not, after all, dead. It is not clear from his notes (where he refers to him as 'My Aunt's persecutor') that Dickens foresaw this resurrection from the beginning, or whether—as seems more likely—it was a mid-narrative brainwave. In his notes Dickens debates with himself whether to introduce the persecutor early or hold him back until a more effective moment in the narrative. He decides, on reflection, to hold him back. What else he held back about the man we can only guess.

The first enigmatic clue the reader gets about the 'persecutor' is from Mr Dick, in conversation with David, in Chapter 17 ('Somebody Turns Up'): 'Soon after' the time that King Charles turned up (i.e. after the fever and psychosis induced by his brother's and the asylum's ill treatment) 'the man first came', he tells David. 'The man' hung about the house by night. When she saw him, Miss Trotwood was painfully affected: she shivered, held on to the palings, wept, and 'gave him money'. Miss Betsey was evidently surprised, as well as distressed, by this apparition. Mr Dick, as he tells David, has since seen the man again.

David dismisses Mr Dick's account as another King Charles's head. But later, in Chapter 23, when Miss Trotwood comes up to London to pay for David's articles, they pass a 'lowering, ill-dressed man' in the street who evidently recognizes Betsey. She certainly recognizes him. 'I don't know what I am to do,' she tells David, 'in a terrified whisper, and pressing my arm' (p. 340). David

sees nothing but an importunate 'sturdy beggar' to be sent
on his way. But the old lady, gathering herself, tells him
she must go off with the ill-dressed man in a coach. She
and David will meet later in St Paul's churchyard. When
they meet, a confused David notes that her purse is empty
of the guineas it formerly contained. What David sees in
London corroborates Mr Dick's story about the mysterious
'man' who preys on Miss Trotwood. But he does not learn
the man's identity until years later. Alarmed by a light
at midnight in his guardian's cottage in Highgate, he
goes across the short distance between their dwellings.
In the garden, he sees and hears 'the man' drinking and
demanding money. 'What have I to do, to free myself for
ever of your visits, but to abandon you to your deserts?'
Miss Trotwood says. Why doesn't she, he asks, tauntingly:
'*You* ask me why!', she replies, 'What a heart you must
have' (p. 669). It would be interesting to know, exactly,
what lies behind that 'why!'

  After the man has gone on his way, Betsey confesses all
to David: 'Trot . . . it's my husband.' She tells the whole
sad story. He wasted her fortune and 'nearly' broke her
heart.

I left him . . . I left him generously. He had been so cruel to me,
that I might have effected a separation on easy terms for myself;
but I did not. He soon made ducks and drakes of what I gave him,
sank lower and lower, married another woman, I believe, became
an adventurer, a gambler, and a cheat. (p. 670)

From this 'grumpy, frumpy, story' we understand there
was no divorce, but a deed of separation. After she had cut
herself off from the Copperfields (her only living relatives,
apparently) and set herself up as a spinster in Dover—the
husband reappeared on the scene. There is a novel's-worth
of incident in these few months of Miss Trotwood's life. If,
however, the man had indeed 'married again' he would,

one assumes, be a bigamist, and in no position to apply any blackmailing pressure at all on his abused former wife. He would be in mortal fear of criminal prosecution. Why, then, is Miss Trotwood so frightened of him? She is, in other departments of her life, a plucky woman well able to fight her corner. She declines to be browbeaten by the much more dangerous Uriah Heep (whom she physically assaults) or the 'murdering' Murdstones (whom she fearlessly tongue-lashes). What hold does her former husband have over her?

The 'persecutor' makes his final appearance in the novel as a corpse. He has died in hospital in Canterbury, and is about to be borne away by a hearse (paid for by Miss Trotwood) to be buried at Hornsey, where—as Betsey tells David—he was born. On his deathbed, it emerges, he sent for Miss Trotwood, and asked her forgiveness. 'Six-and-thirty years ago, this day, my dear', she tells David, 'I was married' (p. 763).

We learn nothing more about the man from Hornsey. But what we do know provokes some teasing speculations. What happened to his second 'wife'? Why was she not in attendance at the hospital, did he not have apologies to make to her? *Was* there a second wife? Did Miss Trotwood really believe he was dead, when—as Mr Dick recalls—he 'first' reappeared in Dover to persecute her? Additionally, there is the odd business of 'Miss' Trotwood's name. Obviously, for informal purposes, people can call themselves what they want. There are no regulations regarding nicknames. If Miss Trotwood wants to call Mr Babley 'Mr Dick', and David Copperfield 'Trotwood' Copperfield, so be it. It is of no more significance than Mr Dombey renaming his servant 'Richards' on the grounds that 'Toodle' is beneath his household dignity. But changing one's name for legal purposes and transactions is not so easy. At the very least, one would need to keep one's solicitor informed. Names

have to be kept straight on legal documents. Since Agnes
carefully calls David 'Trotwood Copperfield', it would seem
that Betsey took the precaution of informing Mr Wickfield
about this matter.

It also seems clear that Miss Trotwood and her husband
were not divorced but separated. Legally, she would still be
known, at least on certain important legal documents, by
his surname, whatever it was. Her legal advisers, Spenlow
and Jorkins, evidently know her only as 'Miss Trotwood'.
Her 'married name' is never brought up. But it would
need to be known about and recorded in order to make
her papers entirely legal. The married name ('Mrs X, also
known as "Miss Trotwood"') would surely also have to be
entered somewhere on her deeds of trust (which Wickfield
has, and which Heep embezzles), if only in parenthesis.

Also, if Miss Trotwood is not divorced, her property
would not be her own but her husband's—unless some
form of legal agreement were entered into with him,
under his legal name, at the time of separation. This may
well be the reason for Miss Trotwood's uncharacteristic
nervousness—a fear that the persecutor will enforce his
conjugal rights and seize the £5,000 portion remaining
to her from her fortune (we learn, later, that she has
prudently secreted £2,000, presumably for just such an
eventuality). Forster's slip about 'Mrs Trotwood' arose,
I would suggest, from a logical but erroneous train of
thought. He recalled, subliminally, that Miss Betsey was
still 'married', and that she must for the legal purposes
which figure so centrally in the plot have used a married
name and that name must therefore have been 'Trotwood'.

Another incidental puzzle is: did 'the persecutor' ever
go to India? Did he in fact ride an elephant and consort
with a baboo or a begum? (He clearly didn't die in
India—as family legend also has it.) 'Emigration' and the
spiritual regeneration that it permits is a major theme

in *David Copperfield*. But unlike Em'ly and Micawber, the persecutor seems an unlikely candidate. His Indian career is, most likely, a flight of Trotwoodian fancy—like the foreign investments in which (to protect Wickfield) she claims to have lost all her money. Miss Trotwood is quite capable of exotic lies in an honest cause.

This hypothesis is supported by one's difficulty in fitting the Indian business into a logical time frame. Miss Trotwood announces her thirty-sixth wedding anniversary at a period (Dora's death) when David is around 26. Presumably, then, the marriage took place 10 years before his birth. Yet, it is said that after the marriage (which must have lasted some years, if the persecutor contrived to squander the greater part of Miss Trotwood's considerable fortune) he went to India (a journey which would have taken many months), where he died 'within ten years' (the news, of course, would have taken many months to return). All this took place before David's birth, and even his parents' wedding. By no manipulation of time schemes can one make this order of events work. We must assume, I think, that the 'persecutor' never went to India. On the other hand, from her shock at his reappearance, we may well assume that Miss Trotwood *thought* him dead.

There is no easy answer to the puzzles which swarm around Miss Trotwood's past, and any attempt at explanation needs to take into account Dickens's working methods. If Dickens, opening his narrative, was uncertain as to who 'the hero' of 'these pages' would be, he may just as well not have determined—at that early stage—who the villain was to be. As a kind of 'defence in depth', Dickens may well have laid the ground for a potential sub-plot, to fall back on if need be.

One can speculate about that unwritten (because unneeded) subplot. There is, in Chapter 33 of *David Copperfield*, a strangely digressive paragraph describing some

proceedings in court in Doctors' Commons (where divorce
business was done at this period) undertaken by Spenlow
and the newly articled David:

Mr. Spenlow and I went into Court, where we had a divorce-
suit coming on, under an ingenious little statute (repealed now,
I believe, but in virtue of which I have seen several marriages
annulled), of which the merits were these. The husband, whose
name was Thomas Benjamin, had taken out his marriage licence
as Thomas only, suppressing the Benjamin, in case he should not
find himself as comfortable as he expected. *Not* finding himself
as comfortable as he expected, or being a little fatigued with his
wife, poor fellow, he now came forward by a friend, after being
married a year or two, and declared that his name was Thomas
Benjamin, and therefore he was not married at all. Which the
Court confirmed, to his great satisfaction. (pp. 465–6)[2]

This little excursus has no relevance to the plot that one
can see. Mr Benjamin never reappears. It seems entirely
by the way. Unless, of course, Dickens were keeping it
in reserve as what I have called a 'fall-back' plot-line. In
this unwritten narrative we might find that, like Thomas
Benjamin, the persecutor 'entraps' eligible women. He
'married' the ancient heiress, Miss Trotwood, using a false,
or imperfect name. The subsequent 'separation'—which
involved a huge pay-off on her part—was not a divorce.
It could not be a divorce, because the couple were never
legally married. In one sense he was still her 'husband' (he
had presumably enjoyed conjugal physical rights). But, in
another sense, she was still a spinster ('unmarried woman
. . . old maid'). Miss Trotwood was never obliged to change
her name back to its maiden form. Since the marriage was
invalid, this had always been her legal name, anyway.

As a gullible victim of this kind of confidence trick, Miss
Trotwood would be terrified of the humiliating publicity of
being exposed, and susceptible to blackmail. Legally, the
persecutor—like Mr Benjamin—would be untouchable.

Not a bigamist, that is, but a serial confidence trickster. His 'second wife' presumably fell victim to the same ruse as Miss Trotwood. She was another dupe. In the imagination one can see an unwritten narrative in which all this would come out. But, in the event, Dickens did not need to fall back on this reserve plot, if that's what it was. Uriah Heep and Mr Murdstone (another serial predator on marriageable ladies) served the novel's needs for villainy quite adequately. Is, then, Miss Trotwood a spinster?— strictly no; but one *can* make a case that she was never anything else.

Postscript: Are Bella and Laura married women?

John Carey and David Grylls have raised in conversation with me other puzzles of a similar nature to the Benjamin– Miss Betsey–man from Hornsey kind. As Professor Carey points out, Bella Wilfer marries the 'Secretary' in *Our Mutual Friend* believing him to be John Rokesmith. She becomes, in good faith, Mrs John Rokesmith. They have a child who is, presumably, baptized and registered in the name Rokesmith. But, of course, John Rokesmith is— legally—John Harmon (alias Julius Handford). All this comes out in the denouement. The penultimate chapter of the novel ('Persons and Things in General') opens: 'Mr. and Mrs. John Harmon's first delightful occupation was to set all matters right that had strayed in any way wrong' (p. 803). Was one of these 'matters' to go through a new wedding under their proper names? Was there no legal reprisal for John Harmon's passing himself off as 'John Rokesmith'? Was their child effectively bastardized for the period that he was a 'Rokesmith'?

The problem in *The Woman in White* is, as Dr Grylls points out, even more perplexing. Walter Hartright and

Marian Halcombe rescue Lady Laura Glyde (née Fairlie) from the asylum where she is known as the patient 'Anne Catherick'. The three of them go into hiding in a 'poor neighbourhood' in the 'Far East' of London (pp. 420, 440). It is 1851, the year of the census. The two women, Hartright tells us, are 'described as my sisters'. Although he does not say so outright (he is, in fact, very vague on the subject) they must all be sheltering under the same assumed name. They know themselves to be in 'serious peril' if Fosco and Glyde track them down. Presumably Walter makes a false return on the census return (as Wilkie Collins did in 1861, to protect his mistress Catherine Graves).

Marian and Walter set themselves to discover the 'Secret'. It will, they believe, lead to the unmasking of the villains and the restitution of Laura. On their part Fosco and Glyde know that Anne has escaped but they do not, at this stage, know that Walter is involved. Nor, of course, do they know where the artist and his two 'sisters' are living. If they did, more vile skulduggery would ensue.

The 'Secret' leads Walter to Mrs Catherick at Welmingham. He evidently introduces himself to her *in propria persona* (she calls him 'Mr Hartright'). Walter discovers that the 'Secret' lies buried in the registers of Old Welmingham church. But before he can get at them Glyde arranges to have him taken up by the magistrates for assault. It is, of course, a set-up. But, we deduce, Walter gives a false address (and possibly a false name) to the authorities. To do otherwise would be to give Fosco and Glyde directions to the whereabouts of his 'sisters', and would surely lead to the incarceration of Laura once more.

Sir Percival Glyde is incinerated in the fire in the church, attempting to destroy the evidence of his illegitimacy (the 'Secret'). Walter, who led the attempt to save his rival's life, is called as a witness at the inquest. Surprisingly (given the fact that Glyde was his closest friend and his fellow conspirator), Fosco is not in attendance at Welmingham. We assume that again Walter gives a false name and address.

Four months later the trio spend a 'fortnight [at] the seaside'. They have 'earned a little holiday' (p. 571), Walter says. When in town, they are now living at Fulham. During their seaside holiday ('the third day from our arrival') Walter confesses to Marian his desire to marry Laura. 'I am so happy' (p. 576), Laura responds. There follows the enigmatic parenthesis: 'Ten days later, we were happier still. We were married . . . In a fortnight more we three were back in London' (p. 576).

Do they then marry at the seaside? There is no time for the banns to be called, so it must be a civil marriage. They could hardly marry at Fulham where, presumably, Laura is known as Walter's 'sister'. What name does Laura Fairlie–Glyde–Catherick marry under? And does she declare herself a 'spinster', or a widow (Lady Laura Glyde)? However mitigated there must be a degree of wilful misrepresentation. Laura is, legally, 'dead'. Corpses cannot marry. And is it, legally, a marriage? Is it in any sense a marriage? The wedding takes place in 1851. It is not until a couple of years later, after Laura has been brought back to life and legality, that she and Walter have their first child, little Walter. When they return to Fulham, do Walter and his 'wife' continue a chaste existence as brother and sister?[3]

The Oxford World's Classics *David Copperfield* is edited by Nina Burgis, with an introduction by Andrew Sanders. The Oxford World's Classics *Our Mutual Friend* is edited by Michael Cotsell. The Oxford World's Classics *The Woman in White* is edited by John Sutherland.

═══

How does Ruth end up in Wales?

═══

Frances Twinn, a graduate student working on the fiction of Elizabeth Gaskell, points to a troubling inconsistency at the heart of *Ruth*. The narrative opens with a depiction of the poor-but-genteel heroine apprenticed to a harsh milliner, Mrs Mason, in 'an assize town in one of the eastern counties'. It is 'many years ago' (p. 3). We should picture, it seems, a sleepy county town like Ipswich or Norwich in the 1830s. The heroine, Ruth Hilton, is an orphan. Her mother had been the daughter of a Norfolk curate—a 'delicate, fine lady' (p. 36); her father had been a farmer—a good-hearted but tragically unlucky man. The delicate Mrs Hilton died early of physical exhaustion, unable to cope with the physical demands of being a farmer's wife. He followed soon after of a broken heart and bankruptcy. Ruth, alone in the world, falls into the unfeeling custody of a 'hard-headed' guardian, who disposes of the waif to Mrs Mason so as to be rid of her, at the small expense of her indenture fee.

At the shire-hall new-year celebrations, 15-year-old Ruth Hilton catches the eye of a 23-year-old sprig of the gentry. In return for the girl's deftly mending the torn dress of his partner (the haughty Miss Duncombe), Henry Bellingham gives Ruth a camellia. The gentleman's trifling gift goes to the humble dressmaker's heart. Over the following six months Bellingham pursues Ruth. She is a beautiful girl—although chronically shy and deferential. It is not clear whether he intends to seduce her or to enjoy some risky flirtation: he is no villain, merely feckless. She is no trollop, merely innocent of the ways of the world. As Mrs Gaskell emphasizes time and again, she has no *mother* to guide her.

On a nostalgic visit to her former home, Ruth is seen in the company of Bellingham by Mrs Mason and dismissed on the spot ('I'll have no slurs on the character of my apprentices . . . I shall write and tell your guardian to-morrow', pp. 54–5). Her guardian, of course, will now disown her—glad to be rid of the expense. Ruth is now that most unfortunate of Victorian women, a 'castaway'. Bellingham at first seems perplexed as to what to do: 'It is very unfortunate; for, you see, I did not like to name it to you before, but, I believe—I have business, in fact, which obliges me to go to town to-morrow—to London, I mean; and I don't know when I shall be able to return' (p. 56).

The news that he too is about to abandon her plunges Ruth into paralytic despair. But, on the spur of the moment, Bellingham sees a solution: 'Ruth, would you go with me to London . . . you must come with me, love, and trust to me.' It is the serpent's invitation. 'Young, and innocent, and motherless'—Ruth succumbs. Bellingham goes off to get the carriage that will carry the young milliner to her eternal shame.

Chapter 4 of Gaskell's novel (which has been rattling along) ends: 'Ruth was little accustomed to oppose the wishes of any one—obedient and docile by nature, and unsuspicious and innocent of any harmful consequences. She entered the carriage, and drove towards London' (p. 61).[1] As Mrs Twinn puts it:

So the reader is left expecting the couple to arrive in London as they turn over the page. Therefore it is with some astonishment that the reader finds himself transported to 'a little mountain village in North Wales.' Why did Gaskell change her mind? Are there any clues that she has intended to do this all along?

It's a good question. Without explanation or any further
mention of London, we find ourselves at the beginning of
Chapter 5 in the Welsh village Mrs Twinn mentions. It
is unnamed, but some 17 miles from 'Pen trê Voelas'—
somewhere in the north of the principality, near Snow-
donia we may guess. It is early July—only two months can
have passed since Chapter 4 (as Mrs Twinn calculates).
It turns out that the inn in which Henry and Ruth are
now staying is familiar to him from his varsity days. He
knows 'its dirt of old', as Gaskell ominously puts it. He and
his fellow undergraduates used to bring 'reading parties'
there.

From the disreputable nature of Mrs Jenny Morgan,
the landlady, it is clear that the inn does not uphold strict
rules of morality among its patrons. 'Young men will be
young men,' Mrs Morgan thinks indulgently when she
apprehends that Ruth is 'not his wife . . . His wife would
have brought her maid, and given herself twice as many
airs about the sitting rooms'. Ruth, presumably, is wearing
gloves, so the ring, or its absence, are invisible to the
innkeeper's sharp eyes. Clearly 'Mrs Bellingham'—as she
will have been introduced—has *some* luggage (at least a
change of clothes and toilet articles) with her, if no maid.
From Mrs Morgan's indulgent reflections, we may assume
that when the young students last came, three years ago,
they brought some loose company ('Cyprians') with them
in addition to their books. Ruth is just such another *belle
amie*.

It is said that the couple intend only 'a week's enjoyment
of that Alpine scenery', although it seems from other
comments that he may be looking for a house to set her
up in. Even in private conversation Ruth still timidly
addresses Bellingham as 'sir', but it is clear they have
slept together and are currently sharing a bed. Although
she does not yet know it, Ruth is already pregnant with

baby Leonard. Bellingham, ominously, is beginning to be
bored with the little dressmaker. It has been the best
part of a week and the evenings drag without livelier
company. But before their relationship can work itself to
the inevitable conclusion, Bellingham falls into a fever and
is repossessed by his vengeful mother, who self-righteously
casts out the little minx who has clearly entrapped her son.

So begins Ruth's long travail as a Victorian lone parent
and the main business of the novel. But the question
remains, why does it begin in North Wales, not London?
It may, of course, be a bad join in the narrative. But there
is a possible explanation, more flattering to Gaskell's art
and her tender sensibility. The first question that strikes
the reader is: did Henry Bellingham *really* have to go to
London? Probably not. His uncertain and stumbling choice
of words ('I *believe*—I have business') and his claim to
have just this moment remembered that he has business
in the capital suggest a spur-of-the-moment brainwave. It
strikes him that, since Ruth is fortuitously homeless and
friendless, now is the time to make his move.

Secondly, what is the route that the couple have taken
in Bellingham's carriage? If they are going from the
general direction of an 'eastern assize town' to northern
Wales, they would almost certainly have to go cross-
country through London. So it would not be illogical for
the carriage to drive, on its first leg, in that direction, as
we are told at the end of Chapter 4. What subsequently
happens in London? First, Bellingham would put up
in some convenient (but discreet) hostelry and do what
seducers do when innocent young things fall into their
clutches. Then, on the next day, he would buy some clothes
and other necessaries for his new mistress (who has
left without luggage—not that her milliner's-apprentice
outfits would be appropriate for her new station in life as
'Mrs Bellingham').

It would be difficult for Bellingham to stay in town—his mother might find out. She might tell Ruth's guardian. The girl is 15—three years over the age of consent for sexual intercourse but six years below the age of consent for marriage in England. It would look bad if Ruth laid a bastard to his charge in the 'assize town' where he lived, and claimed that he had promised marriage. Even if this disaster were averted, Mrs Mason might find out what has happened to one of her charges (she is *in loco parentis*) and make all sorts of trouble. Where would be a convenient place to install the young lady where she might be available, but not publicly visible? As a 23-year-old, Henry has little experience in such worldly matters as setting up a mistress. But, he remembers, there was that place in Wales where, as a student, he and his friends had that jolly time, and where the landlady was so accommodating. Just the ticket! The journey is around 200 miles, and they will arrive in a couple of days in his hired carriage. He will find some remote (and cheaply rented) house for Ruth well out of the world's eye. He can visit her at his discretion. The name 'Bellingham' will mean nothing in rural Wales.

Why did Gaskell not describe the London episode: the defloration of Ruth? Because it was painful and (as with the murder in *Mary Barton*) she did not like painful scenes and would go to some lengths to avoid them. Secondly, it would have been difficult to present Ruth to the reader in such a way as not to make her seem in some part guilty of her own downfall—unless, that is, she also presented Bellingham as a Lovelace-like rapist (something else she did not want to do). Ruth did not have to get in the carriage and go to London. She could have taken her chances with her guardian, explained her innocence to Mrs Mason, even have gone to the local clergyman. Even in the London inn—or house of assignation—where her pearl without price was lost, Ruth did not *have to* give in (assuming that Henry did not force her). A firm 'no' would have sufficed to preserve her virtue. A decent veil is drawn, so that we do not think too ill of the poor motherless child. The ever-motherly Mrs Gaskell will not cast the first stone.[2]

The Oxford World's Classics *Ruth* is edited by Alan Shelston.

What is Henry Esmond's 'great scheme'?

I have read *The History of Henry Esmond* many times and have examined the manuscript and written on changes Thackeray made to it. I have transcribed the notebook which the author compiled for the novel, and have even edited the novel itself (not, unfortunately, for Oxford World's Classics).[1] But I cannot make sense of the Restoration plot which makes up the main business of *Henry Esmond*'s third volume. Nor have I read any account which does make sense of it. Commentators and editors (including myself and the Oxford World's Classics editor) tactfully ignore the problem as something insoluble and best passed over.

The Restoration plot was evidently suggested by that in Scott's *Woodstock*, and in many details follows its original closely. In *Henry Esmond* the hero intends to win Beatrix's (indelibly Jacobite) heart by changing the succession of royal families in England. He will bring the Pretender back from France, arrange a clandestine meeting with Queen Anne, and thus win her support for him as heir. She has, of course, no child of her own to put on the throne. The 'great scheme' is set up and played out in Chapters 8 and 9 of Volume III of *Henry Esmond*.

In Chapter 8, Esmond travels to France. It is May 1714. He goes incognito as 'Monsieur Simon', giving it out to the *monde* in London that he (Mr Esmond) 'was sick, and gone to Hampshire for country air' (p. 398).

He leaves his faithful manservant, John Lockwood, at Castlewood (in Hampshire). 'The circumstance on which Mr Esmond's scheme was founded' is the fact that young Viscount Castlewood, currently resident in France and a fervent Jacobite, 'was born in the same year as the Prince of Wales; had not a little of the Prince's air, height, and figure; and . . . took no small pride in his resemblance to a person so illustrious' (p. 399).

In France 'M. Simon' persuades the Prince and the Viscount to join in the 'scheme'. Esmond prepares the ground by sending back to the London house of the Castlewoods in Kensington Square a portrait of the Viscount, done by Rigaud. In fact, it is a portrait of the Prince. It is 'hung up in the place of honour in her ladyship's drawing-room'. This is a dangerous game the Castlewoods are playing. On 23 June 1714 Parliament posts a reward of £5,000 for anyone discovering the Pretender in England. The authorities were nervous of his reappearing on the scene during the last, tense days of Anne's reign.

Esmond's intention with the Rigaud portrait, clearly enough, is to delude the world as to the facial appearance of the Viscount, Frank. As a further precaution, 'All the old domestics at the little house of Kensington Square were changed.' It was given out that Frank would be returning to England 'about the 17th or 18th day of June, proposing to take horse from Paris immediately, and bringing but a single servant with him'. He has been away for five years. The essence of the 'scheme' is given in a coded message sent on 10 June 1714 which 'told those that had the key, that

the King will take the Viscount Castlewood's passports and travel to England under that lord's name. His Majesty will be at the Lady Castlewood's house in Kensington Square, where his friends may visit him; they are to ask for the Lord Castlewood. (p. 406)

So far, the outline of the 'scheme' is crystal clear. The Prince will come to England impersonating the Viscount Castlewood, who will accompany him as his personal servant. The complications arise in Chapter 9 ('The Original of the Portrait comes to England'). The chapter opens:

'Twas announced in the family that my Lord Castlewood would arrive, having a confidential French gentleman in his suite, who acted as a secretary to his lordship, and who being a Papist, and a foreigner of good family, though now in rather a menial place, would have his meals served in his chamber, and not with the domestics of the house. (p. 408)

This also seems clear enough. The Viscount—in the person of 'Monsieur Baptiste', is to be kept out of the way. It will be assumed by the brighter servants that—Frank Castlewood having converted to Catholicism during his five years in France—M. Baptiste is actually his chaplain.

The unclarity begins with Esmond's riding down with John Lockwood to Rochester, to await 'the king in that very town where his father had last set his foot on the English shore' (p. 409). A room has been reserved in an inn 'for my Lord Castlewood and his servant.' But when the two men appear, Lord Castlewood is Lord Castlewood and the *Prince* is playing the part of M. Baptiste (very badly—he does not take orders well and 'runs after barmaids'). What happened to the business about his taking the Viscount's passports? The Prince has evidently travelled to England under M. Baptiste's name. Confusing.

Confusion intensifies. The three men gallop to London, reaching Kensington at nightfall. Lockwood has been left behind at Rochester to take care of the tired horses. He will follow the next day. The principals arrive at the Castlewood residence—Lord Castlewood *in propria persona*, the Prince still as M. Baptiste, and 'constantly neglecting his part with an inconceivable levity' (p. 413).

Both visitors have, of course, been seen by all the servants of the house gathered to welcome their homecoming master. It may cross their minds that he does not resemble the portrait hanging upstairs. But let that pass.

There then follows the most perplexing passage. Next day, John Lockwood reappears:

Esmond's man, honest John Lockwood, had served his master and the family all his life, and the colonel [i.e. Esmond] knew that he could answer for John's fidelity as for his own. John returned with the horses from Rochester betimes the next morning, and the colonel gave him to understand that on going to Kensington, where he was free of the servants' hall, and indeed courting Mrs. Beatrix's maid, he was to ask no questions, and betray no surprise, but to vouch stoutly that the young gentleman he should see in a red coat there was my Lord Viscount Castlewood, and that his attendant in grey was Monsieur Baptiste the Frenchman. He was to tell his friends in the kitchen such stories as he remembered of my lord viscount's youth at Castlewood . . . Jack's ideas of painting had not been much cultivated during his residence in Flanders with his master; and before my young lord's return, he had been easily got to believe that the picture brought over from Paris, and now hanging in Lady Castlewood's drawing-room, was a perfect likeness of her son, the young lord. And the domestics having all seen the picture many times, and catching but a momentary imperfect glimpse of the two strangers on the night of their arrival, never had a reason to doubt the fidelity of the portrait; and next day, when they saw the original of the piece habited exactly as he was represented in the painting, with the same periwig, ribbon, and uniform of the Guard, quite naturally addressed the gentleman as my Lord Castlewood, my lady viscountess's son.

The secretary of the night previous was now the viscount; the viscount wore the secretary's grey frock . . . (pp. 416–17)

Why switch identities now? If it were necessary, why was not the change done at Rochester, or behind some convenient hedge outside London? And, most confusingly, why did they not stick to the original plan of having the Prince travel as the Viscount? In the above passage, it seems from the opening sentences that John Lockwood is in on the 'scheme'. But then all the business about his being ignorant of art and 'easily got to believe that the picture brought over from France . . . was a perfect likeness of . . . the young lord' indicates that he is *not* in on the 'scheme', but a dupe like the other domestics. But then, later in the chapter (after the Prince has fondled his sweetheart) it is made clear that Lockwood—who fought six campaigns in Flanders with the real Viscount—is quite well aware who 'M. Baptiste' is. And, of course, he was at Rochester when the Viscount and Baptiste disembarked. He must be 'in'.

Throughout July the Prince, in the person of Viscount Castlewood, keeps to his rooms on the pretext of an old war wound breaking out. He has an interview with the terminally ailing Queen in Kensington Palace Gardens (as Viscount Castlewood, paying his respects to the sovereign), and all looks hopeful. But when Frank and Henry confront him with their suspicions that he intends to dishonour Frank's sister Beatrix (who is loyally willing to be dishonoured by her monarch), the Prince flounces out of the safe house in Kensington Square. He has the co-conspirator Bishop Atterbury install him in the house of a curate in nearby Kensington Mall. Here he is known as 'Mr Bates' (p. 448). The reader gathers that, in this character, he is in the habit of going abroad. Presumably a sharp-eyed servant in the Castlewood household might have seen this mysterious personage on the night of his arrival as Monsieur Baptiste, on the next day as the Viscount Castlewood, and now promenading the streets of Kensington as Mr Bates.

A reward of £5,000 awaits any British citizen who identifies the Prince. Short of wearing a crown, the Prince

could hardly make it easier for some Kensington resident
to get rich quick. 'Mr Bates' is meanwhile accompanied
by a Castlewood servant ('Martin') who, from a number
of comments in the narrative, evidently still thinks
the Prince ('Mr Bates') is the Viscount. Stupid Martin,
presumably, is not talking to his old friends at the servants'
hall a few hundred yards away in Kensington Square.
And those servants might wonder where the 'Viscount'
has mysteriously disappeared to, and why he has left
M. Baptiste behind. Some scheme.

On the last day of July, the conspirators decide that it
is 'now or never'. They summon 'Mr George' (yet another
pseudonym for the Prince) to attend on the dying Queen
in her bedchamber, and be proclaimed by her the next
monarch, King James III of England. But 'Mr George'
(alias 'Mr Bates') is not to be found at the curate's house.
Other bedchambers are on his mind. He has gone into
Hampshire (as Viscount Castlewood!) to seduce Beatrix.
Her brother and mother have sent her to the Castlewood
seat in the country, to be away from the attentions of the
Prince. She has foiled them with a secret note to her royal
lover.

Frank and Henry gallop down to Castlewood. They save
Beatrix's honour in the nick of time. Or perhaps they don't
(the narrative is slightly vague on the matter). But when
they return to London with the Prince, it is too late: King
George has been proclaimed: 'all the vain hopes of the
weak and foolish young pretender were blown away' (p.
461). The Prince is smuggled back to the safety of France:
whether as the Viscount Castlewood, M. Baptiste, Mr
Bates, or Mr George, the narrative does not say.

What was Thackeray thinking of in this dog's dinner of
an episode? My guess is that the original 'simple' scheme
('The Pretender impersonates the Viscount') was clouded
in his mind when he came to write it down by the sudden

realization of a fatal flaw. As conceived by Thackeray, the Prince has very imperfect English. This, in fact, is one of the many disqualifications for kingship which emerge during his clandestine six weeks in England. He might take the Viscount's passports, but any inspector— particularly on the English side of the Channel—would quickly realize that this was no English nobleman, but a French impostor. Hence, the plot was changed so that the Prince was smuggled in as M. Baptiste.

On the other hand, a French servant could hardly be smuggled into Kensington Palace for a private interview with the Queen of England. Only a lofty (and loyal) English nobleman would serve that purpose. Hence the change of identities, the day after arrival. That change of identities also validated the business of the Rigaud portrait which Thackeray had gone to some trouble in setting up. The John Lockwood threads were left dangling, but readers pay very little attention to servants. The original 'simple scheme' was overlaid with a fussier scheme. And the fit was somewhat less than perfect.

Why did Thackeray not sort out this mess? Because as he came to the end of the novel, he was in a great hurry. He was leaving for America, and had to prepare for a hectic lecture tour over there.[2] He patched over the bad joins between the two schemes and hoped for the best. Hoped, that is, that readers would not notice. Nor, in general, do they. There are much better things to concentrate on in this wonderful novel than a few hanging threads.

The Oxford World's Classics *The History of Henry Esmond* is edited by Donald Hawes.

Charles Dickens · *Bleak House*

═══

What kills Lady Dedlock?

═══

A recent disagreement between two Dickensian critics
highlights a central puzzle in *Bleak House*. In a 1983 article, entitled 'The Fever of *Bleak House*', Fred Schwarzbach
noted that 'disease plays a central part' in the novel's
plot, 'as both subject and metaphor'.[1] Few readers will
disagree. Many characters in *Bleak House* die, of many
ailments, ranging from opium poisoning, through cerebral
stroke, to that most controversial of causes of death,
'spontaneous combustion'. But 'What is not clear, and
has puzzled modern critics', Schwarzbach notes, 'is why
Dickens has Jo contract smallpox. Should he not have
written instead about cholera, the most feared of all fevers
in mid-Victorian England, which recently had ravaged the
nation in the epidemic of 1848–9?'

Two suggested explanations are offered, both pertinent
to the novel's design. Smallpox (unlike typhus) is contagious and serves a 'symbolic' function by linking all
the otherwise divergent lines of character and action.
'Connection' is a major theme in the novel, and nothing
connects like the pox. Secondly, on the level of plot device,
the disease serves the practical purpose of 'disfiguring
Esther so that no one will notice her resemblance to her
mother.'

In a subsequent article, '"Deadly Stains"; Lady Dedlock's Death', Schwarzbach elaborates this insight, arguing that—although Dickens does not clearly indicate the
fact—it *must* be smallpox that kills Lady Dedlock.[2] The
moment of contagion occurs in Chapter 16 when, disguised

in her servant's clothes, she pays a night-time visit to her lover, Captain Hawdon, resting in his pauper's 'berryin' place'. Dickens accompanies the contagious episode with a charnel-house description of the miasmic infection swirling around the graveyard, and its deadly deposits of 'witch ointment' and 'Tom's [i.e. Tom-all-alone's] slime' (p. 243). In this gothic effusion, Schwarzbach detects a 'key detail' which 'evidently has escaped the notice of modern critics' in the sentence: 'The servant [i.e. Lady Dedlock in her maid's gown] shrinks into a corner—into a corner of that hideous archway, *with its deadly stains contaminating her dress*; and . . . so remains for some moments.' The stains are 'deadly' because they contain the virus (literally 'poison'). Dickens selected the scene for illustration in the serial version of the novel:

Consecrated Ground

Smallpox, as Schwarzbach notes, has 'a variable incubation period', and it is the fever phase of this disease which, we are to assume, eventually kills Lady Dedlock. In her last hours, we are told by eyewitnesses that she is 'hoarse', 'pale', and 'unable to eat'; symptoms compatible with those of the smallpox fever (a sceptic might note, however, that they are symptomatic of much milder ailments than smallpox). Schwarzbach informs us that Victorians believed smallpox could lie dormant until 'a period when the physical system was fatigued or under stress—that is why Jo becomes seriously ill only after Bucket forces him to "move on" ceaselessly.'

Lady Dedlock is certainly under stress in the last two days of her life. Her world collapses with a letter accusing her of killing Tulkinghorn, and a visit from the obnoxious Guppy indicating that her secret past is secret no more. She will shortly be unmasked before the world as a 'harlot' (which she is) and charged as a murderess (which she is not). 'There is no escape but in death' (p. 790), she resolves.

But she does not, in fact, kill herself—or at least not directly. It is morning. Dashing off a letter to her husband (which will induce a paralytic stroke when he reads it), she confesses guilt for everything but the murder, and promises 'I will encumber you no more'. By which we understand, she will disappear without trace. She veils and dresses for the outside weather; it is winter, and bitterly cold. She 'leaves all her jewels and her money' (although she evidently keeps her watch), and slips out into the early morning London streets.

It is not at all apparent at this stage what Lady Dedlock's intentions are—but it is clear enough that she has a plan of some kind. As we reconstruct it, her first intention is to go down to Saint Albans to have a last unseen sight of Esther. She does not intend to speak to her daughter, merely to gaze at her from afar. Why she does not take money sufficient for the train or coach is mysterious. Presumably she thinks that travel on public transport would make her too conspicuous. But, as subsequent events make clear, a well-dressed gentlewoman, walking the winter roads of outer London, is a sight that sticks in observers' minds. The lady is, we deduce, not thinking straight.

For whatever reason, Lady Dedlock resolves to *walk* the twenty-odd miles into Hertfordshire and to Bleak House. When she arrives, many hours later, she discovers that Esther is in fact in London. She evidently gives up hope of having a last sight of her daughter. Lady Dedlock persuades the brickmaker's wife, Jenny, to change clothes with her, and travel on in a northwards direction. This, she hopes, will throw any pursuers off the scent. Jenny's brutish husband is bribed into complicity with the last of Lady Dedlock's valuables, her watch—something that, presumably, she had hoped to give to Esther.

Now dressed less conspicuously in Jenny's clothes, Lady Dedlock retraces her steps, walking back to London. Why, one wonders? Meanwhile, Esther and Bucket are in close pursuit. Conceivably, their paths actually cross on the London–Saint Albans road: they galloping post-haste north, she limping painfully south on the road that is now the A1. Before leaving London, Bucket has cast a shrewd eye over Lady Dedlock's private apartments. He notes, among other things, that she has taken no money or valuables with her ('rum', he thinks). His first deductions are clear. A woman who does not need money is one who is going on her last journey in life, for which there is no charge—the river, that is. Bucket's first stop is by Limehouse, to check if Lady Dedlock has thrown herself in the Thames, off one of the metropolitan bridges favoured by desperate females.

Esther observes Bucket make his discreet enquiries of

the river warden, whose job it is to scoop the day's harvest of corpses out of the water: 'A man yet dank and muddy, in long swollen sodden boots and a hat like them, was called out of a boat, and whispered with Mr Bucket, who went away with him down some slippery steps—as if to look at something secret that he had to show' (pp. 803–4). But the woman's corpse which the warden shows Bucket is, evidently, not that of a gentlewoman, or this particular gentlewoman ('thank God').

Bucket and Esther continue their pursuit of Lady Dedlock, by fast private coach, to the edge of Saint Albans, arriving between five and six in the morning. Lady Dedlock had passed the same way between eight and nine the previous evening. When they arrive at the brickmakers' cottage, Bucket and Esther discover that neither Lady Dedlock nor Jenny is there. The astute Bucket (but not the sweetly unsuspicious Esther) penetrates the 'change of clothes' ruse at once. But for inscrutable reasons of his own, the detective keeps Esther in the dark. (As his notes show, Dickens was in two minds whether to keep the reader in the dark as well, and decided against it.)

Bucket and Esther retrace their steps to London. It is now snowing hard. They arrive back in the capital around four. In Holborn, they pick up Lady Dedlock's trail again at the Snagsby household (Esther still thinks that they are, for reasons she cannot fathom, following Jenny). Woodcourt now joins them. Guster has a letter from Lady Dedlock, which she has been asked to deliver by hand. The girl has also been told to delay any pursuit as best she can. Bucket quickly gets possession of Lady Dedlock's letter, and shakes the truth out of a feebly obstinate Guster.

In her letter Lady Dedlock declares that she has only two objects left in life: 'to elude pursuit, and to be lost.' 'I have no purpose but to die,' she says bleakly. 'Cold, wet, and fatigue, are sufficient causes for my being found dead;

but I shall die of others, though I suffer from these. It was right that all that had sustained me should give way at once and that I should die of terror and my conscience' (p. 841, my emphasis).

Guster, under pressure from the remorseless Bucket, reveals that Lady Dedlock has asked directions to 'the poor burying ground . . . where the man was buried that took the sleeping stuff' (p. 843; i.e. where Hawdon, having committed suicide with an overdose of opium, is buried).[3] One element in Lady Dedlock's plan is now clear; she wishes to be buried as a destitute vagrant alongside her lover. This is why she has taken no money, and disguised herself as a working-class woman. (Although Dickens is too delicate to mention the fact, we have to suppose that she has exchanged her fine silk underclothes with Jenny as well, and discarded her wedding ring and those 'sparkling rings' which so impressed Jo, when she made her earlier visit to the 'berryin' place', p. 243). Her body will be found and, without any identifying marks, deposited without ceremony in a pauper's grave alongside Hawdon's, or so she hopes.[4]

Woodcourt, Bucket, and Esther now hurry to the 'berrying place'. There, beneath the 'horrible arch', lies a body. At last Bucket tells Esther the truth ('They changed clothes at the cottage'), but the distracted girl cannot take the information in.

I saw before me, lying on the step, the mother of the dead child [i.e. Jenny]. She lay there, with one arm creeping round a bar of the iron gate, and seeming to embrace it. She lay there, who had so lately spoken to my mother. She lay there, a distressed, unsheltered, senseless creature. She who had brought my mother's letter, who could give me the only clue to where my mother was; she, who was to guide us to rescue and save her whom we had sought so far, who had come to this condition by some means connected with my mother that I could not follow, and might be passing beyond our reach and help at that moment; she lay there, and they stopped me! I saw, but did not comprehend, the solemn and compassionate look in Mr Woodcourt's face. I saw, but did not comprehend, his touching the other on the breast to keep him back. I saw him stand uncovered in the bitter air, with a reverence for something. But my understanding for all this was gone.

I even heard it said between them:

'Shall she go?'

'She had better go. Her hands should be the first to touch her. They have a higher right than ours.'

I passed on to the gate, and stooped down. I lifted the heavy head, put the long dank hair aside, and turned the face. And it was my mother, cold and dead. (p. 847)

Esther falls ill at this point, and we learn nothing of the inquest, nor what verdict is passed on the death of Lady Dedlock.

Schwarzbach's 'smallpox' thesis is beguiling. Lady Dedlock is, as in coroners' terminology, 'a well nourished woman' with no history of invalidism. *Something*, we assume must have killed her. Those 'filthy stains' are a plausible 'cause of death'. Susan Shatto, in an answering article entitled 'Lady Dedlock and the Plot of *Bleak House*',[5] begs to disagree and gives powerful reasons for her disagreement. While accepting that smallpox infects Jo, Charley, and Esther, she is entirely unconvinced that Lady Dedlock contracts the disease. Nor does she believe that smallpox kills Jo. He finally succumbs to pulmonary tuberculosis, she maintains.

The time-scheme, as Shatto points out, contradicts Schwarzbach's 'fever' hypothesis. There are *two years* intervening between the 'filthy stains' contamination in Chapter 16, and Lady Dedlock's death in Chapter 59. It stretches credulity to imagine that the disease would have remained latent for two years in its host: 'Dickens would

surely [have] known the average period of incubation
[was] usually ten to twelve days, and at the maximum
seventeen days.' It is true that Victorians (as Carlyle's
famous description of the infected shirt in *Past and
Present* indicates) believed that clothing could harbour
disease and spread it to the upper classes. But Lady
Dedlock's servant would have been much more at risk
than the mistress who, only once, borrowed her clothes—
assuming, as is extremely unlikely—she did not wash (and
decontaminate) those clothes after Lady Dedlock returned
them. There is no intervening source of contagion that we
know about.

It is a persuasive refutation. The smallpox hypothesis is
attractive, but unsustainable—unless one assumes wilful
medical ignorance on Dickens's part, and among his
readers. Less persuasive, perhaps, is Shatto's theory of
what *does* kill Lady Dedlock: 'most readers would consider
a forty-two mile journey on foot through a snowstorm
sufficient for a cosseted lady suffering great emotional
stress to grow pale, exhausted, hoarse, miserable, and
ultimately, to die.' If for 'cosseted' one were to read 'well
fed', 'most readers' might not wholeheartedly agree. Lady
Dedlock is in her mid-forties, or just under 50 (Dickens
is delicate about the precise age). We are given no hint
that she is an invalid. In fact, the evidence suggests that
she is anything but a weakling. She has borne a child in
secret and defied conventional morality by none the less
making her way in the world with nothing but her looks
and will to assist her. This, we deduce, is a tough woman.
She is capable of making trips at night in disguise to grave-
yards in slum areas of London. She evidently knows how
to look after herself on the streets. On her last journey to
Saint Albans and back she has had rest, shelter (and some
liquid refreshment) at both the brickmakers' cottage and
in Holborn.

Lady Dedlock obviously *intends* to die by her lover's grave. This is the script she has written for her last act. But death does not come on time simply because it is dramatically 'right' that it should do so—except in fairy stories and melodrama. There is also the strange business of Bucket and Woodcourt's reactions when they see the body on the steps. How—from a distance of many yards—do they *know* it is a corpse? Why do they take their hats off? Woodcourt is a medical man. Noble as the gesture is, holding back until Esther has had time to examine the body of her mother ('she has a higher right') would seem to contravene his Hippocratic oath. Unless, that is, he knew that any medical attention is now entirely useless.

If it were merely exhaustion that had felled Lady Dedlock, the doctor's duty (with the detective at his heels) would be to rush forward, elbowing Esther out of the way if necessary, shouting—'make way, make way, I'm a medical man'. He would feel her pulse, chafe her wrists, apply restoratives and smelling salts, burn feathers under her nose. If there were any flicker of life, he would punch her chest, try artificial respiration, wrap her in warm coverings.

And although exhausted (if it were only exhaustion that had rendered her insensible) there would be every expectation that some life might remain in a healthy, 40-year-old woman after a day-and-a-half's exposure and that the prompt attention of a medical man might revive it. Well-fed, warmly clothed, middle-aged people have survived the London streets longer than that—and do so around us every day.

On her part, Esther assumes the body slumped on the steps is 'senseless', not dead. But Bucket evidently knows better. It is too late. There are a string of clues as to how he knows that the body lying in front of them is lifeless, beyond resuscitation. The fact that she stripped herself of

money and jewels initially persuaded him that the woman
intended to do away with herself, and had a plan for doing
so—quickly and efficiently (when did Lady Dedlock ever
dither?). Hence Bucket's first stop at the river. Having met
a dead end there, Bucket deduced (from the evidence of
Esther's handkerchief in Lady Dedlock's jewel case) that
the mother will have gone to take a last glimpse of her child
in Saint Albans (as she thinks). There are further clues for
Bucket in Lady Dedlock's statement that 'I shall die'—but
not of cold, wet, and fatigue. She has asked directions to
where 'the man was buried that took the sleeping stuff'
(as Guster gratuitously adds). Dickens, evidently, does
not want us to forget that Hawdon took his own life by
overdosing on opium (easily acquired by anyone at this
period). Someone like Lady Dedlock, given to midnight
insomniac walks in London and in Lincolnshire, would
certainly have had a supply of opium or laudanum in
her medicine cabinet. How does Bucket know, from many
yards distant, that Lady Dedlock is dead as a doornail?
Because he has (correctly) worked out that she has killed
herself. How? With the desperate woman's best friend,
opium.

The balance of probability is, we deduce, not that Lady
Dedlock died of delayed smallpox, nor cold and exhaustion,
but that like Hawdon, she poisoned herself. The prospect of
being revived, unmasked as the mother of an illegitimate
child, publicly tried, and haled off to prison for murder
would be too awful. Nor would Lady Dedlock *risk* that
happening.

Why then, do Bucket and Woodcourt not say something?
Bucket—in the business of Jenny's clothes—has shown
an ability to keep facts to himself. There was a particular reason for taciturnity where suicide was concerned.
Nineteenth-century regulations as to the interment of
those guilty of 'felo de se' were savagely punitive. Up to

1823 the suicide was required to be buried at a crossroads, in unconsecrated ground, with a stake through the heart (the barbarous ceremony was, for obvious reasons, rarely carried out). Until 1880 the suicide was required to be buried without rites of Christian sepulture. For this reason magistrates, investigating police, and doctors signing death certificates were generously vague, misleading, or simply silent as to cause of death. As, indeed, Woodcourt is when he is called to Hawdon's body. He does *not want to know* if Hawdon took an overdose:

'He has died,' says the surgeon, 'of an over-dose of opium, there is no doubt. The room is strongly flavoured with it. There is enough here now,' taking an old teapot from Mr Krook, 'to kill a dozen people.'

'Do you think he did it on purpose?' asks Krook.

'Took the over-dose?'

'Yes!' Krook almost smacks his lips with the unction of a horrible interest.

'I can't say. I should think it unlikely, as he has been in the habit of taking so much. But nobody can tell.' (pp. 153–4)

Guster is less circumspect.

The suspicion of suicide explains a little exchange between Jo and 'the servant', Lady Dedlock, in which she is particularly inquisitive on the question of whether Hawdon has been buried in consecrated ground:

'The servant [Lady Dedlock] shrinks into a corner—into a corner of that hideous archway, with its deadly stains contaminating her dress; and putting out her two hands, and passionately telling him to keep away from her, for he is loathsome to her, so remains for some moments. Jo stands staring, and is still staring when she recovers herself.

'Is this place of abomination, consecrated ground?'

'I don't know nothink of consequential ground,' says Jo, still staring.

'Is it blessed?'

'WHICH?' says Jo, in the last degree amazed.
'Is it blessed?'
'I'm blest if I know,' says Jo. (p. 243)

Hawdon, evidently, *does* lie in consecrated ground and had some form of Christian burial, even though he took his own life. Ironically, Lady Dedlock is buried in the Mausoleum in Lincolnshire: separated in death from her lover. But, it is clear, the verdict on her at the Coroner's Inquest cannot have been suicide. Nor would Bucket, or Woodcourt, say anything to put such a thought in the investigating magistrate's mind.

The death of Lady Dedlock is no minor episode in *Bleak House*. Dickens gives it pride of place as a 'number ending', with a vivid 'curtain line' and one of the novel's forty illustrations. It is a narrative highpoint. The reader is bound to be curious as to how she dies, and we have—I think—four options. The smallpox hypothesis is attractive, but medically unsound in ways that Dickens would certainly have been aware of. Exhaustion is more likely, but the timing of the death is unsettlingly convenient— more convenient than such deaths are in real life.

This leads to what one might call the 'melodrama' option. In melodrama, heroines can and do die of such non-pathological conditions as 'broken heart' or 'grief' at precisely the right theatrical moment. In life, 'stress' and 'despair' do kill—but usually in undramatic, protracted, messy, and untimely ways. The melodramatic option is plausible but not flattering to Dickens's 'art', nor does it fit in a novel which is elsewhere so successfully realistic.

The fourth option is that Lady Dedlock, like Hawdon (whose death she in other ways imitates, as I have suggested), did away with herself by the opium which she would surely have to hand in her medicine box. (The drug was not even minimally controlled in Britain until the Pharmacy Act of 1868; before then it was more easily available—and cheaper—than beer.) As with Hawdon, the benevolent authorities gloss over the fact of her suicide— Sir Leicester will not know; Esther will not know; the world will not know. The place in Lincolnshire can have its grand funeral. Of the options, I prefer the fourth, although it is unenforceable by clinching evidence.

The Oxford World's Classics *Bleak House* is edited by Stephen Gill.

Elizabeth Gaskell · *North and South*

═══

What are Mr Hale's 'doubts'?

═══

The Victorians had a soft spot for novels about the 'agony' of religious uncertainty. The most popular, by far, was *Robert Elsmere* (1888) by Mrs Humphry Ward. Mrs Ward's hero is a young Anglican minister, tormented by spiritual anxiety—'doubts'. Specifically, Robert cannot accept Christ's divinity, the biblical miracles, or the 'damnatory psalms'. Yet, the Revd Mr Elsmere 'believes'.

Elsmere is a product of Oxford in the 1850s. The university had been, since Newman's first 'Tract for the Times' in 1833, the epicentre of religious doubt and what Gladstone (reviewing *Robert Elsmere*) called 'the battle of belief'. After much spiritual battling, Elsmere moves towards a Unitarian position on matters of theology. He resigns his country living, and starts a 'settlement' for the poor ('The New Brotherhood') in the East End of London. At the end of the novel he dies of consumption. His monument, the New Brotherhood, lives on.

With its Gladstonian endorsement, *Robert Elsmere* sold by the thousand in Britain and the million in America where, at the height of its popularity, it was given away free with 4-cent bars of soap, on the principle evidently that cleanliness is next to godliness. Since there was at this period no international copyright, Mrs Ward got nothing from the sale of either book or bar.

The Victorian reading public had an insatiable appetite for this kind of fiction. From the 1840s onward there was a regular annual supply of 'novels of faith and doubt', a survey of which is offered in Margaret Maison's

delightfully entitled *Search your Soul, Eustace!* (1961).
The twentieth-century reader does not have much time
for Eustace's soul-searching. If there is one category of
Victorian fiction which has died the death, it is novels of
faith and doubt. Even the greatest of them, *Robert Elsmere*
(to my personal regret), has been unable to hold its place
in the Oxford World's Classics catalogue. *Sic transit.*

Elizabeth Gaskell's *North and South*, although normally categorized an 'industrial novel', pivots on an act
of religious conscience by the heroine's father. The Revd
Mr Hale has been for a quarter of a century a clergyman
in Hampshire. A morally weak, but scrupulous man, Hale
out of the blue informs his appalled daughter that he must
resign his living forthwith. Moreover, he charges the girl
to pass the news on to his invalid wife. He has 'doubts',
Mr Hale explains to Margaret, reiterating the resonant
word three times. 'Doubts, papa! Doubts as to religion?'
(p. 34) his shocked daughter asks. (With a rare flash of
humour, Gaskell observes that Margaret wonders if her
father 'were about to turn Mahometan'.) 'No! not doubts
as to religion; not the slightest injury to that,' Mr Hale
firmly replies.

He will, he tells Margaret, just this once answer any
questions as to his changed views on religion: 'but after
to-night let us never speak of it again.' None the less,
during this single question-and-answer session, Mr Hale
is sadly unspecific as to what his 'painful, miserable
doubts' actually are. The whole point about doubts is
that they can go in any number of directions. If not
Islam, Mr Hale could be moving anywhere on a whole
spectrum of doctrinal positions from high Catholicism to
low Methodism.

Mr Hale does not answer his daughter's barrage of
anxious enquiries directly. Reaching up to his bookshelf he
reads out a long—and not very illuminating—peroration

from 'a Mr Oldfield', a country minister in Derbyshire, 'a hundred and sixty years ago, or more' (p. 34). The Revd Hale's recitation is not easy to follow and even harder to apply to his own case. Oldfield is not a household name, nor was he in 1854 (rarely, incidentally, have Oxford World's Classics notes been so necessary). Oldfield was, with 2,000 others as we discover, ejected from his living in 1662 (on the return of the monarch) on grounds of his refusal to 'conform'.

The only thing to the point which Mr Hale says to Margaret is that the bishop has recently offered him a new living, and the offer crystallized his spiritual uneasiness, and brought it to the pitch of rebellion—or at least resignation. 'I should have had to make a fresh declaration of conformity to the Liturgy' (p. 36), he tells his daughter. This means, apparently, that he would be obliged to make a new affirmation to the Thirty-Nine Articles, as he earlier did at college, at ordination, and on taking over his present living. Even refusing the preferment and staying at Helstone is now beyond him. He must resign.

But why? What precisely is it in the declaration of conformity which causes Mr Hale such agony at this moment? Which of the articles are difficult for him?— presumably those great bones of theological contention, the Apostolic Succession or the Trinity, although one cannot know.[1] He has been at Helstone, as far as we can make out, for going on thirty years. Why resign now? The Oldfield comparison is not apt since he, and the two thousand others, were 'ejected'—driven out. If he just keeps his head down, no one is going to *eject* the vicar of Helstone if he drifts towards a broad, or low-church position. As long as he does nothing wilfully provocative, he has considerable freedom to redefine his personal position on matters of faith and conscience. The only person who can eject Mr Hale is the vicar of Helstone.

He is, as we gather, a conscientious and caring parish priest much loved by his 'people'.

Mr Hale is an Oxford man (a significant detail), and has evidently kept in touch with his alma mater. His old tutor at 'Plymouth College' (Exeter College, we apprehend, from the geographical clue), Mr Bell, has connections in the north of England and has arranged for him to be a private tutor in 'Milton-Northern' (Manchester we apprehend) in 'Darkshire' (Lancashire, self-evidently).

A less pliant young lady than Margaret Hale might bridle at all this. For obscure reasons, she was obliged to leave home at the age of 9 and was billeted on relatives in London. The Shaws were kind enough—but they were not her beloved parents. In the interim, the Revd Mr Hale and his wife lavished their attention on her feckless brother Frederick—who after participating in a naval mutiny has been forced to join the Spanish army. A Spanish bride is in prospect. Now, at last, Margaret has returned to rural Helstone, a Hampshire village which she loves. She is a nubile 18 and, as she fondly thinks, is being prepared for a suitable marriage. Now she discovers—after only three months at home—that her father is intent on packing her off to the satanic mills of Darkshire. None the less, she does her duty—taking charge of the household from the incompetent hands of her invalid and neurotic mother whom the Revd Mr Hale, for all his 'conscience', has left entirely in the dark as to his intentions.

On the face of it, Mr Hale's 'agony' seems a mirror image of Robert Elsmere's, as does his drift towards Unitarianism—Christianity based on a 'human' conception of Christ, and ritual stripped to its minimal and most 'rational' form. With its intellectual core at Oxford, 'doubt' pulled mid-century Anglicans in two opposite directions. Rome and Newman was one; Manchester and the arch-Unitarian, James Martineau, was the other. Mrs

Gaskell's husband, William, was of course a Manchester Unitarian, as was she. Mr Hale too, we assume, will gravitate towards Martineau and Unitarianism, although it is not made entirely clear in the novel that he does so. His son Frederick (another 'rebel') gravitates towards Catholicism.[2]

Tempting as the comparison with Robert Elsmere is, Angus Easson specifically warns us in his notes to the Oxford World's Classics edition not to jump to it. The novels, he reminds us, are divided by almost thirty years—decades which were momentous for the Victorian Church. Elizabeth Gaskell did not intend a 'novel of religious doubt' of the kind popular later in the nineteenth century, but more of a 'crisis of conscience' novel. Mr Hale's dilemma is not, specifically, theological but temporal. He cannot accept that the Church of England has any right to *compel* men's beliefs. His position is akin to that of the rebellious dissenters of the seventeenth century. It is coercion, not doubt, which principally agonizes him.

Easson has tracked down the sources and the actual book from which Mr Hale lengthily quotes to Margaret. John Oldfield (1627?–82) was an obscure Derbyshire rector, ejected in 1662 under the Uniformity Act. Mr Hale quotes him as cited in a later text, *The Apology of Theophilus Lindsey* (1774). Lindsey—a dissenter even more obscure than Oldfield—was one of the founders of what later became Manchester Unitarianism. Angus Easson, as far as I am aware, is the only reader to have cracked this nut. Until he wrote an article on it in the *Review of English Studies*,[3] the Oldfield–Lindsey business was a secret between him and Elizabeth Gaskell. Few readers of the 1850s, and fewer in the 1990s, will pick up the intricate allusion to remote texts of forgotten religious controversies. Elizabeth Gaskell, it seems, was playing a very deep game. But what game, and why?

It is the more tantalizing since, after he leaves Helstone, Mr Hale seems to have no religion whatsoever. Over the next three years, during which he is a central personage in the novel, we never know what church in Milton he attends; what religious company he consorts with; whether or not he takes Communion. In one sense, this disinclination to specify could be temperamental— a Gaskellian trait. She is characteristically vague on a number of crucial narrative occasions. There is part of her, apparently, which thinks it bad form to be too direct about such personal matters as religion and health. When, for instance, Mrs Hale falls ill, Margaret alone is told by Mr Donaldson what fatal ailment she has: 'He spoke two short sentences in a low voice, watching her all the time.' Margaret blanches, and exclaims: 'Oh, my God, my God! but this is terrible. How shall I bear it? Such a deadly disease! no hope!' (p. 127). Mrs Hale is a long time dying, and we are given close descriptions of her 'spasms'. But what, specifically, the 'deadly disease' is we know no more than what Mr Hale's 'miserable and painful doubts' are.

One can, however, profitably pursue the puzzling religious doubts. Elizabeth Gaskell is insistent about the contemporaneousness of her 1854 narrative. It is, on the face of it, odd that in the late 1840s–early 1850s Mr Hale (MA Oxon.) should evoke obscure martyrs of 180 years ago. There were nearer martyrs than John Oldfield to evoke. Richard Hale (55 at the time of his death) must, we calculate, have been a student at Oxford in the 1820s at the same time as Newman and Keble. He would certainly, as a bright young undergraduate with a religious vocation, have come into contact with 'Oxford's agony'. He would have been immersed in the debate on Tractarian 'doubts' and the spiritual counter-movements which were tearing the university apart, and with it the Church of England.

Moreover (as the first readers of *North and South* would

have appreciated), there were some notorious novels on the subject of religious doubt written alongside Elizabeth Gaskell's. In 1849, five years before *North and South*, J. A. Froude published *The Nemesis of Faith*, 'the most notorious religious novel of the century', as it has been called. Its literally incendiary impact can be indicated by a brief summary:

> The story is told in confessional autobiographical form. Markham Sutherland, a young Oxford undergraduate, prepares for ordination in the Anglican Church, but is agonized by doubts which are expressed in a series of letters to a friend, Arthur, in the early 1840s. He cannot believe in the savage God of the Old Testament. At his family's urging and after six months' inward struggle, he takes orders, but resolves only to give ethical, not religious instruction. He is denounced by his co-religionists and obliged to give up his living. At this point of the narrative, Markham's epistolary record becomes the 'Confessions of a Sceptic', comprising straight theological disquisition . . . The novel was publicly burned (for its manifest blasphemy) at Oxford by William Sewell.[4]

Sewell was a fellow of Exeter College, who had written his own novel strenuously opposing 'doubt', *Hawkstone, A Tale of and for England* (1845), tilting principally at Newman (fellow at Oriel). Newman—shortly after going over to Rome—weighed in with *his* novel about 'doubt', *Loss and Gain, the Story of a Convert* (1848).

If one accepts the Plymouth College–Exeter College link, one could argue that Mr Bell—the Revd Hale's mentor and intimate friend—must have taken dinner several nights a week with the choleric Revd Sewell, and have heard his colleague's thunderous denunciations of 'atheist' Froude and 'apostate' Newman. It is, of course, probable that the Mancunian Bell is a covert Unitarian— uncomfortable in his faith, but unwilling to discommode himself by any act of rebellion that would mean no more

sinecure, no more high table, no more good college wine.
Best say nothing and put up with Sewell's nightly rant.

The Nemesis of Faith was not, in Angus Easson's term
'popular'—indeed, it was sufficiently unpopular in some
quarters to be incinerated; a rare distinction it shares
with Hardy's *Jude the Obscure*. But Froude's novel was
certainly well known, and it is inconceivable that the
inmates of Helstone's vicarage would not have heard of
it, even if they had not read it. Helstone (which has a
railway service) must be very cut off, and Mr Hale must
be very out of it in 1850, if he has not heard of the
current book-burnings in the Anglican Church. And any
well-informed Victorian reading about Mr Hale's doubts
in 1854 would, one may be sure, recall the Oxford furore
provoked by Newman, Froude, and Sewell. There was,
surely, no need for Mr Hale to go back 180 years to
find precedents for his 'doubts' and his act of conscience.
Markham Sutherland gives up his living, on what look
like remarkably similar grounds. Why, then, is Elizabeth
Gaskell not as forthright on the subject of Mr Hale's doubts
as Froude is? The question relates to another area of
referential fogginess in *North and South*: that concerning
'Milton-Northern' and 'Darkshire'. These locations are,
self-evidently, Manchester and Lancashire. Why not, then,
use the proper names? *North and South* was Elizabeth
Gaskell's third novel. Her first, *Mary Barton*, is boldly
subtitled 'A Manchester Story' and introduces any number
of actual urban locations. Why this topographical mas-
querade in *North and South*?

In order to makes sense of the veiled names, it is necessary to consider the journal for which Gaskell's novel was
first written. Unlike *Mary Barton* (which was published
first in two volumes), *North and South* was serialized
in *Household Words*, a 2*d.* weekly journal 'conducted' by
Charles Dickens. It followed hard on Dickens's own serial

for the paper, *Hard Times*. Both novels are 'social problem' novels (sometimes called 'Condition of England' novels) set in the industrial north, around Manchester. And both were directly inspired by the bitter Preston Strike of 1854, in which textile-mill workers demanded a raise in their hourly rate of pay and the masters locked them out for months, precipitating great hardship and the eventual collapse of the workers' action. *Hard Times*'s 'Coketown' is an amalgam of Manchester and Preston. Although no strike features directly in the narrative, union agitators from London are shown working up the mill-hands to an act of desperation.

In *North and South* Gaskell pivots her story on a strike (see, for example, the chapter 'What is a Strike?'). The conflict between 'Masters and Men' makes up the central events of the narrative. And, in a larger sense, Gaskell's novel is a meditation on civil disobedience—in the form of industrial action, military mutiny, and religious dissent. But, no more than Dickens in *Hard Times*, does she directly mention the great Preston strike—something that must have been in the forefront of the mind of every British reader of both novels. As Dickens masked Preston-Manchester as 'Coketown' she masks the conurbation as 'Milton-Northern' (i.e. 'a northern mill town').

North and South obliquely alludes to Preston and to the Oxford religious controversies of the time in discreet but— for the wideawake reader of the 1850s—transparent codes. Both Dickens and Gaskell are doing, in these 'problem novels', what fiction, in an expert's hands, does very effectively—writing about 'the problem' without directly naming it, but in such a way that it does not have to be named. It is analogous to what in gunnery is, I believe, called 'aiming off'—having your shells land a little to the side of the target. It is clear that this 'aiming off' was deliberate on Gaskell's part in the matter of Mr Hale's doubts. When she began writing, Dickens specifically warned his author to play down Mr Hale's religious doubts:

This is the place [in the narrative] where we agreed that there should be a great condensation, and a considerable compression, where Mr Hale states his doubts to Margaret . . . What I would recommend—and did recommend—is, to make the scene between Margaret and her father relative to his leaving the church and their destination being Milton-Northern, as short as you can find it in your heart to make it.[5]

Dickens gives as the reasons for this curtailing 'the mechanical necessities of *Household Words*', but this is clearly a pretext. As Easson points out, Dickens 'shied away' from 'doctrinal controversy' in his paper. He did not want a *Nemesis of Faith* and some zealot burning copies of *Household Words*, God forbid! As with Preston, some decent muffling was in order. *Household Words* had a broad-based 'family' readership, as its name implied: the kind of readership which required caution on the perennially divisive and sensitive topics of sex, religion, and politics. He was not imposing a total suppression. A little 'aiming off' would do it.

Mrs Gaskell duly did as tactfully instructed and, in the matter of Mr Hale's doubts, alluded to what she meant, rather than plunging into the religious disputes of the 1840s. Intelligent readers would fill in the blanks without difficulty. What one concludes is that we lose a lot in Victorian fiction by not reading Victorian daily newspapers. With *North and South*, modern readers are in the position of their great-great-grandchildren watching a rerun of *Our Friends in the North* in—say—2098. Without, that is, having followed the 1984 coal strike on the evening television news, or without knowing—from personal and painful acquaintance—what the stresses of the Thatcherite 'enterprise culture' meant for those who lived through it and had their lives turned upside down.

Doubtless those future watchers of the television mini-series will, with the advantage of a century's historical hindsight, see the drama more clearly than we do. But that hand-in-glove intimacy with the present, and that precious ability to intuit what the author *means* (but is not directly saying) will be lost.

The Oxford World's Classics *North and South* is edited by Angus Easson, revised by Sally Shuttleworth.

Name Games

An Oxford World's Classics reader, John Cameron, writes to ask if I have noticed that between pages 102 and 135 of *Oliver Twist*

there are lots of references to Jack Dawkins (the Artful Dodger) and Charley Bates. Bates is referred to variously as Mr Charles Bates, Charley Bates, Charley, and, most equivocally, *Master Bates*. Out of 28 references, he is called 'Master Bates' 7 times. Dawkins, on the other hand, is called Jack Dawkins, John Dawkins, Dodger, Mr Dawkins but never 'Master Dawkins'. Is Dickens having a joke at the expense of his readers, I wonder? Or is this just a figment of my own suspicious mind?

Other suspicious readers and some critics have wondered whether Dickens is making an off-colour joke with 'Master Bates'.[1] There is no doubt that Dickens often uses embedded word-association in the names of his characters. Murdstone and Merdle, for instance, combine the overtones of the French *merde* ('shit') and 'murder'. Murdstone is a stony-hearted murderer; Merdle deals with 'filthy' lucre. 'Uriah Heep' brings with it, every time the name and its owner crop up in *David Copperfield*, a subliminal vision of a heap of ordure ('uria' is defined in the dictionary as 'urine' and 'urea', even less attractively, as 'the solid component of mammalian urine'). Likewise, Carker and 'cack' (a slang term for excrement). Dickens, we may deduce, would not flinch from 'Master Bates—masturbates' on grounds of taste. But the objection to its being deliberate is that the schoolboy joke ('This is Mr and Mrs Bates, and their son Master Bates')—although current from time immemorial—would seem *below* the author of *Oliver Twist*.

Dickens's mastery of the art of nomenclature is most

striking in his creation of new names that carry with
them suggestions that we cannot quite pin down. Of all the
Victorian novelists, he is the most original coiner of names.
The originality has not pleased every reader. Thackeray
observed while *David Copperfield* was still coming out: 'I
quarrel with his [Dickens's] Art in many respects; which I
don't think represents Nature duly; for instance Micawber
appears to me an exaggeration of a man, as his name is
of a name.'[2] Philip Collins once told me that there are
no Scottish names in Dickens, with the possible exception
of the less-than-his-best M'Choakumchild in *Hard Times*
or Mrs MacStinger in *Dombey and Son*. But 'Micawber'
has a certain Scottishness to the ear, if not the eye, and
it is not impossible to hear (if not see) it as a bastard
variant of 'MacIvor' (a prominent and heroic name in
Scott's *Waverley*, and ironically appropriate for the great
Wilkins).

Quilp is—for reasons which are hard to express—
horribly sinister; Gargery is vaguely reassuring; Rosa
Bud is perhaps too obviously virginal (although we may
suspect the Blakean worm at work within); Estella is cold,
distant, and starlike ('Stella' would be less so); Biddy is
biddable (but not, alas, to her suitor Pip); Bounderby is
a bounder; Scrooge (with the echo of 'screw') is miserly;
and Cratchit catches, by its onomatopoeia, the weary
scratch of the clerk's pen on paper. Dombey, Dorrit, and
Jarndyce are pregnant with suggestive but ultimately
elusive associations. Sometimes Dickens was prepared
to load the name of a character with private reference:
he called his wicked Jew by an Irish name, because—
for reasons that only a psychoanalyst could fathom—he
associated the merry old gentleman with a young gent,
Bob Fagin, one of his workmates in the blacking factory.
He called the wife- and horse-beating villain of *Great
Expectations* 'Bentley' after the 'Brigand of Burlington

Street', the publisher Richard Bentley, whom he conceived to have robbed him when a young author.

Occasionally a literary echo can be picked up in Dickens. Esther Summerson is, presumably, so-called by allusion to that other famous foundling, Tom Jones, whose father we discover on almost the last page, was called 'Summer'. Hence Tom is Summer's son. The haughty Sir John Chester in *Barnaby Rudge* recalls Lord Chesterfield, whose doctrine of 'manners maketh nobleman' Dickens despised. 'Humouristic' names often figure in the Ben Jonson-loving author's fiction. Hence the paralysed-by-rank Dedlock, and Gradgrind, the grinder out of graduates (although after some thought, Dickens gave him the 'doubting' Christian name Thomas, leaving open a small aperture for future redemption).[3]

I suspect that the 'Master Bates' acoustic pun was accidental, although it may have been unconsciously revolving in Dickens's mind (hence the obsessive seven usages). Richard Altick suspects that Thackeray's 'naughty joke' in *Pendennis* was similarly accidental or unconscious.[4] In that novel, Thackeray called the purest of maiden heroines Laura Bell. This happened to be the name of one of the most notorious courtesans of the mid-Victorian age. Putting it into *Pendennis* would be like John Updike naming the heroine of his next novel 'Heidi Fleiss'. In 1848, however, when Thackeray began serializing his novel, she was not as notorious as she was later to become. It may have been, as the twentieth-century disclaimer routinely puts it, 'entirely coincidental'.

According to Henry James, Thackeray is 'perfect' in the devising of comic, or otherwise meaningful names for his characters. Nowhere is this perfection more evident than in his Bunyan-titled novel *Vanity Fair*. Becky is sharp both by name and by nature. The Scott allusion (to Jewish Rebecca and Saxon Rowena in *Ivanhoe*) carries, as Kathleen Tillotson notes, a slight but tingling racial charge.[5] Amelia recalls Fielding's passively good wife in the eponymous novel. Dobbin is the steady-as-she-goes carthorse who gets there in the end. George Osborne combines the Christian name of the author's abhorred 'first gentleman of Europe', and a buried anagram of 'snob' (Thackeray invented the term, in his great 'snobonomy', *The Snobs of England*, 1846–7).

Thackeray hit his title and main elements of *Vanity Fair*'s plot while holidaying at Brighton (the Prince Regent's favourite holiday resort). Brighton and Sussex inspired many of the names. The 'Southdown' family is headed by its sheepishly docile (and plain) Lady Jane. The Crawleys (Crawley is a small town near Brighton) are so named for their hundreds of years of sucking up ('crawling') to those in power. The Crawleys always, however, 'rat' at the wrong time, as Chapter 7, summarizing the family history, makes clear. Dominating this complex of Brighton names is the Marquis of Steyne—with its combination of the grand esplanade and 'stain'—appropriate for this most morally spattered of noblemen.

In his later fiction Thackeray curbed his propensity for meaningful or prophetic names. But Arthur Pendennis ('Pen') is, in his nickname at least, the embodiment of hopeful authorship. It would have pleased Thackeray to think that, a century later, the most powerful society of authors would be called 'PEN'. The young swell, and would-be seducer of women, is called 'Foker' (which may be as near an improper pun as Thackeray would consciously allow himself); the future doctor in *Pendennis* is called 'Huxter' (or 'huckster'). In *Esmond* Rachel is so called because, like her biblical namesake, she must faithfully wait many years and outlive a husband before she can be united with her true love (in Virginia—some hopes!). Beatrix was originally (in the manuscript of the novel) called 'Beatrice'—the young girl worshipped from her fourteenth year, Dante fashion, from afar by the older hero. In Thackeray's next full-length novel, the Newcomes are so called because they are both a *nouveau riche* and an *arriviste* family. By this middle stage of his career Thackeray is more consistently realistic in his naming practices. By the time of his last completed novel, *The Adventures of Philip*, he has adopted the 'muscular school' habit of using ostentatiously democratic surnames: Philip Firmin belongs with Tom Brown, Lance Smith, and Guy Livingstone. Trollope guys the Guy Livingstone fashion in the title of his 1861 novel, *The Struggles of Brown, Jones, and Robinson* (one of his weakest efforts). These manly ('firm') heroes are emblematic of the 'best of Britishness' (see Hughes's eulogy on the 'Browns of England' in the opening chapters of *Tom Brown's Schooldays*). In shorter fiction, to the end of his career Thackeray confected aptly descriptive names. We know, from the moment we hear the name, that Mr Batchelor will not win the girl in *Lovel the Widower* and that Lovel (love-all) will.

Henry James uses Thackeray's mastery in the 'science of names' as a stick with which to beat Trollope's clumsiness.[6] James specifically cites, from *Barchester Towers*, the doctor Mr Rerechild and the Revd Mr Quiverful (with his many children) as examples of Trollope at his most heavy-handed (compare Quiverful, for example, to Thackeray's delightfully philoprogenitive 'the Revd Felix Rabbits'). One could cite in support of James's criticism Trollope's litigious barrister Samuel Dockwrath (in *Orley Farm*), his brewers Bungall and Tappitt (in *Rachel Ray*), his lethal physician Dr Fillgrave (in *Doctor Thorne*), his arch-feminist Baroness Banmann (in *Is he Popenjoy?*), and the breeches-maker Neefit (in *Ralph the Heir*). These, particularly the last, are groan-making.

None the less, even in *Barchester* one can find a bundle of wittily apposite names. There is Miss Trefoil (an amateur botanist), 'old Scalpen' (the retired apothecary and tooth-drawer), farmer Subsoil, and Mr Finnie (the cold-blooded attorney). Mr Plomacy, although we are never informed of the fact, must have a first name beginning with 'D'—he is so unfailingly diplomatic. The peas-in-a-pod doctors, Sir Lamda Mewnew and Sir Omicron Pie, have their names made up of the eleventh to sixteenth letters of the Greek alphabet—a little Hippocratic joke. Mr Arabin's curious name can be glossed as 'a rabin' (or 'religious teacher'), and strikes one as just right for the man.

According to James, Trollope's indicative names are acceptable when they are attached to background characters (like Dickens's generic 'Barnacles'), but they jar when those characters (as do Neefit and Quiverful) move to the foreground of the action. 'We can believe in the name [of Quiverful] as we believe in the [fourteen] children, but we cannot manage the combination,' James concludes.[7] James is aware (as not all modern readers may be) of the joke in Mr Quiverful's name—the allusion to Psalm 127: 4–5: 'As arrows are in the hand of a mighty man: so are children of the youth. Happy is the man that hath his quiver full of them.'

Mrs Proudie, James concedes, is an excellent name. But is the pronunciation as in 'proud' or 'prude'? Trollope never tells us, letting both adjectives hover over the proud and prudish lady. Other felicities can be found in the ranks of Trollope's principal characters. Augustus Melmotte, in *The Way We Live Now*, is imperious, cosmopolitan, and rootless, like the hero of Maturin's novel *Melmoth the Wanderer* (there are fainter echoes of the common Jewish name 'Malamud'). Quintus Slide is a slithery journalist's name (in *Phineas Finn*) that Thackeray himself might be proud of. Johnny Eames (the faithful lover in *The Small House at Allington* and *The Last Chronicle of Barset*) is so

called, I believe, in deference to that favourite Horatian
tag of both Thackeray's and Trollope's:

servetur ad imum
Qualis ab incepto processerit, et sibi constet.[8]

Eames is faithful to Lily Dale *ad imum* ('to the last'). But
why, one wonders, did Trollope pick up that obnoxious
Thackeray name for his most admirably dogged hero,
Josiah Crawley (in *The Last Chronicle of Barset*)? The
Revd Mr Crawley is no crawler, but it may be that bowing
the knee to proud bishops called Proudie sticks in his craw.
The obnoxious Thackerayan tinge in 'Crawley' is none the
less disturbing, as is the Shakespearian tinge of 'Shylock'
in Sherlock Holmes.

Trollope is responsible for the funniest joke by an
author about his own name in Victorian fiction. Apropos of
Obadiah Slope, in *Barchester Towers*, the narrator notes
that the clergyman may be descended from 'that eminent
physician who assisted at the birth of Mr T. Shandy' (I. 25).
Trollope here refers to an unsavoury episode in the early
chapters of Sterne's *The Life and Opinions of Tristram
Shandy*. In Volume II, chapter 9 of Sterne's narrative,
the 'man-midwife', Dr Slop, is introduced, accompanied
by a maladroit servant, Obadiah. Slop is short, fat, and 'a
Papist'. The name alludes to his besmirched appearance
(he is introduced, having just fallen in the mud). Many
chapters and much salacious detail is devoted to the
subsequent delivery of the hero at Dr Slop's 'obstetrick
hand'. 'For euphony' an 'e' has been added to 'Slop(e)' we
are told. The euphonious 'e' introduces an overtone of both
'slippery' and 'trimmer'. Mr Slope is no Catholic, but an
evangelical Protestant. As David Skilton has noted, the
remark about other great men having added an 'e' to their
surname 'for euphony' evidently refers to Trollop(e)'s own
surname.[9] It's amusingly sly. Trollope, especially at school,

must have put up with much badinage. ('Hey, Anthony! Is your mother a trollop?')

George Eliot's names are frequently 'loaded' with literary or other implications. 'Adam Bede' incarnates Adamic rural strength and venerable Christian integrity. Hetty Sorrel's surname recalls a bitter (forbidden) fruit. 'Hetty' throws back the echo 'petty' and 'pretty'. In *Middlemarch* Mr Brooke babbles—especially after two glasses of sherry. Unfortunately, his name is bequeathed for part of the book to his niece Dorothea, who does not babble, although Celia may be said to do so. Lydgate's fall is like the fall of the princes about whom John Lydgate wrote. Edward Casaubon's name has tantalized generations of commentators with its apparently over-determined allusion to the seventeenth-century French scholar, Isaac Casaubon. Ladislaw (originally pronounced 'Ladislav') is the slave of ladies. Gwendolen Harleth, the heroine of *Daniel Deronda*, is a woman who sells her body to a man she does not love. Her surname evokes Richardson's Clarissa Harlowe, and through her, 'harlot'.

Elizabeth Gaskell has a good ear for a naturalistic sounding name, but an odd preference for the '-on' suffix: as in Jem Wilson and John Barton (in *Mary Barton*), Mr and Mrs Thornton (in *North and South*), Ruth Hilton and Mr Benson (in *Ruth*), Sylvia Robson (in *Sylvia's Lovers*), and Molly Gibson and her father Mr Gibson (in *Wives and Daughters*). Mrs Gaskell's maiden name was Stevenson. The Brontës, as David Lodge has noted, have a tendency towards powerfully elemental names: Jane Eyre (air), Helen Burns (fire), St John Rivers (water), Lucy Snowe (frozen water), Heathcliff (heath and cliff), Robert Gerard Moore (moor), Helstone (stone).[10]

Wilkie Collins usually invents names with no superficially obvious loadings. An exception is the right-hearted Walter Hartright in Collins's *The Woman in White*. Like the wavering Waverley in Scott's novel, or the *toujours l'audace* Lady Audley in Mrs Braddon's sensation novel, Walter's character is encapsulated in his Dudley Dogood name. More to my taste are Collins's out-and-out surrealistic names, such as the tract-dropping Drusilla Clack in *The Moonstone* or Ozias Midwinter, the Creole hero of *Armadale* (a novel which is remarkable for having five characters called Allan Armadale).

Thomas Hardy typically flavours his names with regional associations, but occasionally adds tinctures from other sources. In *Tess of the d'Urbervilles: A Pure Woman*, his 'pure man' is called 'Angel Clare' and plays a harp, which may be an allusion too far. 'Durbeyfield' has, to my ear, a meaningful echo of 'dirty-field'. An exception to Hardy's usual realism where names are concerned is *Far from the Madding Crowd*, in which the oak-like hero is called 'Gabriel Oak', the flashy soldier who abducts the beautiful woman 'Sergeant Troy' (provoking a little war by so doing), and the woman who is lusted after by three men 'Bathsheba'. And did any Victorian novelist come up with a better name for a flirt than 'Fancy Day' (in *Under the Greenwood Tree*)?

Names have values embodied in them. They carry baggage. It is noticeable, for example, that characters named after middle-sized (particularly northern) English towns are invariably strong people in Victorian fiction, although not always nice: see, for example, Edward Rochester (*Jane Eyre*), George Warrington (*Pendennis*), Stephen Blackpool (*Hard Times*), John Halifax (*John Halifax, Gentleman*), and Arthur Huntingdon (*The Tenant of Wildfell Hall*). Villains are rarely called Frank (an exception is the utter cad Frank Levison in *East Lynne*). 'Fred', on the other hand, seems to bring with it associations of weakness: as in Fred Vincy (*Middlemarch*) and Fred Neville (*An Eye for an Eye*), two of the weakest-kneed heroes to be found in the novel of the period. Latin names in Trollope's fiction (see Adolphus Crosbie, Undecimus Scott, Augustus Melmotte, and the Revd Joseph Emilius) are invariably dubious. His elder brother was called Adolphus, and—'a student of Draco'—beat Anthony mercilessly when they were boys at school together. Jasper is not a reassuring name, and from its overtones alone I deduce that John Jasper did indeed murder Edwin Drood. It could, however, be a case of 'give a dog a bad name and hang him'.

Charles Dickens · *A Tale of Two Cities*

Where does Sydney Carton get his chloroform?

Before Sydney Carton can do the far better thing than he has ever done he is obliged (rather ignobly) to disable his double, Charles Darnay, with an anaesthetic and have him smuggled insensibly out of Revolutionary France to the safety of England. Carton's plan is complicated by the fact that, in reprisal for the Evremonde crimes (testified to, unwillingly, by his father-in-law, Dr Manette), Charles has been sentenced to death. The young aristo is being held in the impregnable 'black prison of the Conciergerie' (p. 428), closely guarded by fanatic sentinels, until—in a few hours—Madame Guillotine does her bloody work and there is one Evremonde the less.

Carton lays his plot with care. First he pays a call on a sinister Parisian apothecary:

> traversing with the decided step of one who remembered the way well, several dark and dirty streets—much dirtier than usual, for the best public thoroughfares remained uncleansed in those times of terror—he stopped at a chemist's shop, which the owner was closing with his own hands. A small, dim, crooked shop, kept in a tortuous, up-hill thoroughfare, by a small, dim, crooked man. (p. 386)

Carton gives the crooked chemist a prescription which he has written himself. '"Whew!" the chemist whistled, as he read it. "Hi! hi! hi!".' (That 'Whew!', incidentally, strikes one as un-Gallic.) As he fills the prescription in 'certain small packets' the chemist accompanies it with a warning:

'You will be careful to keep them separate, citizen? You
know the consequences of mixing them.' 'Perfectly,' Carton
answers, in what we take to be flawless French. The
second, and more dangerous part of the plan follows.
Carton has recognized the turnkey at the Conciergerie
as a former Old Bailey spy, Barsad (he is also, by fantastic
coincidence, Miss Pross's scapegrace brother Solomon).
Armed with this information, Carton is able to blackmail
Barsad to smuggle him into Darnay's solitary cell on his
day of doom.

As the Oxford World's Classics notes point out, con-
demned prisoners were allowed to write a 'last' letter—a
privilege equivalent to the English prisoner's 'hearty' last
breakfast. It is on this pretext that Carton comes to the
jail. Once in the cell, by sheer peremptoriness the young
lawyer cajoles a mystified Darnay to change outer clothes,
cravat, and boots with him and to shake out his hair
from its 'queue', to look more like his (Sydney Carton's).
Darnay does as he is told; without having the faintest
idea, apparently, what purpose his visitor has in mind
with these instructions. Fear has paralysed him. 'The
prisoner was like a young child in his hands' (p. 433), as
the narrative records.

Their outer dress exchanged, Carton instructs Darnay
to take down a letter to his (Carton's) dictation. Meanwhile, the Englishman stands over the sitting prisoner,
'with his hand in his breast'. 'What is it in your hand?' Darnay asks. Carton does not answer but merely commands
'Write on.' The words he dictates seem of little significance.
But while uttering them, Carton's hand 'slowly and softly
moved down close to the writer's face'. Darnay breaks
off from writing, with a 'vacant' look; 'What vapour is
that?' he asks. 'Vapour?' Carton echoes. 'Something that
crossed me' (p. 435), Darnay says. It was nothing, he is
told. An increasingly distracted Darnay writes on—his

breathing becoming heavier. Again Carton's hand crosses 'slowly and softly' across the other man's face. Darnay's writing deteriorates into 'unintelligible signs' and, 'within a minute or so, he was stretched insensible on the ground' (p. 435).

Darnay uses the term 'vapour', which indicates fumes rising off a liquid, as opposed to wholly airborne 'gas'. We assume that Carton is administering some narcotic. We may also note that, whatever it is, it works extremely fast—a couple of minutes is all it takes—and is practically odourless. Carton now puts on the remainder of the prisoner's clothes and summons Barsad to take out the insensible young Frenchman—who will, of course, be mistaken for a fainted Sydney Carton by any suspicious guard. It was too much for the young man. Carton instructs Barsad that the unconscious Darnay be taken to Mr Lorry and given 'no restorative but air'. And, he adds, tell Lorry 'to remember my words of last night, and his promise of last night, and drive away!' (p. 436), taking Darnay and Lucie to safety in England.

A swarm of questions hover round this scene. First, how does Sydney Carton know so much about dubious French apothecaries and the dubious chemical substances they purvey? The clue is given in an early exchange with Stryver. The two lawyers were schoolboys together at Shrewsbury. Since those days, Carton ruefully observes, 'you have fallen into your rank, and I have fallen into mine. Even when we were fellow-students in the Student-Quarter of Paris, picking up French, and French law, and other French crumbs that we didn't get much good of, you were always somewhere, and I was always—nowhere' (p. 105).

This period of study in Paris explains how it is that Carton can speak the language well enough to pass for a Frenchman (the chemist calls him 'Citizen'). And, we assume, among the 'crumbs' the two young dogs picked up was a knowledge of illicit pharmacology. Students don't change much. Carton 'remembers' the chemist's location well because he went there often as a young man. In passing, we may be curious as to why—alongside the obvious drugs a licentious law student might want ('recreational' substances, and nostrums for venereal disease)—Carton should have made himself so knowledgeable about 'Mickey Finns', or 'knockout drops', as they are called in pulp fiction.

The overriding question is—what is this unnamed 'vapour', a couple of whiffs of which renders Darnay rapidly unconscious—but not life-threateningly so? The Oxford World's Classics notes tentatively suggest that it is 'Sulphuric ether'. This was one of the varieties of 'laughing gas' that became commonly used in the mid-nineteenth century (the other was nitrous oxide). Andrew Sanders's note is on the right lines, but chemically wrong. The substance Carton uses is quite clearly chloroform.

Reference either to ether or chloroform would, of course, have been entirely appropriate for the 1859–60 period in which *A Tale of Two Cities* was written and published, but entirely inappropriate to the French Revolutionary period in which the narrative is set. The history of 'inhalation anaesthetics' in the mid-nineteenth century is a matter of medical-historical record. In 1846 it was successfully demonstrated in America, by an American dentist called Morton, that sulphuric ether could be used to anaesthetize patients undergoing operations. Hitherto the only anaesthetic available to surgeons or dentists was mesmerism. Enthusiasts believed in it, many (particularly those about to undergo radical surgery) were sceptical. There could be no doubt that ether, properly applied, rendered the subject wholly unconscious, deadened the pain of operation, and represented little risk to recovery.

Morton's discovery was picked up by the English medical establishment in late 1846 and triggered what has been called an 'Ethereal Epidemic'.[1] Although ether (and chloroform) had been around for some time as compounds, and their properties recorded, the realization that they could be safely used for surgery was one of the most exciting medical breakthroughs of the century.

In the first six months of 1847 the *Lancet* published 112 articles on 'ether anaesthesia'. The Scottish physician James Simpson made a worldwide reputation, and earned himself a knighthood and a place in the *DNB* as an advocate of the ether-anaesthetic technique in the late 1840s. Exciting breakthrough though it was, ether had some shortcomings as an ideal inhalation-anaesthetic. As a 'laughing gas', it was widely abused and popularly associated with 'drunkenness', in much the same way that aerosol-based nitrous oxide and ether-based glue are today. For the physician ether was difficult, being a gas, to administer. Effectively, it could only be done with the full co-operation of the patient, either through a mask or by breathing in from a beaker with a covering over the head.

There were obvious difficulties with delirious patients, infant patients, or patients thrashing about in pain. These problems were remedied with the innovation of chloroform. Chloroform could be easily produced, in liquid form, by the mixture of various agents (hence the 'several packets' which the chemist gives to Sydney Carton). It could be stored, ready for use, as a stable, room-temperature, 'ponderous' liquid. A few drops on cloth (the amount could be accurately measured) would suffice, as it vaporized, to render the patient unconscious. All that was required by way of co-operation was that the subject should breathe. In addition to being easier to administer, chloroform was extremely efficient and produced controllable unconsciousness quicker than sulphuric ether. Nor did it have any attractions for the drug-abuser. No one was tempted to take chloroform for kicks. Nor can chloroform be abused as a sedative, or as a means of suicide.

Dr John Snow publicly demonstrated the efficacy of chloroform to his fellow professionals in November 1847. They were persuaded of its superiority. By the end of the decade, as Alison Winter reports, chloroform had entirely replaced sulphuric ether as the inhalation-anaesthetic of choice. Chloroform was publicized to the British middle classes in the most effective way, when Snow used it in the delivery of two of Queen Victoria's children in April 1853 and April 1857. It was now an anaesthetic with a royal warrant. Snow died in 1858, and in the same year his great posthumous work, *Chloroform and other Anaesthetics*, was published.

Dickens's journals took a keen interest in the chloroform phenomenon. There were three articles in *Household Words* in the years leading up to *A Tale of Two Cities*: 'Some Account of Chloroform', by Percival Leigh (10 May 1851); 'Chloroform', by Henry Morley (23 April 1853); and 'Chloroform', by William Overend Priestley— one of Simpson's assistants—on the eve of publication of Dickens's novel (12 February 1859). Priestley's article hailed the drug ('this cup of Lethe') as a medical advance as momentous as Harvey's discovery of the circulation of the blood and Jenner's invention of vaccination. Dickens must have edited the article.

It seems incontrovertible that Dickens was thinking of chloroform in the Conciergerie scene in *A Tale of Two Cities*, written 1858–9, although he prudently doesn't identify Carton's drug by name. We are led to suppose that Carton has prepared the mixture before coming to the prison, secreting it on his person in a small pocket-flask, or as lint wrapped in greased paper. While leaning over Darnay, he passes the open flask (or uncovered lint) in front of his unsuspecting victim's face. A couple of passes does it. The vapour does its work, as efficiently as it doubtless did on Queen Victoria.

Although it is not named, every Victorian reader of 1859–60, bombarded as the public had been with descriptions of the new wonder drug, would have known what Dickens was writing about in this scene. One concludes that Sydney Carton should really have studied medicine rather than law. He is fully sixty years ahead of the British medical establishment. This use of chloroform—a drug not used as an inhalation-anaesthetic until 1847—seems, on the face of it, wildly anachronistic. It is equivalent to Jude Fawley and Sue Bridehead sharing a joint, or Tess Durbeyfield dropping some acid with her fellow milkmaids.

Novelists of the late 1850s and early 1860s were, however, entranced by the plot opportunities which chloroform offered, and be hanged to any anachronism. Thackeray in *Philip* (1860) similarly uses the drug to engineer a dramatic climax to his novel. As it happened, Thackeray was very interested in chloroform for personal reasons. He was considering an operation to relieve the stricture of the urethra which had tormented him for years. Without anaesthetic, such an operation would be hideously painful. In 1860 he published an article, 'Under Chloroform', in the *Cornhill Magazine* (of which he was the editor), in which he clearly outlines the surgical benefits of the anaesthetic.

Philip was first serialized in *Cornhill*. The novel's last section is set in the 1840s. Dr Firmin, the hero's worthless father, has been packed off to America, from where he sends back a number of products with which he hopes to make his fortune. They include, among other quite plainly crazy inventions, 'a cask of petroleum from Virginia' (that will never catch on!), and a small flask of chloroform ('this was what Dr Firmin chose to call his discovery'.

Rather surprisingly, Thackeray seems to imply that the name of the drug originated with one of his fictional personages). The 'Little Nurse'—a good woman who was seduced by Firmin years earlier—takes possession of this bottle of chloroform, and is instructed by her mentor, Dr Goodenough, how to use it.[2]

As it happens, she does not use it for medicinal ends. Instead, she employs it to knock out a villainous defrocked clergyman who is blackmailing the hero, Philip, with a money order on which Dr Firmin has forged his son's signature. While he is dozy from drink, the 'Little Nurse' passes a cloth, on which she has dropped some liquid chloroform, in front of his face. When he is 'under' she steals the bill, and Philip is safe. I would guess that Thackeray, as even great novelists are prone to do, 'borrowed' this chloroforming from *A Tale of Two Cities*, published a few months earlier. Thackeray, however, knew—when he wasn't changing history for fictional purposes—that what had been imported from America in 1846 was not chloroform but sulphuric ether. He also knew that the use of chloroform as an inhalation-anaesthetic had been pioneered not by a quack like Dr Firmin, but by the eminently (indeed royally) respectable British physician, Dr John Snow. Thackeray therefore added the following editorial footnote to the letter in which Dr Firmin announces his 'discovery' of what he calls 'chloroform':

'*Ether* was first employed, I believe, in America; and I hope the reader will excuse the substitution of Chloroform in this instance.—W.M.T.'[3]

One does forgive the author of *Philip* because it would have been impractical for the Little Nurse to have administered a gas like ether. Chloroform was required. Thackeray admits his anachronism, and craves the reader's indulgence, which is readily granted. On his part, Dickens fudges the

Judith and Holofernes

issue (and avoids the necessity of an embarrassing footnote) by never actually mentioning chloroform, although every wide-awake reader of 1859 would have realized what Carton had in his breast pocket.

In his 1859 novel, *The Woman in White*, set in 1851, Wilkie Collins also draws on the chloroform mania (the novel followed on *A Tale of Two Cities* as the lead serial in *All the Year Round*). In the crisis of Collins's narrative, at Blackwater Park, Count Fosco engineers the dismissal of the family physician Mr Dawson and takes personal charge of the neurasthenic Laura and the delirious Marian. Collins makes the point that Fosco has a 'vast knowledge of chemistry' and is well up with medical innovation in the 1850s. As she later recalls, Fosco contrived to render Laura senseless, in order to abduct her to his hideaway in St John's Wood, where vile things will be done to her. He does so by offering her a restorative, as (typically) she turns faint on being told that Marian is not to accompany her:

she hastily took the bottle of salts from Count Fosco, and smelt at it. Her head became giddy on the instant. The Count caught the bottle as it dropped out of her hand; and the last impression of which she was conscious was that he held it to her nostrils again. (p. 435)

It is clear that Fosco has spiked the smelling-salts with chloroform, although the drug's name is not mentioned. It is not, as in *A Tale of Two Cities* and *Philip*, an outright anachronism, although one does rather wonder at the Count's being so far ahead of the Queen's physician in these matters.

Does Dickens have any warrant for chloroform's being available to his hero in France in 1793, some fifty-four years before it was available to Dr Snow? A very small warrant. As the *OED* indicates, 'chloroform' was originally

a French word and was current in French usage as early
as the 1830s. If the word circulated in earlier decades in
France, why should not the anaesthetic itself? It is a straw,
but it is something on which to build narrative plausibility.

Postscript: What is Carton doing in France?

There is an incidental puzzle in *A Tale of Two Cities*
which Kenneth Fielding points out. How do all the English nationals and sympathizers—Lorry, Lucie, Manette,
Carton—have free right of entrance to and departure
from France, a country with which England is at war?
After a period of great turbulence, hostilities broke out
between the two countries in January 1793. It is clear
from internal references (to such things as the king's death
in December of that year, see pp. 259–60, and Andrew
Sanders's chronology of historical events in the Oxford
World's Classics edition) that the climax of the novel is
taking place in the last months of 1793.

The free passage of these English visitors in wartime
France can be explained by a historical oddity in the history of passports. They were introduced to allow nationals
privileged entrance to and exit from countries at war with
each other and to control such aliens while they were
within the borders. Passports did not serve, as they do today, to enable civilians unhindered passage during time of
peace. Until the twentieth century passports were largely
dispensed with during times of peace and normality. It is
clear from his last conversations with Lorry that Carton is
in possession of a certain 'certificate' which enables him 'at
any time to pass the barrier [of the city of Paris] and the
frontier'. There is some slightly mystifying conversation
about these 'papers', but they are, evidently, 'letters of
introduction'. This system of monitoring aliens was in the

process of being superseded by strict passport controls, which required registration with the authorities. The new passport system was introduced by the Revolutionary government, culminating in the statute of September 1797. Doubtless, as a prudent man of law, Carton had letters of introduction drawn up with the authorities before coming to France, but has caught wind of sinister changes in the offing.[4]

The Oxford World's Classics *A Tale of Two Cities* is edited by Andrew Sanders. The Oxford World's Classics *The Woman in White* is edited by John Sutherland.

Wilkie Collins · *The Woman in White*

Why doesn't Laura tell her own story?

The Woman in White opens with Walter Hartright's startlingly original declaration of how the subsequent narrative will be laid out:

As the Judge might once have heard it, so the Reader shall hear it now. No circumstance of importance, from the beginning to the end of the disclosure, shall be related on hearsay evidence. When the writer of these introductory lines (Walter Hartright by name) happens to be more closely connected than others with the incidents to be recorded, he will describe them in his own person. When his experience fails, he will retire from the position of narrator; and his task will be continued, from the point at which he has left it off, by other persons who can speak to the circumstances under notice from their own knowledge, just as clearly and positively as he has spoken before them. (p. 5)

Wilkie Collins's reportage style of narration was to be central in the evolution of the 'Sensation Novel', and its influence can still be felt as far afield as contemporary docufiction. *The Woman in White* is, in terms of its narrative technique, one of the most innovative novels of the nineteenth century.

As Hartright arranges the evidence, there are ten narrators or 'witnesses'. Hartright himself and Marian Halcombe tell the main lines of the story. Their account is supported by testimony from: Count Ottavio Baldassore Fosco; Vincent Gilmore (the Fairlie solicitor); Frederick Fairlie, Esq. of Limmeridge House; Eliza Michelson, housekeeper at Blackwater Park; Hester Pinhorn, cook in the service of Count Fosco; Alfred Goodricke (the doctor who signed the death certificate of 'Laura'; Jane Gould (who laid out the body); and Mrs Catherick (mother of the 'Woman in White').

As the critic David Grylls has pointed out to me, one witness's evidence is mysteriously missing—and that the most important person of all. Laura Fairlie (subsequently Laura Glyde, and Laura Hartright) is not called on. Why? It's a damaging omission, since the abduction of Laura, and the theft of her identity, is at the heart of the story. She is, needless to say, the person 'more closely connected than others with the incidents' that make up *The Woman in White*. It is true that after her rescue from the asylum Laura is traumatized. But by the end of the narrative (the period in which Walter is putting together his account) she is alert and wholly *compos mentis*. Yet with her alone, the reader has to be satisfied with 'hearsay evidence'.

Dr Grylls suggests that the mysterious silence of Laura can be linked to sexual *pudeur*. Her experiences as wife to the degenerate Glyde are held back from the respectable reader, lest they offend like undraped piano legs in the drawing-room. A useful way of testing this hypothesis is through the 1997 television adaptation of *The Woman in White*—a dramatization which wilfully reinserted the sexual explicitness which, the scriptwriters assumed, Collins had been reluctantly obliged to leave out in deference to his stuffy Victorian age.

The dramatization confined itself to two ninety-minute segments and necessarily streamlined the three-volume novel narrative. Blackwater Park was merged with Limmeridge. The encounter with the woman in white on Hampstead Heath (which Dickens thought one of the two best scenes in literature) was sacrificed. A host of secondary characters were dropped. Regrettably, the end of Fosco (stretched out on the Paris morgue slab, like a cod in a fishmonger's) was dropped. The heroines were made not half-sisters but sisters (Marian Halcombe became 'Marian Fairlie'). This was a pity, since Collins's main point in making them half-sisters was to open the way to Walter's being able to marry Marian after the delicate Laura dies, as the reader perceives she soon must. As deceased wife's sister, Marian 'Fairlie' would be forbidden fruit.

Most arresting, however, were the changes that the televisers made to sexual plot and motivation. Sir Percival Glyde was transformed into a monster of depravity. Shortly after marriage, he takes the servant Margaret Porcher as his mistress. And the 'secret' which can ruin him (in the book, it is disinheriting illegitimacy) was changed to paedophilia. Anne Catherick's mother had been mistress to the Fairlie girls' father; Glyde had made 12-year-old Anne Catherick his mistress. Glyde is that most detested of modern criminals, a child-abuser. It was his molestations that drove Anne mad.

In fact, the dates—in so far as we can reconstruct them from Collins's narrative—fit the television scenario rather neatly. The 'prehistory' of *The Woman in White* goes thus. In July 1803 Sir Percival Glyde's parents 'married' (in fact, since his mother, Cecilia Jane Elster, was already married, the union was invalid—this is to be the great 'secret' in the subsequent narrative). The Glyde parents died abroad, at some point between 1825 and New Year 1827. In March 1804 young Percival Glyde was born abroad. Around 1825 Marian Halcombe was born. Her father died soon after. In autumn 1826 Philip Fairlie vacationed at Varneck Hall near Southampton, where he had an affair with a married woman of the lower orders, Mrs Jane Anne Catherick. From this union, in June 1827, Anne Catherick was born, the illegitimate daughter of Mrs Catherick and Philip Fairlie. In 1827

Sir Percival Glyde committed his forgery at Welmingham, falsifying evidence of his parents' 'marriage', to protect his title and inheritance. In the summer of 1827 Philip Fairlie married the widowed Mrs Halcombe. On 27 March 1829 Laura Fairlie was born, the only child of Philip and Mrs Fairlie (formerly Halcombe), and half-sister to Marian. In 1838 Anne Catherick came to school for a brief period at Limmeridge, where she developed her lifelong fixation on Mrs Fairlie. In November 1847 Philip Fairlie died, leaving his daughter Laura and his stepdaughter Marian Halcombe orphans. Before dying, he obtained a promise from Laura that she would marry Percival Glyde. In the interval between his death and Laura's marriage, he left the girls in the care of his younger unmarried brother, Frederick, at Limmeridge. In 1847 Percival Glyde committed Anne Catherick to a private lunatic asylum, from which she escapes to have her midnight meeting with Walter on Hampstead Heath in August 1849. With this wonderful scene the novel proper begins.

It is quite feasible that in 1838–9, when Anne was 12 years old and at Limmeridge, a villainous 34-year-old Sir Percival might have had his evil way with her. And that Glyde might have gone on to blackmail Philip Fairlie with the threat of exposing him as the father of Anne. The price of Glyde's silence?—The hand (and wealth) of Laura when she comes of age. Collins gives not the slightest hint of such a sub-plot, but, as I say, it fits chronologically and has a certain plausibility.

Other aspects of the television characterization of Glyde are implausible. The dalliance with Margaret Porcher, for instance. In the novel, this woman is grossly unappealing. She is the 'largest and the fattest' of the housemaids at Blackwater, with a 'fat shapeless face' (p. 208). She is 'the most awkward, slatternly, and obstinate servant in the house', with an idiotic, slow-witted grin, and great red arms (p. 298). Glyde would need to be degenerate indeed, if Porcher were his taste in sexual diversion.

What do we know about Glyde's 'tastes', and his conduct as a husband? What clues, if any, do we have as to the bedroom activities of Sir Percival and Lady Glyde? There are some tantalizing fragments of evidence in the novel. The letters which Laura sends Marian over the six months of her wedding trip on the Continent notably lack the 'usual moral transformation which is insensibly wrought in a young, fresh, sensitive woman by her marriage . . . it is always Laura Fairlie who has been writing to me for the last six months, and never Lady Glyde' (p. 203). From which we may deduce that the marriage is blank. None the less, when she finally arrives, Marian notes that: 'There is more colour, and more decision and roundness of outline in her face than there used to be; and her figure seems more firmly set, and more sure and easy in all its movements than it was in her maiden days' (p. 213). From which we deduce that, like Tess, Laura is a maiden no more. The marriage *has* been consummated. Miss Fairlie has become Lady Glyde in more than name.

Laura declines to enter into any details on the subject of her marriage, even with Marian (p. 214). None the less, some hints slip through. In the tremendous scene in which Laura refuses to sign the document making over her property, Sir Percival savagely (and in the presence of Marian) accuses his wife of making 'a virtue of necessity by marrying *me*'—by which the swine implies that she did not come to the marriage bed pure (p. 250). This raises some interesting speculations. In a later confidence with Marian, Laura recalls that when they were in Rome, only a few weeks married, Percival used to 'leave me alone at night, to go among the Opera people' (p. 263)— a clear euphemism for courtesans (nothing in Collins's description of Glyde suggests any musical taste).

Percival's dry cough, lean looks, bald head, advanced years (he is 46), and swishing cane suggest a certain bedroom sadism. But the broadest clue we have to the married life of the Glydes is given in the unbuttoned man-to-man talk of Sir Percival and Fosco, smoking, drinking, and chatting late into the night. Collins is obliged to use all his sensationalist's ingenuity to set this scene up so that we (and the women among his readership) may plausibly overhear this conversation. He does so magnificently. Marian literally 'eavesdrops'. First, she is made to strip off her silk gown and the 'white and cumbersome parts of my underclothing' (her petticoats). She then clambers out, with only a thin cloak over her exciting undress, to perch precariously on a windowsill over a verandah under which Glyde and Fosco are talking.

Fosco quizzes Glyde as to the conditions which obstruct their getting hold of her £20,000 fortune. 'In the case of Lady Glyde's death,' Fosco asks:

'what do you get then?'
  'If she leaves no children—'
  'Which she is likely to do?'
  'Which she is not in the least likely to do—'
  'Yes?'
  'Why, then I get her twenty thousand pounds.'
  'Paid down?'
  'Paid down.' (p. 333)

How would adult Victorian readers take 'not in the least likely to'? In one of five ways. They might assume that Glyde was using some form of contraception. Or they might assume that even if Glyde (as would be in character) brutally took his conjugal rights over the honeymoon, he now has no use for his insipid wife. The tender-hearted might assume that the marriage has *never* been consummated; that Laura will, eventually, come to Walter still pure—a white bride (she is, on all the evidence, fertile enough: they have their little Walter within a year of marriage). Cynics and 'men of the world' might assume that the worldly Percival Glyde is (like Walter in *My Secret Life*) sterile as the result of venereal disease (who knows what infections he may have picked up from those Roman 'Opera people'?).

Collins cunningly leaves all these options open. Had Laura been made to speak, that openness would have been compromised. If, like other 'witnesses', she were to give the 'whole truth' as she (alone) knows it, Lady Glyde would have had to say something more tangible about the marriage, and what kind of husband Sir Percival was to her. David Grylls, I think, is right. Laura is silenced to preserve the interesting aura of sexual ambiguity that hovers around her career in the novel. Like the other 'Woman in White', Laura remains a woman of mystery.

The Oxford World's Classics *The Woman in White* is edited by John Sutherland.

===

Why was Pip not invited to Joe's wedding?

===

Malcolm Hurwitt writes to ask 'if you are aware of the puzzle which I feel exists in *Great Expectations*? It may be described as "Why was not Pip invited to the Wedding?".' Mr Hurwitt goes on:

At the end of Chapter 57 Pip has decided to go to his old home to propose marriage to Biddy, Joe Gargery's housekeeper. At the end of the first section of Chapter 58 he meets Joe and Biddy and discovers that it is their wedding day. He collapses from the shock. He had not even been informed of it, yet he was Joe's brother-in-law; he was on good terms with them; Joe had recently nursed him through a long and serious illness and had secretly paid off his debts. There had always been a deep and warm affection between Pip and Joe in spite of and perhaps partly because of the strictness of Pip's sister, Joe's first wife. There was no closer relative, yet Pip had not been invited to the wedding nor even told of it. However little fuss Joe and Biddy wanted, it is hard to understand why Pip had not been let in on the secret.

It is, as Mr Hurwitt rightly says, odd; and it gets odder the closer one looks at the episode. After Magwitch's euthanasia, during a 'cold and dusty spring' (p. 453), Pip falls into a 'fever'—the dreaded 'jail-fever', as we apprehend. (The *OED* defines the disease as 'a virulent type of typhus-fever, formerly endemic in closed jails, and frequent in ships and other confined places.') The illness is the last of Magwitch's gifts to Pip, and the most fatal.

Pip has—in the intoxication of his 'expectations'—run up debts of some £123 with a jeweller, and is now summonsed for debt. Two bailiffs call on his rooms in the Temple; either he must pay the money or surrender his person (this is the era before the reform of laws on personal debt). The usual sequence of events was that the debtor would be held in a 'sponging house'—under house arrest, and given a last chance to pay (or 'expunge') his bills. Failing this last chance, he would be carried off to prison. If he settled his account (not necessarily in full), the sponging house would collect its cut.

Were he in health, Pip would presumably go to the house with the bailiffs and shoot off desperate letters to all his friends, requesting aid. But the young man is now too ill to be moved. The arresting officers know jail fever when they see it, and they refrain from carting his insensible body into captivity. As a debtor, of course, there is no question of calling in a doctor (who would pay the guinea fee?). He is left to die or recover as fate pleases.

Pip falls into a delirium in which he evidently remains for several weeks. When he comes round, it is the last day of May. Joe has been taking care of him, he discovers. This 'gentle Christian man' (p. 458) was summoned by letter, from his village home down by the marshes. Who, one wonders, sent the letter telling Joe of Pip's plight? It cannot be Herbert, who has gone off to Egypt with his bride. It cannot be Pip's slatternly, thieving, and illiterate maidservant. It can hardly be the bailiffs who have come to take him away. They would not know Joe's address, nor his relationship to Pip. Conceivably, Pip himself might have babbled out something in his semi-consciousness and later forgotten doing it, but this is unlikely. It must, one assumes, have been either Wemmick or Jaggers who sent the letter to Joe. But the kind-hearted Wemmick would surely not have left Pip to die alone and untended in his apartment. Hard-hearted Jaggers, on the other hand, might feel obliged to contact the 'next of kin' (which Joe is), as a point of professional etiquette but would not trouble himself to attend his former client's bedside at any risk to his own health or legal safety.

One can reconstruct the scene. It is quite plausible that Jaggers would have sent a clerk round to Pip's rooms in the Temple, just to see the lie of the land. The man reported back and Jaggers sent a letter, possibly unsigned, to Joe. Jaggers, of course, would still be nervous about being involved in a prosecution arising from the (clearly felonious) conspiracy to smuggle Magwitch out of the country. He is a cautious lawyer. Jaggers knows everything about Pip; more, in fact, than the young man knows about himself. He would certainly have Joe Gargery's address in his files. If he wrote the letter, Jaggers would also, doubtless, add the detail that Pip was being distrained for debt and precisely how much debt.

This last supposition would clear up another little mystery: namely, how it is that Joe happens to be able to pay the very substantial sum of £123. 'Ready money' is, of course, the only form of payment the bailiffs would accept at this stage of the game. As the receipt he leaves for Pip indicates, Joe paid the debt in full in cash, while in London. The country blacksmith would not, of course, have a bank account in town. Nor would he have one in the country. Like Silas Marner, Joe would keep his savings under a floorboard. Those savings would be made up of the sovereigns, florins, half-crowns, and the smaller silver he received over the years for his smithy work. Unless forewarned, he would not bring this treasure to London with him. It is hard to credit that he has much more than £123 in his life's savings. He may even have had to borrow from Biddy's savings to make up the sum of Pip's jeweller's debt.

As June draws on Pip makes a rapid recovery. Early in the month Joe departs precipitately, leaving a cryptic

letter ('Not wishful to intrude I have departured fur you
are well again dear Pip and will do better without . . .
Jo . . . P. S. Ever the best of friends'). Joe also leaves
the receipt for payment of the jeweller's bill and the
bailiff's costs. 'Down to that moment', Pip ruefully says,
'I had vainly supposed that my creditor had withdrawn or
suspended proceedings until I should be quite recovered.
I had never dreamed of Joe's having paid the money; but,
Joe had paid it, and the receipt was in his name' (p. 466).

It is still June when Pip makes his sudden decision to
go down to the village and propose marriage to Biddy.
On his part Joe must, of course, have known that *he* (Joe
Gargery) was going to be married to Biddy when he came
up to London. He must surely have sent love-letters to his
intended in the country, together with bulletins about Pip's
health and when he expected to 'departure' London. Banns
would have had to be called in the village church. And it
is doubtless to prepare for his imminent wedding day that
Joe has rushed back—without explanation to Pip. Joe's
letter hints that he is not entirely keen that Pip should
follow him. It would, for instance, have been easy to add
a 'coddleshell' or another 'P. S.' saying something like: 'do
come and see us soon.'

Joe's conversational exchanges with the convalescent
Pip are hilariously circumlocutory. But, conceivably, he
did try on at least one occasion to broach the subject of
his impending nuptials. On resuming consciousness, after
his long delirium, the first question Pip asks is 'How long,
dear Joe?':

'Which you meantersay, Pip, how long have your illness lasted,
dear old chap?'
   'Yes, Joe.'
   'It's the end of May, Pip. To-morrow is the first of June.'
   'And have you been here all the time, dear Joe?'
   'Pretty nigh, old chap. For, as I says to Biddy when the news

of your being ill were brought by letter, which it were brought
by the post and being formerly single he is now married though
underpaid for a deal of walking and shoe-leather, but wealth were
not a object on his part, and marriage were the great wish of his
hart—' (p. 458)

At this point, Pip interrupts, bringing Joe—as he
thinks—back to the point. But, conceivably, 'marriage . . .
the great wish of his hart' *is* Joe's point. It is not the
postman's marriage that he really wants to talk about so
much as his own imminent union with Biddy. Had his wits
been recovered Pip might have been suspicious about the
relationship between Joe and Biddy. Joe's new literacy—
his ability to read and write—argues close intimacy.

Biddy is not (as Mr Hurwitt says) Joe's housekeeper at
this point of the narrative. After the death of Mrs Gargery
no housekeeper is required and Joe and Biddy agree that
it would not be respectable for her to stay in the house of
an unmarried man—even a man twenty years older than
her. Nor, until a decent interval elapses, can Joe remarry.
Biddy leaves to take up a post as the village schoolteacher.
There will, of course, be a tied-house with the position.

When Pip comes down to the village, he stays at the
Blue Boar. Everyone at the inn knows about his reduced
'expectations' and he is lodged in a poor room, at the
top of the house. The innkeeper and his staff would, one
imagines, surely know of an impending wedding in their
small community. But, if they know, nothing is said to Pip
about his brother-in-law's big day.

The forge and Joe's house are near the village, but on
his early morning walk Pip does not go there. He returns
instead to his hotel for breakfast, and who should he meet
but Pumblechook. The merchant pompously upbraids Pip
for 'ingratitood'. The two men do not, however, mention
what one would have thought to be matters of more direct
interest. Their mutual assailant Orlick, for instance—now

in custody at the county jail. More curiously, Pumblechook does not mention the wedding, which is, as we later learn, taking place at that very moment. Joe is a relative of both Pip and Pumblechook. And Pumblechook does talk about 'Joseph' at great length. Surely—as a relative, a neighbour, a village dignitary, and an old family friend—he would have been invited to the wedding? If not, surely, his wrath against Joseph's 'ingratitood' would have been even more virulent than against Pip's. He would certainly not have kept his peace on the subject. We have to assume that Pumblechook does not know of the wedding, any more than Pip does. What is going on?

Pip first calls at the school—which is mysteriously closed. He arrives at the forge:

Almost fearing, without knowing why, to come in view of the forge, I saw it at last, and saw that it was closed. No gleam of fire, no glittering shower of sparks, no roar of bellows; all shut up, and still.

But, the house was not deserted, and the best parlour seemed to be in use, for there were white curtains fluttering in its window, and the window was open and gay with flowers. I went softly towards it, meaning to peep over the flowers, when Joe and Biddy stood before me, arm in arm.

At first Biddy gave a cry, as if she thought it was my apparition, but in another moment she was in my embrace. I wept to see her, and she wept to see me; I, because she looked so fresh and pleasant; she, because I looked so worn and white.

'But, dear Biddy, how smart you are!'

'Yes, dear Pip.'

'And Joe, how smart *you* are!'

'Yes, dear old Pip, old chap.'

I looked at both of them, from one to the other, and then—

'It's my wedding-day,' cried Biddy, in a burst of happiness, 'and I am married to Joe!' (p. 472)

Evidently Joe and Biddy were married at crack of dawn. There has been no breakfast, no reception, no wedding guests. Who were the witnesses? Who was the best man?

Can one make any sense of this perplexing episode? One can dismiss out of hand the usual motive for a hole-in-corner wedding; namely, that Biddy is pregnant (little Pip turns up much later, well beyond the nine-month mark). There is, I think, a more likely explanation. Joe can never have been prosperous, and never less so than at the moment. He has taken two months off work to look after Pip. Clearing Pip's debts may conceivably have put him in debt himself. While in London, he had further financial burdens—squaring the bailiffs, day-to-day living expenses, and the cost of medical attention for Pip. Biddy can only be earning a pittance at the school. What these two good people have done, we apprehend, is to cancel their wedding party (for which they had prudently saved) and had a 'paupers' wedding'. There is no feast, no honeymoon because, having given their all to Pip, they can no longer afford such luxuries. Their marriage contrasts with the sumptuous and sterile party which never was at Satis House. That was an affair with all the trappings of the marriage ceremony but no union, this a union without trappings.

Pip's ignorance of the wedding is a puzzle—but not, I think insoluble, nor deleterious to our respect for Dickens's artistry. Clearly Pip was not invited because there was no party to invite him to. Nor was he told of the wedding, because of the embarrassment of having to explain why there was no party. The money saved up for it had been spent on his jewellers' debts. Why make the young fellow feel even more guilty than he already does?[1]

The Oxford World's Classics *Great Expectations* is edited by Margaret Cardwell with an introduction by Kate Flint.

George Eliot · *The Mill on the Floss*

———

Should we change the end of The Mill on the Floss?

———

In *Can Jane Eyre Be Happy?* I drew attention, as have other commentators, to troubling improbabilities in the tremendous watery climax to Eliot's novel. Among other things, I pointed to: (1) the meteorological improbability of a flash flood of the torrential nature which Eliot describes in the low-lying, flat countryside around St Ogg's. As Gordon Haight neatly put it—if all the twenty-five inches of rain that falls on Lincolnshire in a year were to fall in a single night, it would not produce the biblical deluge Eliot portrays at the end of *The Mill on the Floss*; (2) the physical improbability of the large, wooden lump of machinery which rushes down on the flood current to crush Tom and Maggie, 'overtaking' their boat. This is against the laws of hydrodynamics. Large wooden objects do not float faster than smaller objects in the same stream.

These problems were confronted and solved (after a fashion) by the adaptors of Eliot's novel for television. The programme went out on BBC Television on 1 January 1997. Maggie was played by Emily Watson, and the screenplay was done by Hugh Stoddart. Stoddart and his collaborators evidently decided in their story conferences that the climactic flood scenes, as written by George Eliot, were unfilmable—whatever 1990s special-effects magic was drawn on.

It would, of course, have been possible to make a small change to Eliot's narrative by having Tom and Maggie's

'It is coming, Maggie!' Tom said, in a deep hoarse voice, loosing the
oars and clasping her.

boat snag on some obstacle (a submerged tree branch, for example). But there remained other improbabilities and impossibilities—evident in the foregoing illustration from the 'Cabinet' Edition. Why doesn't the boat, as depicted above, tip over? Why isn't the boat moving? Why is the 'wooden machinery' riding so high in the water? The whole thing looks and feels entirely *wrong*.

Although elsewhere faithful to the main lines of Eliot's narrative, Stoddart completely changed the ending. As I saw the TV version (for reasons that will become clear, one has to be rather subjective in one's speculations), there *was* a flood. But it was more a quiet seep of water over low banks, turning the water-meadow outside the Tulliver Mill into a huge, still, millpond. On the mirror-like surface of this pond at midday, as it seemed (the scene in the novel takes place at stormy night, and still-stormy early dawn), Maggie sculled her way to the mill. Tom—from a top window—saw his rescuer and, using the rope with which grain was hoisted to the top of the building, lowered himself down. But he became tangled in the rope and fell into the (glassily still) water. For mysterious reasons, he sank like a stone. Maggie, on impulse, jumped in— converting the episode into what looked like a double suicide. The dramatization ended with an underwater sequence of the two Tullivers, a coiling umbilical rope around them, going to the bottom. Neither seemed to be making any attempt to swim or regain the surface.

In an eerie way it was—if untrue to Eliot—effectively enigmatic. The reviewer in *The Times*, Peter Barnard, was entranced by the scene:

It is one thing to describe in words Maggie trying to rescue Tom but deciding once his life is clearly gone, to die with him. To do so in a television sequence underwater is quite another. But the combination of Graham Teakston's directing, Hugh Stoddart's script, and Emily Watson's ability to make her face act for her achieved that feat and the result was a moment of real dramatic brilliance.[1]

A moment of melodramatic improbability on the page became a moment of 'real dramatic brilliance' on screen. But, even to achieve this 'brilliance', is an adaptor licensed to make changes of this radical kind to Eliot's text?

The main objection one would make to Stoddart's changed ending is that it is manifestly false to Maggie's character, as conceived by her creator. Maggie has, we remember, already contemplated suicide in Bob Jakins's parlour, just before the flood, and rejected it as the solution to her overwhelming problems (it is at this moment that she feels the swirling water round her ankles). Just as the television version takes all the storm out of the flood—making it no more dramatic than a leaking cistern—so it siphons all the life-force out of Maggie in her last moments. When she bravely accepts fate, in the form of the great mass of wooden machinery looming down on them, it is as an acceptance of God's will, and she stands up—as the accused in court stands up to receive sentence. Supinely letting herself sink to the bottom of a pond seems wholly out of character.

Is there any way out of this narrative impasse? I thought not. George Eliot had written herself into a box and all we could do was cavil or sympathize. A solution to the problems of the ending of *The Mill on the Floss* came, however, from an Oxford World's Classics reader, Mr Mark Tatam, of Hall Farm, Gainsborough, Lincolnshire. Mr Tatam's letter to me (dated 4 January 1998) began:

Dear Professor Sutherland, I have been greatly enjoying your book *Can Jane Eyre Be Happy?* I hope you will forgive my presumption in writing to you, not as a literary critic but as a farmer living close to 'St Ogg's' [i.e. Gainsborough]. In the spirit of your own writing, I would like to suggest that George Eliot's hydrodynamics do, if you will excuse the phrase, 'hold water' quite well.

Mr Tatam firmly—and rather chauvinistically—locates the action of George Eliot's novel around Gainsborough, in Lincolnshire (as have other authorities—although I think there is a strong infusion of Coventry, where Eliot was brought up).[2] Historically, the area around Gainsborough has been transformed over the century by the practice of 'warping'—controlled flooding so as to leave a sediment of rich silt on the bordering agricultural land. At the time George Eliot was writing, the land was much lower: 'well below mean sea level' (as Mr Tatam points out). Gainsborough lies alongside the Trent, which is tidal in this region. Mr Tatam goes on:

You quote Gordon Haight as saying that the necessary rise could not occur 'if the whole twenty-five inch rainfall of Lincolnshire had dropped there in one night'. This is, of course, misleading . . . what if the Trent is in flood and then meets an extreme Spring tide coming the other way? A cousin farming on the banks of the Trent nearby assures me that a very powerful backing up action occurs that even now, after vast sums of money have been spent on bank raising and flood defences, can be quite frightening . . . A breach of the Trent bank by both river and tide would have spilled vast quantities of water onto the land twenty or more feet below. The low hills beyond would have stopped the waters from spreading more than a few miles. My cousin assures me that he has seen excavators and straw stacks totally submerged from even minor flood problems, even though the land level is now higher than it was because of the effects of warping. The once-in-sixty years flood proposed by Eliot would certainly cause the rapid and deep flooding she suggests.

Mr Tatam offers a remarkably welcome explanation in so far as it makes more plausible what Eliot herself wrote. Mr Tatam's follow-up explanation for the paradoxical hydrodynamics of the last scene is, I think, even more satisfactory than his suggestions about the plausibility of the flash flood around St Ogg's:

Finally the question of the wooden machinery rushing down on the boat. Whilst this takes a little more reconstructing, it is certainly not impossible. The famous Trent *Aegir* is an example of the odd things that can happen when outflowing river meets incoming tide. Given a massively swollen river, a very high and powerful spring tide, and the effects of the Trent bank bursting and water flooding out onto the land below, massively complex and powerful swirls, eddies, cross-currents and undercurrents can develop. In tidal water the undercurrents may often be going in the opposite direction to the top flow. It would be quite possible for the Tullivers' shallow boat, affected only by the top current, to be swept away by a 'huge mass' being dragged along by the undertow.[3]

Not everyone will agree with Mr Tatam—but his points are extraordinarily well taken. Better than any academic critic I have come across, he reads the ending of *The Mill on the Floss*, through his formidable expertise as a Lincolnshireman, in such a way that Eliot's text *makes sense*. I am glad (even though I have been comprehensively corrected) to have inspired this display of Oxford World's Classics reader power. Should we change the end of *The Mill on the Floss*? Not now, we shouldn't.

Postscript: Is Maggie Tulliver a murderer?

In conversation with me, Dinah Birch, who has written the introduction to the Oxford World's Classics *The Mill on the Floss*, agreed in finding Mr Tatam's *Aegir* thesis plausible, adding that it was additionally satisfying in mirroring Maggie's 'massively complex and powerful swirls' of emotion in these last chapters. This was something entirely missing in the placid 'millpond' climax of the television dramatization.

Dr Birch offered another puzzle. Does Maggie 'murder' Tom? Had she not gone to the Mill—but simply saved herself (or put herself out to save the Jakins family), Tom would presumably have weathered out the flood in sturdy Dorlcote Mill. The building has manifestly survived the great flood of sixty years before and would doubtless survive this one too. Had Maggie not gone to the Mill, had she not induced Tom to get into the boat (instead of herself taking refuge in the Mill), he—and conceivably both of them—would have lived through the deluge. There is, of course, a lot of repressed violence in the sibling relationship, going back to Maggie's 'killing' (by negligence—or was it?) Tom's rabbits, and Tom's sadistic interference with her love-affair with Philip Wakem. At some subconscious level, has Maggie resolved that he (and she) must die? As they go under, is she to be pictured with a stranglehold round him, in the same way that Bradley Headstone takes Rogue Riderhood to the bottom in his 'ring of iron'?

The Oxford World's Classics *The Mill on the Floss* is edited by Gordon Haight, with an introduction by Dinah Birch.

===

How long is Alice in Wonderland for?

===

The above is a minor puzzle among those in the most puzzle-packed of Victorian narratives, *Alice's Adventures in Wonderland*. The story opens:

Alice was beginning to get very tired of sitting by her sister on the bank, and of having nothing to do: once or twice she had peeped into the book her sister was reading, but it had no pictures or conversations in it, 'and what is the use of a book,' thought Alice, 'without pictures or conversations?'

So she was considering, in her own mind (as well as she could, for the hot day made her feel very sleepy and stupid), whether the pleasure of making a daisy-chain would be worth the trouble of getting up and picking the daisies, when suddenly a White Rabbit with pink eyes ran close by her. (p. 9)

It is, we apprehend, gloriously high summer. The 'hot day', the daisies, and the dress in which Tenniel portrays the little girl confirm this seasonal dating. It would be logical to assume the setting in Carroll's mind was 4 July 1862; the day, that is, when Charles Lutwidge Dodgson took Alice Liddell, and her sisters Lorina and Edith, on the boating trip on the Cherwell. On that day, as literary history records, *Alice's Adventures in Wonderland* was conceived as an entertainment by the maths don for his young guests.

The vegetation which Carroll describes and Tenniel pictures confirms the midsummer setting: the 'great thistle' behind which Alice hides from the puppy, or the harebells around the mushroom on which the caterpillar sits. Similarly high-summery are the open-air 'mad tea-party', and the roses in bloom, about which the Queen of Hearts is so tyrannical. This, one confidently gathers, is a July–August story.

How, then, does one make sense of the end? In her dream Alice is growing embarrassingly during the peremptory trial presided over by the King and Queen of Hearts. Defying the ordinance that 'all persons more than a mile high should leave the court', she stays on to hear sentence passed:

'Off with her head!' the Queen shouted at the top of her voice. Nobody moved.

'Who cares for *you*?' said Alice, (she had grown to her full size by this time.) 'You're nothing but a pack of cards!'

At this the whole pack rose up into the air, and came flying down upon her; she gave a little scream, half of fright and half of anger, and tried to beat them off, and found herself lying on the bank, with her head in the lap of her sister, who was gently brushing away some dead leaves that had fluttered down from the trees upon her face.

'Wake up, Alice dear!' said her sister. 'Why, what a long sleep you've had!' (pp. 109–10)

After Alice has gone off home, her older sister remains sitting on the bank, thinking about Wonderland. She also foresees 'how this same little sister of hers would, in the after-time, be herself a woman'. How the adult Alice would, at some distant point in time, entertain her own children with her dream of Wonderland, 'and find a pleasure in all their simple joys, remembering her own child-life, and the happy summer days'.

So the story ends, with the phrase 'summer days' that seems so appropriate for all the preceding narrative. All, that is, except for that detail about what it was that woke Alice up: 'some dead leaves that had fluttered down from the trees on to her face.' The leaves of brown, as the song tells us, come fluttering down in September and in the rain.

Alice goes to sleep in midsummer and wakes up in autumn, in the sere and yellow leaf of the year. Her sister's exclamation is apposite: 'Why, what a long sleep you've had!' Rip van Alice, one might think. How can one make sense of this? The most attractive hypothesis is that *Alice* is not just the story of a summer afternoon. It is an allegory of the transitions accompanying puberty: the growing-pains which intervene between a little girl's childhood and her young womanhood. This transition is remarkably rapid in physiological terms: it happens in just a few months. The child grows, as we say, 'overnight'—by which we mean in just a few months. Carroll, it seems, plays with the same kind of metaphorical foreshortening in his story. Alice goes down the rabbit hole a little girl, and comes out—if not an adult woman—a pubescent girl on the brink of womanhood. How long has she been asleep? A few minutes and an epoch.

The Oxford World's Classics *Alice's Adventures in Wonderland* is edited by Roger Lancelyn Green.

═══

Does Dickens know his train signals?

═══

Departing from his normal practice, Dickens offers at the end of the serialized *Our Mutual Friend* a 'Postscript: in lieu of Preface'.[1] This afterword reminds readers of what most of them must have well known—that there almost was no concluding part of the novel. Everything after Chapter 51 was, in a sense, a 'postscript', because thereafter Mr Charles Dickens was living on borrowed time.

Our Mutual Friend was serialized from May 1864 to November 1865. As Dickens recalls:

On Friday the Ninth [of June] in the present year [1865], Mr and Mrs Boffin (in their manuscript dress of receiving Mr and Mrs Lammle at breakfast) were on the South Eastern Railway with me, in a terribly destructive accident. When I had done what I could to help others, I climbed back into my carriage—nearly turned over a viaduct, and caught aslant upon the turn—to extricate the worthy couple. They were much soiled, but otherwise unhurt . . . I remember with devout thankfulness that I can never be much nearer parting company with my readers for ever than I was then, until there shall be written against my life, the two words with which I have this day closed this book:—THE END. (p. 822)

Dickens gives here a vivid thumbnail account of the terrible Staplehurst accident, in which ten less fortunate passengers perished and forty were seriously injured. The 2.38 train from Folkestone to London (Dickens had been in France) crashed at speed on a viaduct under repair. The

system of red-flag warnings (it was daylight) had failed.
Dickens's was the only one of seven first-class carriages not
to fall off the viaduct. In the above, semi-comic account,
Dickens omits to mention his own heroic conduct in aiding
the injured and dying. He also omits to mention that, in
addition to Mr and Mrs Boffin, his mistress Miss Ellen
Ternan and her mother were in the train with him.

The trauma of the Staplehurst accident may well have
shortened Dickens's life. It certainly made him nervous
about trains. As his son Henry recalled, after Staplehurst,
'I have seen him sometimes in a railway carriage when
there was a slight jolt. When that happened he was almost
in a state of panic and gripped the seat with both hands.'[2]
The Boffin–Lammle breakfast episode Dickens mentions
as carrying with him occurs in Book IV, Chapter 2 ('The
Golden Dustman rises a little').

Oddly enough, there is a railway scene a few chapters
earlier in which—as we may think—a terrible rail accident
is eerily forecast. It occurs at the end of Book III, Chapter
9. Bella Wilfer and 'the secretary' (John Rokesmith) have
come to Betty Higden's pauper's funeral, near Henley on
Thames. After her conversation with Lizzie Hexam, in
which the two young ladies strike up a friendship, Bella
and Rokesmith make their way back to the railway station
and the train that will carry them back to London. It is
night as they approach the station on foot. From the fact
that they can see the signal-lights, they must be coming to
the station in the same direction as the train is travelling
(i.e. up-line):

The railway, at this point, knowingly shutting a green eye and
opening a red one, they had to run for it. As Bella could not
run easily so wrapped up, the Secretary had to help her. When
she took her opposite place in the carriage corner, the brightness
in her face was so charming to behold, that on her exclaiming,
'What beautiful stars and what a glorious night!' the Secretary

said 'Yes,' but seemed to prefer to see the night and the stars in the light of her lovely little countenance, to looking out of [the] window.

O boofer lady, fascinating boofer lady! If I were but legally executor of Johnny's will! If I had but the right to pay your legacy and to take your receipt!—Something to this purpose surely mingled with the blast of the train as it cleared the stations, all knowingly shutting up their green eyes and opening their red ones when they prepared to let the boofer lady pass. (pp. 530–1)

One notes the slight, but palpable, differences in Victorian rail travel from ours. Because they wore bulkier clothes than us (particularly crinolined women) and had a baffling array of carriages to choose from (three 'classes', 'ladies only', 'smoking'—i.e. gentlemen only), simply alighting and descending from the train were complex operations and might take some minutes. To warn passengers, Victorian stations had a 'departure bell' (not to be confused with the whistle, which was a signal for the driver). Dickens specifically mentions this bell, in a later railway scene in *Our Mutual Friend*, where Bradley Headstone has his epileptic fit.

Getting on board was, as I have said, a much more fussy business than it was to become in the twentieth century. And once aboard and settled inside the appropriate carriage, the dim, oil-fuelled lights would allow one to see the stars outside (all modern travellers can see by night are their own reflections—the interior being so much brighter than the exterior). Steam engines give a warning blast as they move off—or sound a warning toot from their whistles as they thunder through stations.

But one thing has not changed over the last 130 years: red means stop and green means go. How, then, should we understand the description of the signals in the above passage? Victorians, of course, did not have the profusion of highway traffic-lights that we have. They did not have the Highway Code drummed into them as kindergarten pedestrians. It might be that they, in general, had as little sense of railway signalling codes as most present-day sea travellers do of whether red stands for starboard or green for port.

In the above passage, Dickens clearly describes what looks like a dangerously wrong sequence. Modern passengers, seeing a red platform signal-light come on, would assume that there was no need to 'run for it'. The train will only leave when the light turns to green. That is when you would run. No driver will drive his train through a red light. And in Dickens's final sentences, the business of the railway stations 'all knowingly shutting up their green eyes and opening their red ones when they prepared to let the boofer lady pass' would seem to lay the ground for any number of Staplehursts.

Is Bella's beauty so radiant as to have disoriented the signals, so they do not know their red from their green? Is there, perhaps, some play with the symbolism of Othello's green-eyed monster or Macbeth's bleeding eye of day which overrides the signalling codes of the Great Western Railway (which the couple are evidently riding, if they have been to Henley and back)? However ingenious, it is hard to make headway here with the traditional literary associations of red and green.

The most satisfactory explanation of this problem is given by T. S. Lascelles, in his article 'A Railway Signal Puzzle in *Our Mutual Friend*'.[3] Lascelles argues that 'Dickens had seen and correctly observed the old time-interval system of train working'. The explication of how the 'old time-interval system' worked is complicated, but basically as follows. This signalling system was developed before the electric telegraph allowed stations to know that a train was coming, or what other traffic might be on the line. All that the managers of the station knew, for certain, was that a train had arrived when they saw it come in. A technique was thus devised by which, when a train drew in, the green signalling lamp would (by the dropping of a filter over the lens of a bright oil-lamp) turn red. It would remain red for a 'safe' period after the train had departed—say ten minutes. The red signal did not indicate to the driver waiting at the station 'don't go'; it indicated 'we shall ensure no one follows you too closely, so leave at your discretion—but don't wait too long'. The signal-light would not be placed at the head of the platform, but in the middle, where it would be more visible to the majority of passengers and to incoming trains.

What, above all, had to be avoided was an incoming train—particularly a 'through' train—crashing into one which had already halted at the station, or that was still moving slowly out of the station. For this reason the signal-light at the rear-end of the station to the oncoming train, the first light the driver would see, needed to be red as well. And it, like the front light, would stay red for some time after the train ahead left. So when Rokesmith and Bella see the red light, this, as Lascelles points out, is no guarantee that the train in the Henley on Thames station is still waiting—it could be just gone, or about to leave. All that it indicates is that a train is in the vicinity. On modern stations, a green light following a red means a train is coming—stand by. When the time-interval system operated, a green light did not mean a train was coming; 'all it could definitely mean was that the previous train had gone by so many minutes'.

The Lascelles explanation, counterfactual as it seems to us and extremely hard to grasp, is satisfying, although not without some difficulties in the application. As Lascelles notes, Dickens was extraordinarily observant. It must have struck him, however, that in the 1860s the time interval system of signalling was extremely antique.

The Great Western Railway began experimenting with electrical-telegraphic signalling techniques in the late 1830s, and they were universal a decade later. As Lascelles notes: 'as electric telegraphy spread, the "time interval" gave place to the "space" interval and what was called . . . the "block system"', which resulted in the signalling conventions we are familiar with today. If, as Dickens noted, *Our Mutual Friend* was set 'in these very times of ours', the time-interval system would have been a thing of the distant past. As Lascelles points out, the line which Bella and John travel on to Henley on Thames opened in 1857, with up-to-date telegraphic signalling (of the kind familiar to us). The 'time-interval' system had no place on this line. One can make sense of the red–green signalling paradox only by recourse to a chronological paradox: one of Dickens's many time-warp effects. Bella and John are not only travelling at unimpeded speed, they are travelling thirty years in the past.

The Oxford World's Classics *Our Mutual Friend* is edited by Michael Cotsell.

Wilkie Collins · *The Moonstone*

Is Franklin Blake a thief and a rapist?

The Moonstone has an honoured place in literary history as, to quote no less an authority than T. S. Eliot, 'the first, longest and best of English detective novels'. Many detective novels have been written since Eliot's accolade (offered, it is pleasing to note, in the first World's Classics edition of *The Moonstone*).[1] But Collins's novel still retains the power to delight and to surprise.

The story, a version of the 'locked room mystery', hinges on a jewel theft. A fabulous Indian gem, the Moonstone, is left to Rachel Verinder. So nervous is she on getting possession of it that she keeps it safely secreted in her bedroom suite at night. None the less, it is stolen. The thief must be someone in the household. Sergeant Cuff of Scotland Yard is called in. There is a likely looking clue. Whoever stole the diamond must have brushed against some wet paint on the door to Rachel's boudoir. But the incriminatingly stained garment is never found. Rachel's maid, Rosanna Spearman, is a prime suspect; she has a criminal past. But Rosanna is now a reformed character and her alibi holds up. Cuff declares himself defeated and goes into retirement in Dorking, where he will devote himself to the cultivation of roses.

There are two rather strange *sequelae* to the mystery. Rachel, who seemed to be in love with Franklin, will have nothing more to do with him after the theft. And Rosanna commits suicide, throwing herself into some conveniently nearby quicksands. But of the diamond, there is no sign. The denouement, when it comes, very late in the narrative, is a bombshell. A year later Franklin returns from a trip 'wandering in the East' (still heartbroken) to the grand Verinder house in Yorkshire. Here he comes by Rosanna's suicide note. It appears the poor woman loved him— hopelessly, of course. She discovered Franklin's paint-stained nightgown on his unmade bed the morning after the theft and realized that he must have been in her mistress's rooms the night before. Whether to steal gems or embraces she does not, of course, know. Out of love, she hides the incriminating article. And out of hopeless love, she later kills herself.

All this is a mystery to Franklin. He *knows* he was not in Rachel's boudoir that night. None the less, an even greater shock awaits him on his reunion with a still-frigid Rachel. Despite her coolness:

I could resist it no longer—I caught her in my arms, and covered her face with kisses.

There was a moment when I thought the kisses were returned . . . [then] with a cry which was like a cry of horror—with a strength which I doubt if I could have resisted if I had tried—she thrust me back from her. I saw merciless anger in her eyes; I saw merciless contempt on her lips. She looked me over, from head to foot, as she might have looked at a stranger who had insulted her.

'You coward!' she said. 'You mean, miserable, heartless coward!' (p. 380)

What does she mean? She tells him: '*You villain, I saw you take the Diamond with my own eyes!*' He came into her boudoir at one o'clock at night and took the gem ('I saw the gleam of the stone between your finger and thumb', p. 387). She saw his face, quite clearly. But Franklin still knows he did not do it. To cut Collins's entertainingly long story short—Franklin was sleepwalking. Why did his

unconscious self want to 'steal' the jewel? Because he knew
there were dangerous burglars about (the Indians), and he
did not think the diamond safe in Rachel's room. Another,
more villainous occupant of the house, was observing
him and purloined from the 'thief' what Franklin would
never know he had stolen. Had Rosanna not hidden his
nightgown Franklin would, of course, have been arrested
by Sergeant Cuff.

The Victorians were fascinated by somnambulism. In
the medical authority which Collins cites on page 433,
John Elliotson's *Human Physiology* (1840), there are a
large number of examples of sleepwalking and sleep-
talking described. But I would guess that Collins was
inspired principally by a report in *The Times*, 18 September 1866, at a period when he was beginning to write
The Moonstone (serialized, January–August 1868). Entitled 'Somnambulism Extraordinary', the newspaper story
records that:

At a farmhouse in the vicinity of Guildford, a few evenings ago,
a large roll of butter was brought in at tea. The careful wife
proceeded to cut the butter in two in order that one half of it
might only remain on the table. The knife grated upon something
in the centre of the butter, and in the very heart of the lump
she found a gold watch and chain, very carefully rolled up, but
not enveloped in paper or any other covering. At this juncture
Sarah B——, the domestic, entered the room, and uttering a
sharp exclamation, darted off again precipitately. Scarce had the
farmer time to remark upon Sarah's strange conduct than she
returned, breathless, with haste and anxiety, ejaculating, 'It's
mine, mum! it's mine!' Mrs —— remembered to have heard Sarah
say that she had been left a gold watch and chain by a deceased
relative, that she was always in terror of losing it, that she did
not wear it, as not suitable for a person in her station of life,
and that for safety she kept it locked up in her box under her
clothes. Sarah declared that she had been in the habit, when
under the influence of strong emotion, of walking in her sleep.

On the previous Monday she had been reading in the newspaper some dreadful tales of burglary with violence. On the same night she had a most vivid dream. She thought the house had been entered by burglars, and that she saw them through a chink in the door enter her master and mistress's room. She tried to scream, but could not, and although very anxious for her master and mistress's welfare, her thoughts seemed to revert in spite of everything to the necessity of saving her watch. At length she dreamed that she hit upon an expedient. She quietly got out of bed, unlocked her box, took out the watch, slipped on her dress, and softly glided down stairs and made her way to the dairy. She there took a roll of butter of the Saturday's making, wound the chain around the watch, and deftly inserted both watch and chain in the very centre of the butter, making up the roll precisely in the form that it was before. She then thought she passed swiftly upstairs, and reached her room unmolested. On inspecting the watch found in the butter, she had no hesitation in declaring that it was hers! Farmer —— and his wife accordingly handed over to Sarah B—— the watch and chain.

Many such stories are to be found in the newspapers and psychological writing of the period. But it was not just the curious pranks that somnambulists got up to which interested Victorians. Much as with Multiple Personality Disorder for us today, the condition raised teasing ethical, moral, and legal questions. Was someone like Franklin a 'thief', or not responsible for his actions? Was the somnambulist an 'automaton' or what some French psychologists called an *automate conscient*?

There was a relevant case, a few years earlier, described in Roger Smith's *Trial by Medicine*:

In 1862, Esther Griggs threw one of her children through a closed window, believing the house to be on fire. A passing policeman stated that she had a nightmare which caused her to try to save her children. Though arrested, she never faced trial as the grand jury did not find a true bill against her, presumably on the ground that she had behaved as an automaton.[2]

So, too, might Franklin claim that he was an automaton, not a conscious agent, when he 'stole' the diamond—although it might be difficult to persuade a jury. There are, however, other rather trickier legal complications. Rosanna's first assumption is that Franklin sneaked into Rachel's bedroom at one o'clock in the morning for a more probable reason than jewel theft ('I shall not tell you in plain words what was the first suspicion that crossed my mind, when I had made that discovery. You would only be angry', p. 353). When he sees Rachel again, after his long travels, despite her clear distaste for him, he cannot help himself: 'I could resist it no longer—I caught her in my arms, and covered her face with kisses' (p. 380). He may on that fateful night have had a strong unconscious urge to protect the diamond. But he has other, stronger, unconscious urges. What would a somnambulant Franklin do if he found himself in the boudoir of an unclothed Rachel? Would he, all unconscious, behave with the propriety of a Victorian gentleman? He doesn't behave like one, even when conscious.

This relates to an oddity in the novel. Why does Rachel not inform on him? There are three possible reasons. She loves him so much, she will protect his grand felony (a felony which robs her grievously). This is unlikely. Less unlikely is that she does not want to have to explain why she did not shriek out the first moment she espied him in her room. Why didn't she? Because she was not intending to offer any resistance to him when he came to her bed, as she thought he must have been meaning to. To have shouted out after he had been in her room for some minutes might give rise to awkward questions.

The third possible reason for Rachel's silence is the most speculative but in many ways the most interesting. Suppose he did make love to a sleepy Rachel—and she acquiesced, rather as Tess acquiesces (as we may assume)

to Alec in Hardy's novel? Then, as he rose, she realized he
was unconscious; then he took the jewel—the other and
less valuable jewel, as we may think. She could not, in
such circumstances, say anything. Even if poor Rosanna
were to go to prison for the crime (as looks quite likely,
for a while). And would Franklin have been, in such a
circumstance, a 'rapist' or merely a lucky somnambulist?

Postscript: Who is the real thief?

Jonathan Grossman writes to say that a student, Beth
Steinberg, working on *The Moonstone*,

wrote a wonderful paper for my Victorian fiction class that might
be thought of as this puzzle: 'How do the Indians get away
with the Moonstone and the murder?' Her brilliantly executed
argument revolves around the idea that the Indian explorer
Murthwaite abets their getaway in his (and the novel's) final
letter. This makes good sense because Murthwaite, self-named
'semi-savage', rather sides with the Indians throughout the novel.
Ms Steinberg argues that Murthwaite's letter effectively puts the
British authorities off the scent of the murderers (the British are
after all the law in India) by saying that the three men have
gone their separate ways as mendicant, anonymous pilgrims.
This stymies any further pursuit of the murderers: 'The track
of the doomed men through the ranks of their fellow mortals was
obliterated.'

Like Professor Grossman, I am impressed and half-
convinced by Ms Steinberg's ingenious speculation. More
so since Murthwaite, on the evening that the Moonstone
is stolen, has a longish conversation with the Indians in
their native language. And what is he doing at Frizinghall
anyway?

The Oxford World's Classics *The Moonstone* is edited by Anthea
Trodd.

===

Elms, limes, or does it matter?

===

George Eliot's huge canvas in *Middlemarch* allows the author the opportunity for luxuriant scene painting. One location, central to the narrative, is described in loving detail—Mr and Mrs Casaubon's married home. Although—as a beneficed clergyman—he has the Lowick living, Edward Casaubon lets the rectory and lives in the nearby manor-house (inherited on the death of his elder brother).[1] We are given an estate agent's eye-view of Lowick Manor when Dorothea, a bride to be, calls to inspect her future home, on a 'grey but dry November morning', in Chapter 9:

It had a small park, with a fine old oak here and there, and an avenue of limes towards the south-west front, with a sunk fence between park and pleasure ground, so that from the drawing-room windows the glance swept uninterruptedly along a slope of greensward till the limes ended in a level of corn and pastures, which often seemed to melt into a lake under the setting sun. This was the happy side of the house . . . (p. 71)

It is not entirely clear to the mind's eye, but it seems that a ha-ha has been banked up to hide the public thoroughfare from which one turns down the private avenue of limes to approach the manor house. As one looks out from the windows of the house, the road is invisible. For the person looking out of its windows the prospect gives the impression of a huge estate, rather than a modest country house surrounded by working farms.

On this first visit Dorothea chooses the room that is to be her 'boudoir', or private retiring room. It is upstairs, with a large bow window, and 'looks down the avenue of limes'—due west. Obviously, before the advent of artificial lighting, west-facing rooms were a desirable interior feature, allowing as they did a longer enjoyment of daylight. Candlelit evenings, even in a prosperous household like Lowick, would be dim affairs; and in summer the flames would make the rooms hot and (given the fact that tallow rather than wax would be used for all but special occasions) smelly. The detail is something to which the nineteenth-century reader would be better attuned than we are. So well attuned, indeed, that it would not need pointing out. Our Victorian predecessors would also pick up (as we do not) the joke in Lady Catherine de Bourgh's remark, on visiting the Bennets' house for the first time, that 'This must be a most inconvenient sitting room for the evening, in summer; the windows are full west' (p. 312). Inconvenient because, as a lady somewhat far gone in the vale of years, she would (like Blanche Dubois) prefer to avoid the strong light of day illuminating her features. Candles are so much friendlier.

Dorothea Casaubon's west-facing boudoir and the west-ward avenue figure recurrently in key scenes in the later narrative. When Ladislaw returns to Middlemarch and informs Dorothea of his intention to take up work with Mr Brooke, Casaubon senses danger. He writes his cold letter of severance, declaring war, as it were, on his young cousin, with Dorothea the prize to the victor. Mr Casaubon dispatches his frigid letter in the morning, after what is evidently a tense night in the marital bedroom (if, that is, Dorothea is sleeping with her husband and not by herself in her boudoir):

Meanwhile Dorothea's mind was innocently at work towards the further embitterment of her husband; dwelling, with a sympathy that grew to agitation, on what Will had told her about his parents and grand-parents. Any private hours in her day were usually spent in her blue-green boudoir, and she had come to be very fond of its pallid quaintness. Nothing had been outwardly altered there; but while the summer had gradually advanced over the western fields beyond the avenue of elms, the bare room had gathered within it those memories of an inward life which fill the air as with a cloud of good or bad angels . . . (p. 367)

One thing has, however, been 'outwardly altered'. The lime-trees have become elms. Elms and limes are, as trees go, very different to the eye—at least when in full leaf. One assumes that when Dorothea made her first visit in grey November the avenue was leafless and—as often happens—the trees less easily identified without their foliage. Even though the elm's is rougher-barked than the lime's, one trunk looks very like another to all but the forester's eye. Now it is verdant summer.

This explanation, however, is dashed by the next appearance of the avenue. It is another crisis in Dorothea's life. She is now a widow, and has taken the painful decision to renounce Will, whom she now realizes she loves:

One morning, about eleven, Dorothea was seated in her boudoir with a map of the land attached to the manor and other papers before her . . . She had not yet applied herself to her work, but was seated with her hands folded on her lap, looking out along the avenue of limes to the distant fields. Every leaf was at rest in the sunshine, the familiar scene was changeless, and seemed to represent the prospect of her life . . . (p. 532)

'Changeless'? The limes which became elms are limes once more.

The final appearance of the westward prospect is one of the most admired and familiar moments of the novel. After her long night-time vigil, Dorothea, as dawn breaks, resolves to dedicate herself to a life of duty, now truly understood and stripped of all girlish idealism:

It had taken long for her to come to that question, and there was light piercing into the room. She opened her curtains, and looked out towards the bit of road that lay in view, with fields beyond, outside the entrance-gates. On the road there was a man with a bundle on his back and a woman carrying her baby; in the field she could see figures moving—perhaps the shepherd with his dog. Far off in the bending sky was the pearly light; and she felt the largeness of the world and the manifold wakings of men to labour and endurance. She was a part of that involuntary, palpitating life, and could neither look out on it from her luxurious shelter as a mere spectator, nor hide her eyes in selfish complaining. (p. 776)

It is a high point, perhaps the highest point, in Eliot's novel. But, playing the part of the 'mere spectator', the reader may wonder about the topography of the scene Dorothea looks out on. She is, as before, looking westwards (whether from her boudoir, or the marital bedroom is not clear)—although 'pearly light' suggests an easterly prospect towards the sunrise. The avenue of limes or elms has disappeared. And the road, which was previously concealed by the ha-ha, has reappeared. Or possibly, it is just the gap where the ha-ha is broken to allow the turn-in from the road. It would be only ten yards or so, and it is hard to think of the family being visible for more than a glimpsed second or two.

If Coleridge, halfway through 'This lime-tree Bower my Prison', referred to the embowering tree as an elm, it would be troubling. Eliot's lime/elm variations are almost invisible in the narrative backdrop. But, once perceived, they unsettle us. Readers will have their own responses, and some may opt for a 'silent emendation' of 'elms' to 'limes' on page 367. No editor, as far as I know, has done it—for the likely reason that no editor has noticed (the anomaly was pointed out to me by the Eliot scholar Margaret Harris, and was pointed out to her by a sharp-eyed undergraduate). For me, the elm–lime confusion 'humanizes' a narrator who might otherwise seem divinely infallible. I like to see George Eliot make tiny mistakes (which, frankly, matter not a jot in themselves) because it makes her a little more like me and less like the Oracle at Delphi.

Can one ascertain what trees *really* border the avenue? English elm (*Ulmus procera*) is most commonly a hedging tree. In the early nineteenth century (when *Middlemarch* is set) landowners encouraged their tenant farmers to plant them, and reserved the timber rights as an eventual cash crop. Elm is not favoured as a decorative border tree for park avenues, because of its tendency to throw out lots of suckers. The small-leaved lime (*Tilia cordata*) or linden (it has no connection with the citrus fruit) was commonly used for avenues in the early nineteenth century. A lime-bordered avenue is prominent, for example, at Donwell Abbey in *Emma*, as the company saunter through Mr Knightley's grounds in mid-June:

It was hot; and after walking some time over the gardens in a scattered, dispersed way, scarcely any three together, they insensibly followed one another to the delicious shade of a broad short avenue of limes, which stretching beyond the garden at an equal distance from the river, seemed the finish of the pleasure grounds. (p. 325)

Lime grows quickly, is handsome looking, and can be readily clipped or pollarded. The wood is of little use for timber (although it does, apparently, have some use for sculpting or carving). My guess is that Lowick Manor's avenue is bordered by limes, and there is a stand of elms beyond in the farmer's 'westward fields'. Dorothea's eye has momentarily confused the two.

The Oxford World's Classics *Middlemarch* is edited by David Carroll, with an introduction by Felicia Bonaparte. The Oxford World's Classics *Emma* is edited by James Kinsley, with an introduction by Terry Castle.

===

How criminal is Melmotte and when is he criminalized?

===

Novelists, from Henry Fielding to Jeffrey Archer, are perennially fascinated by great swindlers—the most adventurous of criminals. For the Victorians, the most notorious such 'buccaneer' was John Sadleir (1814–56). One of the few financier-criminals (along with Robert Maxwell) to earn an entry in the *DNB*, the Irish-born Sadleir rose to fame, power, and high political office on the immense bubble of speculative wealth created by his fraudulent banking activities. When the Tipperary Bank collapsed in February 1856, Sadleir was found to have embezzled £200,000 of its funds and to have ruined legions of widows and children. A couple of days later his body was found on Hampstead Heath, alongside a phial of prussic acid.

Sadleir's meteoric rise, Luciferian fall, and dramatic self-destruction inspired Merdle in *Little Dorrit*, the swindler hero in Charles Lever's *Davenport Dunn* (1859), and—at least partly—Melmotte in *The Way We Live Now* (not least, in regard to the prussic acid). How criminal is Augustus Melmotte? Simply persuading fools (even foolish widows) to part with their money is not necessarily felonious. There is one born every minute, and if the Sadleirs, Merdles, Maxwells, and Melmottes of the world do not fleece them someone else will. Is Anthony Trollope's villain a confidence trickster, or something more serious? Is he a rogue, or an 'arch-criminal'? The question, if one tries to balance all the available evidence, is a lot trickier than it may seem.

The central issue is Pickering Park. Following the tangled career of this property through the long length of *The Way We Live Now* clarifies what is, I think, a significant change of intention by Trollope during the three-months' composition of his novel. Close examination of this issue also highlights that familiar feature of his writing methods—a reluctance to go back and change what he had earlier written. For Trollope, once on paper the narrative was marble. If subsequent problems in consistency or logic arose, Trollope relied on running repair work—a kind of narrative jury-rigging. He did it well and one would not want to catch him out. But uncovering this kind of repair work increases one's respect for his peculiarly fluent genius.

We are introduced to Pickering Park in Chapter 13. A possession of the Longestaffes, it is, like the family's other, and larger, Suffolk property, Caversham, and their town-house in Bruton Street, 'encumbered'. The Longestaffes are 'old' gentry whose income comes from land and they are hard up in these modern times, when big money is made by gambling in the city. Mr Adolphus Longestaffe is keen to sell Pickering so that he can 'disembarrass' Caversham, where his family live (when they are in the country) and where he is squire.

The *nouveau riche* Mr Melmotte is keen to buy (or at least acquire) Pickering as a dowry for his daughter Marie, with which to bribe Lord Nidderdale—his prospective marital target. As the father-in-law of a belted lord, the great financier's campaign to conquer English high society will be usefully advanced. Melmotte is, of course, rather less than keen to pay for Pickering Park, unless he has to. But, keen or not, Mr Adolphus Longestaffe cannot sell the property to Melmotte without the express consent of his

son and heir, the dissolute Adolphus ('Dolly')—an habitué
of the Beargarden Club. Nor, on his part, can Dolly sell
without the consent of his father, who has a life interest
in the estate. Their minds must meet. As Mr Longestaffe
ruefully tells Melmotte, Dolly 'never does do anything that
I wish' (i. 115). Their minds will not meet. There is an
impasse on Pickering Park and the matter is dropped. But,
to raise a few thousands, Mr Longestaffe gives Augustus
Melmotte the title deeds to the London house (in Bruton
Street, as we later learn). What Melmotte subsequently
does with these deeds we never learn (unless I have missed
the detail).

This transaction with the Bruton Street deeds takes
place in mid-April. In mid-June it seems that Dolly has
been brought round on the other matter. More specifically, he has bargained with his father that, after the
outstanding £30,000 mortgage debt on Pickering Park is
paid off, he should receive, cash down, half of the balance,
namely £25,000. Mr Longestaffe's fond hope was that the
whole £50,000 should be applied to Caversham's debt. In
course of time Dolly will reap the benefits when he inherits
Caversham. But Dolly wants 'ready' ('rhino', as they call
it at the Beargarden).

In Chapter 35 (published some six months after Chapter
13 in the novel's serial run) we learn that a paragraph
has appeared in the London newspapers, 'telling the
world that Mr Melmotte had bought Pickering Park,
the magnificent Sussex property of Adolphus Longestaffe,
Esq., of Caversham'. And so it was, the narrator confirms:
'the father and son, who never had agreed before, and who
now had come to no agreement in the presence of each
other, had each considered that their affairs would be safe
in the hands of so great a man as Mr Melmotte, and had
been brought to terms' (i. 325). The awkward phraseology
of 'no agreement in the presence of each other' sticks in

the mind. The business was conducted by correspondence or through an intermediary, we assume. It is not, however, a detail we linger on. A lot is happening at this point in the book.

Augustus Melmotte now takes over Pickering Park as its new owner. Masons and carpenters, 'by the dozen' move in. Ten chapters later (Chapter 45), we are vouchsafed some extra details:

Pickering had been purchased and the title-deeds made over to Mr. Melmotte; but the £80,000 had not been paid,—had not been absolutely paid, though of course Mr. Melmotte's note assenting to the terms was security sufficient for any reasonable man. The property had been mortgaged, though not heavily, and Mr. Melmotte had no doubt satisfied the mortgagee; but there was still a sum of £50,000 to come, of which Dolly was to have one half . . . (i. 422–3)

There is a significant new twist in the account of the earlier negotiations for the sale. Although it was said earlier that the arrangements had been made without the parties meeting, now we are told that Dolly 'had actually gone down to Caversham to arrange the terms with his father'. However one reads it, the versions are contradictory—though again all this is on the level of background detail and can be comfortably overlooked. Of course, if we think about it, the Longestaffes in their meeting at Caversham have discussed the disposition of the title deeds, on which joint assent, by writing, was strictly required. Dolly is now reported to have been very happy with the 'arrangement' he made with his father at Caversham, so long as he gets his £25,000 (the next day, he fondly hopes). All this takes place in the period between mid-June and early July—the zenith of 'Melmotte's glory'. It is a crowded month for the 'great financier'. On 8 July he is to host a magnificent banquet for the Emperor of China, and two days later he will be elected member of

Parliament for Westminster. A fortnight later—after a fall like Lucifer's—he will kill himself, leaving behind a faint aroma of almonds and some unbelievably vast debts.

In Chapter 45 we are told that Mr Longestaffe has 'let his [Bruton Street] house for a month [i.e. mid-June to mid-July] to the great financier' (i. 421). This is the first we have heard of the arrangement—which is to be of vital narrative significance. One deduces, although one is not told, that Mr Melmotte has taken over the Longestaffe house as a temporary refuge from the works being carried out in his Grosvenor Square mansion in preparation for the Emperor of China banquet. None the less, despite the chaotic remodelling going on around them, the Melmottes manifestly continue living in Grosvenor Square, right up to the eve of the banquet. It is from Grosvenor Square, for example, that Marie makes her ill-fated elopement with Felix. After the banquet, the Melmottes seem to have moved lock, stock, and barrel into the Bruton Street house. It is there that Melmotte beats his daughter, and it is in the Bruton Street study that he finally poisons himself.

The whole question of the move of residence is blurred—and not made any clearer by the reader's (but not Trollope's, apparently) recollection of those Bruton Street title deeds. There is, legally, no need for Melmotte to rent Bruton Street; it is his to do as he likes with. A new phase in the Pickering saga begins in Chapter 58, where Dolly—enraged by the fact that he has not yet received so much as a ten-pound note—recruits a sharp lawyer, Mr Squercum, to pursue his interest. At this point in the narrative (during the early days of July) the idea is introduced that Melmotte has committed 'forgery' to gain possession of Pickering Park. Forged what? Why should he have had to forge anything? Rumours claim he has forged title deeds—which is clearly absurd tittle-tattle. Subsequently, it emerges that he is thought to have

forged Dolly's letter, assenting (in mid-June) to the making
over of the title deeds of Pickering Park, directed to Mr
Longestaffe's dilatory lawyers, Slow and Bideawhile. This
is later confirmed by the narrator, in Chapter 73, shortly
before Melmotte kills himself.

It is not, as presented by Trollope, an easy morsel of
information for the reader to swallow. Melmotte, we are
asked to believe, forged Dolly's signature to a blank letter
of assent, which he found in a drawer, in mid-June, in
a desk used by Mr Longestaffe, in Bruton Street, in a
study which contained two desks, the other of which was
reserved for Mr Melmotte's use, in which he (on his part)
keeps documents so confidential that he is obliged to eat
them before doing away with himself. He evidently also
keeps a handy phial of prussic acid in the desk drawer. Mr
Longestaffe, of course, being the owner of the house and
the two desks, would have a master-key to the receptacle
of the great financier's darkest secrets.

At this point, scepticism crowds in. The tissue of
narrative invention is so flimsy that one can poke holes
in it at almost any point. Is it conceivable that Dolly and
his father, coming to their meeting of minds at Caversham
in mid-June (long before we are told the son has his
own lawyer—an afterthought) would not have touched
on the business of the deeds? Would not their handing
over or holding the deeds back have been a central part of
any 'arrangement'? The notion that Slow and Bideawhile
would not have notified Dolly of the transfer of these
documents (representing £80,000 of his inheritance) is
similarly incredible. A witnessed statement would have
been required for the title deeds and property to be passed
over. Melmotte could not have paid off the mortgage holder,
were he not the titled owner.

On his part, Dolly cannot sign away his property
with a casual, unwitnessed, letter. Nor would lawyers

as respectable as Slow and Bideawhile fail to keep their
client informed of what they were doing with a stream
of missives—among which would be their bill, detailing
the transfer of the deeds. This business with the forged
letter is supposed to have taken place in mid-June, at the
time of the newspaper announcement. But Dolly is clearly
aware, in Chapter 35, that the deeds *have* been made
over. Melmotte's workmen would hardly have descended
on the place, nor could the mortgagee have been paid off by
Melmotte, otherwise. All that worried Dolly at that point
was not that the deeds had gone but that his £25,000 was
slow in coming.

The business about the blank letter, left conveniently
in Melmotte's temporary residence (at a time when he
was not residing there), is highly implausible, as is the
account of the financier's housing generally. Melmotte
would surely have kept confidential documents locked in
his safe in Abchurch Lane, or in Grosvenor Square—not
in a study shared with someone whom he was criminally
defrauding. And what—before the sale of Pickering Park
was in prospect—was Mr Longestaffe doing with a blank
lawyer's letter of consent (naming Melmotte as purchaser)
in his desk drawer in Bruton Street? Is he perhaps a
clairvoyant?

Trollope gets round this problem very awkwardly.
Retroactively (in Chapter 45) he has Melmotte living
simultaneously in Bruton Street and Grosvenor Square,
from mid-June onwards. And, in order to get Longestaffe
(or his current business correspondence) into Bruton
Street—a house we were told in Chapter 35 that he has
entirely vacated—Trollope tells us (in Chapter 73) that Mr
Longestaffe has been given *carte blanche* to use this study
whenever he wishes: 'Oh dear yes! Mr. Longestaffe could
come whenever he pleased. He, Melmotte, always left the
house at ten and never returned till six. The ladies would

never enter that room. The servants were to regard Mr. Longestaffe quite as master of the house as far as that room was concerned' (ii. 118).

We never actually see Longestaffe occupying Bruton Street while the Melmottes occupy it—but we are to assume he *did*—inconvenient as such an arrangement would be to all parties. Convenience, of course, is hardly served by there being two desks in the shared study. Mr Melmotte has the key for one, and Mr Longestaffe the key to the other. And in *his* desk, Mr Longestaffe secretes the unsigned lawyer's letter. And then, with no other motive than curiosity, Mr Melmotte forces the lock—breaking it in the process—and discovers—to his immense convenience—the blank letter, awaiting only his forged addition.

One could go on poking holes, but the improbabilities are legion. One recalls one of Trollope's aphorisms in the novel: 'A liar has many points in his favour,—but he has this against him, that unless he devote more time to the management of his lies than life will generally allow, he cannot make them tally' (ii. 254–5). So too with narrators who try to change their plots as they go along. To make the late stages of the novel's narrative tally with the earlier, Trollope has to convince us that Dolly and his father are criminally negligent of their property, that lawyers do not answer letters or draw up contracts, that both Melmotte and Mr Longestaffe contrive to live in two places at once and conduct their very personal business matters in the same office, leaving sensitive documents for each other to happen on. That, just on the off-chance of finding something valuable, Melmotte takes a jemmy to his landlord's furniture.

What happened? Trollope's notes for the novel offer a clue. In his early scheme, Trollope clearly meant Melmotte to be a great confidence trickster—less a villain than a swindler who plays on the gullibility of the English public; a kind of Volpone *de nos jours*. Subsequently—around the middle of his composition—a darker and more feloniously criminal conception of the 'great financier' emerged. In a chapter plan for the novel, as it was evolving, it is clear that Trollope was toying with the idea of climaxing the book with a great trial—Melmotte in the dock at the Old Bailey for forgery.[1] This was to happen around Chapters 71–7. But after projecting this end for the novel, Trollope decided instead on suicide. The evidence is that he began seriously to think of this turn of plot around Chapter 45. He added, as he went along, details that would make the forgery retrospectively plausible—beginning with the lease, and ending with the business of the two desks in the shared study. In a novel less crowded with distracting incident than *The Way We Live Now*, the improbabilities might have protruded fatally. As it is, the reader has so much else to think about that Trollope's fumble passes unnoticed, or if noticed, not dwelt upon.

The Oxford World's Classics *The Way We Live Now* is edited by John Sutherland.

═══

Jules Verne and the English Sunday

═══

Verne's most famous story has a wonderful narrative 'gimmick'. Phileas Fogg lays a bet with his fellow Reform Club members that he can—using the latest transport systems (as advertised in the *Daily Telegraph*)—circumnavigate the globe in 'eighty days or less; in nineteen hundred and twenty hours, or a hundred and fifteen thousand two hundred minutes' (p. 20). He will leave England on 2 October, and return on—or before—'Saturday, the 21st of December, 1872', at a quarter-to-nine. This narrative idea was supposedly inspired by the advertising material of Thomas Cook, catering for the first generation of world 'tourists'.

The story which Verne builds on the 'eighty days' gimmick is wonderfully entertaining. And it ends with a fine *coup de théâtre*. By dint of ingenuity, lavish outlay of money, pluck, and sheer will, Phileas and his comic, but omnicompetent 'man', Passepartout, make it back to England in the nick of time. But at this moment Phileas is falsely arrested for bank-robbery (like tourism, one of the modern world's new growth industries).

He misses the deadline by minutes. To console himself he decides that he will marry the Oriental beauty, Aouda. Passepartout is sent out to arrange things with the clergyman. Then, the following day—again with only minutes to spare—Passepartout rushes back to Fogg's grand mansion in Savile Row. It is, he announces, a day earlier than they think:

Three minutes later, [Passepartout] was back in Savile Row, staggering, completely out of breath, into Mr Fogg's room.

He couldn't speak.

'But what's the matter?'

'Master's . . . ' spluttered Passepartout, '. . . wedding . . . impossible.'

'Impossible?'

'Impossible . . . tomorrow.'

'But why?'

'Tomorrow . . . Sunday!'

'Monday,' said Mr Fogg.

'No . . . Today . . . Saturday.'

'Saturday? Impossible!'

'Yes, YES, YES!' screamed Passepartout. 'Your calculations were a day out! We arrived 24 hours early. But there are only ten minutes left!' (p. 200)

The two men rush the 576 yards to the Reform Club, arriving breathless but just under the wire, as the club clock pendulum beats the sixtieth second, marking the deadline.

As the editor of the Oxford World's Classics edition points out, Jules Verne is engagingly slapdash about the fine detail of his narrative. He mixes up East and West, left and right, and there are many chronological and geographical slips. And striking at the heart of the plot is the business about the 'phantom day'. Fogg, that is, does not undertake to go round the world in '80 days'; but 'within' 80 days—in 79 days, that is. It is an analogous confusion to that currently raging about the new millennium: as pedants love to point out, it will not start on 1 January 2000, but on 1 January 2001— long after all the celebrations have ended and the site at Greenwich is once more a rubbish dump.

Verne's wonderful idea (at least for readers on this side of the Channel) is damaged by another implausibility, attributable to a Gallic incomprehension of the English 'weekend'. Arrived and detained by the police at Liverpool, Fogg dashes to the station and orders a special train to London.

There were several high-speed engines with steam up. But given the traffic arrangements, the special train couldn't leave the station until three o'clock.

At 3 p.m., Philcas Fogg, having mentioned to the driver a certain bonus to be won, was heading for London together with the young woman and his faithful servant.

Liverpool to London had to be covered in five and a half hours: perfectly possible when the line is clear all the way. But there were unavoidable delays—and when the gentleman got to the terminus, 8.50 was striking on all the clocks of London.

Having completed his journey round the world, Phileas Fogg had arrived five minutes late.

He had lost. (p. 191)

He must also have lost a large part of his formidable powers of observation if he cannot tell the difference between Friday night and Saturday night, at a London railway station. Nor have noticed that the Saturday train service differs from that of other days of the week. Fogg, we remember, is a man whose 'sole pastimes were reading the newspapers and playing whist'. Obviously no papers have come to his notice on his six hours' train journey.

Most improbable is that, during the hours of daylight the next day, Fogg should be under the illusion that it is Sunday. Even if the papers were not delivered, the sounds (or lack of them) from the street outside would surely have alerted him. In Britain in 1872 Saturday was not as distinctively different from Friday as it was to become in the twentieth century, with the extension of the English weekend and the five-day working week. But Sunday—oppressed by the iron pieties of the Lord's Day Observance Society—was uniquely grim. Fogg and Passepartout would have to be deaf, dumb, and blind not to notice the graveyard stillness of the English Sunday. Or not, in this case, to notice that it was *not* Sunday, but bustling Saturday, with open shops (Savile Row then, as now, was the Mecca of English gentleman's tailoring), busy places of entertainment, postal deliveries (banned on Sunday by the LDOS), and hectic traffic.

This is an implausibility which would, I think, tend to slip by the French reader (it would have been easily remedied, had Verne noticed it, by having the eightieth day fall midweek). The implausibility will, increasingly, slip by the British reader after the 1990s, with the innovation of Sunday Trading, and the homogenization of the British week. But for those older readers who can remember the full awfulness of the Victorian Sunday, a phenomenon which lasted well into the last decades of the twentieth century, the ending of Verne's romance will always ring false.

The Oxford World's Classics *Around the World in Eighty Days* is translated and edited by William Butcher.

Mark Twain · *Huckleberry Finn*

===

What happens to Jim's family?

===

The most discussed anomaly in *Huckleberry Finn*'s narrative has been satisfactorily explained away by modern critical commentary. In Chapter 8, Huck meets up with his fellow runaway, the slave Jim, on Jackson's Island. Jim explains why it is he has run away. He overheard Miss Watson, his owner, planning to sell him in New Orleans, for $800, 'and lit out mighty quick, I tell you' (p. 41). He has hidden on the island, waiting for a raft to carry him downriver. He intends to go some twenty-five miles downstream, then hide on the Illinois side of the Mississippi. That is, he will go south, not north or east.

The question is, why doesn't Jim just go across into Illinois, which is not a slave state, only a few hundred yards from Jackson's Island where he and Huck are hiding? Why go further into the dangerous south? The question is picked up by Huck in Chapter 20, throwing his new companions the 'Duke' and the 'Dauphin', off the trail:

They asked us considerable many questions; wanted to know what we covered up the raft that way for, and laid by in the day-time instead of running—was Jim a runaway nigger? Says I—

'Goodness sakes, would a runaway nigger run *south*?'
No, they allowed he wouldn't. (p. 116)

It looks, on the face of it, like a lapse of logic. Rather as if Liza, in *Uncle Tom's Cabin*, instead of crossing the ice-floes to the other side of the Ohio had decided to float down on

one, further into the slave-owning territory she is trying
to escape. But, as commentators have made clear, Jim's
decision is a wise one on closer inspection. The western
part of Ohio, bordering the Mississippi, was notoriously
dangerous for runaway slaves. They might be captured
by bounty hunters, who did a thriving trade in returning
runaways (illegal as the business was). They could be held
as indentured labourers for a year until reclaimed; and
even then be returned.

The safest strategy, which Jim has evidently worked out,
is to drift south to Cairo, then go north (as best he can)
on the upstream tributary and get deep into Ohio, where
the underground railway is established and he can travel
on to freedom. Of course, events intervene when he and
Huck arrive at Cairo and this plan is foiled. But it is, none
the less, the best plan and, we may assume, no blunder on
Mark Twain's part.

There is another problem which is less tractable. In
Chapter 16 we learn that Jim is not—as the reader
previously was led to believe—a single man. The raft is
approaching Cairo. Jim is excited, because he sees this city
as his jumping-off place for freedom. Huck is increasingly
gloomy at the thought that he is abetting in the robbery
of Miss Watson, assisting the escape of $800-worth of her
property:

I got to feeling so mean and so miserable I most wished I was
dead. I fidgeted up and down the raft, abusing myself to myself,
and Jim was fidgeting up and down past me. We neither of us
could keep still. Every time he danced around and says, 'Dah's
Cairo!' it went through me like a shot, and I thought if it *was*
Cairo I reckoned I would die of miserableness.

Jim talked out loud all the time while I was talking to myself.
He was saying how the first thing he would do when he got to
a free State he would go to saving up money and never spend
a single cent, and when he got enough he would buy his wife,

which was owned on a farm close to where Miss Watson lived; and then they would both work to buy the two children, and if their master wouldn't sell them, they'd get an Ab'litionist to go and steal them.

It most froze me to hear such talk. He wouldn't ever dared to talk such talk in his life before. Just see what a difference it made in him the minute he judged was about free. It was according to the old saying, 'Give a nigger an inch and he'll take an ell.' (p. 82)

We learn a little more about Jim's family in Chapter 23. His children are called Elizabeth and Johnny. He gives a pathetic description of how, after 'Lizabeth recovered from the scarlet fever, he slapped her for not paying attention to him. Then he discovered, the disease had made her deaf:

'Oh, Huck, I bust out a cryin' en grab her up in my arms, en say, "Oh, do po' little thing! de Lord God Almighty fogive po' ole Jim, kaze he never gwyne to fogive hisself as long's he live!" Oh she was plumb deef en dumb, Huck, plumb deef and dumb—en I'd ben a-treat'n her so!' (p. 142)

It is, arguably, the most moving section of the novel.

Nothing more is said of Jim's family. In 'Chapter the Last' Jim discovers he is free, is taken from his chains, 'given all he wanted to eat, and a good time . . . and Tom give Jim forty dollars for being prisoner'. No mule is forthcoming, but

Jim was pleased most to death, and busted out, and says:
    'Dah, now, Huck, what I tell you?—what I tell you up dah on Jackson islan'? I *tole* you I got a hairy breas', en what's de sign un it; en I *tole* you I ben rich wunst, en gwineter be rich *agin*.' (p. 261)

Jim's former richness was the possession of $14, as we recall. He is now $36 better off. His estimated value is $800. How is he going to buy his wife and children? The narrative ignores this question, in its wrap-up of events. The novel ends with Huck's determination to 'light out for the territory ahead of the rest, because Aunt Sally she's going to adopt me and sivilize me, and I can't stand it. I been there before.' So the novel ends. And what of Jim, his wife, 'Lizabeth, and Johnny? Obviously Jim will never have the wherewithal to buy them. Huck might loan or give him the money from his $6,000 treasure; which would make a nice romantic ending. It is, as best we can guess, the late 1840s or early 1850s.[1] If Jim can wait fifteen years, the Civil War will unite his family (the romantic Tom will be fighting for the South, realistic Huck for the North). His best hope, probably, is some 'Ab'litionist'.

There is currently much discussion about the propriety of suppressing *Huckleberry Finn* on the grounds of its profuse (and disquieting) use of the 'N—— word'. Personally I can tolerate this evidently accurate depiction of the callous vernacular of the place and period more easily than Twain's indifference (and the anaesthetized indifference his narrative induces in us, its readers) to Jim's still-enslaved family.

The Oxford World's Classics *Huckleberry Finn* is edited by Emory Elliott.

Leo Tolstoy · *Anna Karenina*

What English novel is Anna reading?

If Tolstoy's novel *Anna Karenina* had ended a fifth of the way through, at the end of Chapter 29, we would have a bittersweet short story with a happy ending. In this chapter Anna is returning from Moscow to her home, her beloved son Seriozha, and her less-than-beloved husband, Alexei, in Saint Petersburg. She has been in the capital to sort out the marriage problems of her hapless sister-in-law, Dolly.

In Moscow, Anna has fallen under the spell of the dashing cavalry officer, Count Vronsky. But she has not surrendered to temptation. She is still a virtuous wife and matron. By no means entirely happy: but virtuous.

She now travels back to St Petersburg by train, at night, accompanied by her maid, Annushka. 'Well, that's all over, thank Heaven!' Anna thinks as she enters her 'dimly lit' carriage: 'Thank Heaven, tomorrow I shall see Seriozha and Alex Alexandrovich again and my good accustomed life will go on as of old':

With the same preoccupied mind she had had all that day, Anna prepared with pleasure and great deliberation for the journey. With her deft little hands she unlocked her red bag, took out a small pillow which she placed against her knees, and locked the bag again; then she carefully wrapped up her feet and sat down comfortably. An invalid lady was already going to bed. Two other ladies began talking to Anna. One, a fat old woman, while wrapping up her feet, remarked upon the heating of the carriage. Anna said a few words in answer, but not foreseeing anything interesting from the conversation asked her maid to get out her reading-lamp, fixed it to the arm of her seat, and took a paper-knife and an English novel from her handbag. At first she could not read. For a while the bustle of people moving about disturbed her, and when the train had finally started it was impossible not to listen to the noises; then there was the snow, beating against the window on her left, to which it stuck, and the sight of the guard, who passed through the carriage closely wrapped up and covered with snow on one side; also the conversation about the awful snow-storm which was raging outside distracted her attention. And so it went on and on: the same jolting and knocking, the same beating of the snow on the window-pane, the same rapid changes from steaming heat to cold, and back again to heat, the gleam of the same faces through the semi-darkness, and the same voices,—but at last Anna began to read and to follow what she read. Annushka was already dozing, her broad hands, with a hole in one of the gloves, holding the red bag on her lap. Anna read and understood, but it was unpleasant to read, that is to say, to follow the reflection of other people's lives. She was too eager to live herself. When she read how the heroine of the novel nursed a sick man, she wanted to move about the sick-room with noiseless footsteps; when she read of a member of Parliament making a speech, she wished to make that speech; when she read how Lady Mary rode to hounds, teased her sister-in-law, and astonished everybody by her boldness—she wanted to do it herself. But there was nothing to be done, so she forced herself to read, while her little hand played with the smooth paper-knife.

The hero of the novel had nearly attained to his English happiness of a baronetcy and an estate, and Anna wanted to go to the estate with him, when she suddenly felt that he must have been ashamed, and that she was ashamed of the same thing,—but what was she ashamed of? 'What am I ashamed of?' she asked herself with indignant surprise. She put down her book, leaned back, and clasped the paper-knife tightly in both hands. There was nothing to be ashamed of. (pp. 99–100)

It's a wonderfully evoked scene—familiar to anyone who has travelled through the night by train, yet strange, in many of its physical details, to a non-Russian reader (how should we visualize that movable 'reading lamp', for example, hung on the arm of Anna's seat?). Vladimir Nabokov, when a lecturer at Cornell University, used to give a whole lecture to his American undergraduates based on this passage. 'Any ass can assimilate the main points of Tolstoy's attitude toward adultery,' Nabokov asserted, 'but in order to enjoy Tolstoy's art the good reader must wish to visualize, for instance, the arrangement of a railway carriage on the Moscow–Petersburg train as it was a hundred years ago.'[1]

The passage is shot through with omens—trains will not be lucky for Anna. But the attention of the English-speaking reader will be particularly drawn to the 'English novel' whose pages Anna is cutting and reading. We are given precise and detailed descriptions of its narrative. What, then, is it? Surely we can identify it by title? A. N. Wilson, in his life of Tolstoy, is in no doubt that Anna has in her hands a novel by Anthony Trollope.[2] Tolstoy wrote *Anna Karenina* between 1873 and 1878, and it is known that during this period he read and admired Trollope's equally massive novel of parliamentary life, *The Prime Minister*. That novel, published in England in June 1876 (although it cannot have been translated into Russian until a few months later), had a momentous influence on *Anna Karenina*. Trollope's narrative climaxes, brilliantly, with the suicide of the villainous Ferdinand Lopez, in front of a speeding train. There are other such deaths in Victorian fiction (notably Carker's in *Dombey and Son*). But it is likely that the climax of Tolstoy's novel—Anna's self-immolation at Nizhny railway station—is directly indebted to *The Prime Minister*.

There is, however, no scene in *The Prime Minister* in which Lopez makes a speech in Parliament. That episode seems to belong to an earlier Trollope novel, *Phineas Finn, the Irish Member* (1869), whose narrative revolves around the hero's initial failure to make a good maiden speech to the House, and his eventual success in doing so. And the business about Lady Mary riding to hounds and teasing her sister-in-law seems to allude to still another Trollope novel, *Is he Popenjoy?* (1878), where the spirited heroine, Lady Mary Germain (née Gresley), outrages her husband's straitlaced sisters by dancing and hunting. Mary Germain's husband, however, attains his Englishman's idea of happiness not in the form of a 'baronetcy and an estate', but the unexpected legacy of a marquisate and an estate. Tolstoy's 'baronetcy' seems to be a recollection of Trollope's *The Claverings* (1867), in which the hero, Harry, unexpectedly inherits a baronetcy, an estate (and some of the attendant guilt which Tolstoy mentions) when his distant cousins are drowned sailing. As for the business of the heroine nursing a sick man— that would seem to be an allusion to a quite different novel—Charlotte Yonge's sensational best-seller of 1853 *The Heir of Redclyffe*, in which the Byronic hero, Guy, is nursed on his lingering deathbed by his young wife Amy, and gradually repents his wild ways under her tender ministrations.

What, then, is Tolstoy aiming at with this mélange of bits and pieces of English fiction? What the Russian writer is doing, I suggest, is something rather chauvinistic. It was Virginia Woolf who claimed that there was only one 'adult' novel written in Victorian England—*Middlemarch* (a novel that Tolstoy seems not to have read). The mass of English Victorian novels, particularly with their sugar-stick endings and generally optimistic view of life, were essentially *juvenile*, Woolf thought. Henry James made much the same point when he talked, at the end of the century, of the tyranny of the young reader over the adult novelist.

The point that Tolstoy makes is, I think, that Anna

is not reading an English novel so much as 'English fiction'—with all its falsities and its childish addiction to 'happiness', particularly happy endings. To paraphrase the famous opening of *Anna Karenina*, all happy novels are alike, so it does not really matter *which* particular English novel the heroine is reading. What Anna is reading, we apprehend, is a generic English novel—a novel that never existed, but which typifies the genre. And to represent the quintessence of English fiction Tolstoy amalgamates a variety of works by that most English of English novelists, Anthony Trollope, the 'Chronicler of Barsetshire', with a dash of Miss Yonge. He, Count Leo Tolstoy, will write a different kind of novel: one that is harder, sadder, more realistic—Russian, in a word. A novel that does not succumb to the debilitating 'English idea'. 'Expect no pernicious "English happiness" in this Russian novel,' is the implicit warning.

What English novel, then, is Anna Karenina reading? All of them and none of them.

The Oxford World's Classics *Anna Karenina* is translated by Louise and Aylmer Maude, with an introduction and notes by Gareth Jones.

═══

Why are there no public conveniences in Casterbridge?

═══

The furmity-woman is Michael Henchard's albatross, or the equivalent of Macbeth's witches. Whenever she appears on the scene, bad things happen to the Mayor of Casterbridge. It is at the furmity-woman's marquee that her rum-laced drink drives Henchard to the wild act of selling his wife Susan and his daughter Elizabeth-Jane for five guineas—precipitating the long series of events which will, twenty-two years later, lead to his final disgrace and wretched extinction.

Henchard first meets this ominous figure at the Weydon-Priors annual fair (located as Weyhill in Hampshire). The date of the encounter is around 1828 (a period of historical significance—the main part of the narrative pivots around the mid-1840s repeal of the Corn Laws; as the story opens, Wessex is still enjoying its protected prosperity as the granary of England). The fair, as a harvest festival with distant pagan origins, takes place in the hot mid-September (the fifteenth, as we can work out from Henchard's great oath the next day). Its main attractions are 'peep-shows, toy-stands, wax-works, inspired monsters, disinterested medical men, who travelled for the public good, thimble-riggers, nick-nack vendors, and readers of Fate' (p. 8). Liquid refreshments are also on offer.

On her first appearance the furmity-woman is thriving, if unappetizing. She is in her physical prime and at the zenith of her fortunes:

A haggish creature of about fifty presided, in a white apron, which, as it threw an air of respectability over her as far as it extended, was made so wide as to reach nearly round her waist. She slowly stirred the contents of the pot. The dull scrape of her large spoon was audible throughout the tent as she thus kept from burning the mixture of corn in the grain, flour, milk, raisins, currants, and what not, that composed the antiquated slop in which she dealt. (pp. 8–9)

The antiquated slop is a traditional rural beverage. Otherwise known as 'furmenty', its liquid base is wheat boiled in milk. In its unadulterated form, furmity is non-alcoholic. But, of course, the furmity-woman is lacing her drink with strong liquor. As she later admits, she is a 'land smuggler'. Her rum and brandy will be contraband bought from sea smugglers. We should assume that, in addition to her fairground business—which is nomadic and takes her all round Wessex, she sells smuggled liquor to the inns and public houses on her circuit. We do not know what town she comes from, and where she has her base; probably it is on the coast, somewhere like Portsmouth.[1] As the century progresses, more rigorously imposed licensing laws, and a more efficient customs and excise, will ruin her. Like Michael Henchard in his palmy Casterbridge days, hers is a prosperity whose days are numbered. The future is with the licensed marquee at the Weydon-Priors fair, selling 'Good Home-brewed Beer, Ale and Cider'. Its canvas has a pure, 'milk-hued' aspect. The furmity-seller's large tent has an appropriately soiled canvas. Hardy wants us to recall Hogarth's Gin Lane and Beer Street.

After his terrible deed, Michael Henchard wakes up in the melancholy depths of remorseful hangover. His first thought is, 'Did I tell my name to anybody last night, or didn't I tell my name?' (p. 18). He decides he didn't (this seems to have been the case; nor did Susan divulge her married name to onlookers). Henchard then swears his terrible abstinence oath, and goes off to 'far distant' Casterbridge.

Eighteen years later, to the day, Susan and Elizabeth-Jane return to Weydon-Priors. They find the fair 'considerably dwindled' (p. 22). So too has the business of the furmity-seller dwindled. She is now 'an old woman haggard, wrinkled, and almost in rags . . . now tentless, dirty, owning no tables or benches, and having scarce any customers except two small whitey-brown boys' (p. 23). The furmity-seller vouchsafes some details of her personal history to the two ladies:

'I've stood in this fair-ground maid, wife, and widow, these nine and thirty year, and in that time have known what it was to do business with the richest stomachs in the land! Ma'am, you'd hardly believe that I was once the owner of a great pavilion tent that was the attraction of the fair. Nobody could come—nobody could go, without having a dish of Mrs. Goodenough's furmity.' (p. 24)

She even, as she says, 'knowed the taste of the coarse shameless females'—which suggests that in addition to being a bootlegger, Mrs Goodenough may have dabbled in abortion (an overdose of strong liquor and a hot bath was a favoured remedy for young girls in trouble).

More to the point, can she remember the wife-sale eighteen years ago? Only very dimly, it transpires. She now has no clear mental picture of Michael Henchard, beyond his workman's corduroy and hay-trusser's tools. But she does vaguely recall that he came back to the next year's fair (i.e. seventeen years' since), 'and told me quite private-like that if a woman ever asked for him,' she was to say 'he had gone to—where?—Casterbridge' (p. 25).

Two years pass—with immense personal and professional consequences for Michael Henchard, corn factor and Mayor of Casterbridge. In Chapter 28, with his business collapsing around his ears, Henchard goes to take the chair at petty sessions. He is a magistrate by virtue of his late mayorship. There is only one case to be heard, that of 'an old woman of mottled countenance' and greasy clothes— 'The steeped aspect of a woman as a whole showed her to be no native of the country-side or even of a country town' (p. 199). She has drifted in to Casterbridge as so much vagrant refuse from a conurbation like Bristol, we gather.

The court proceedings open with the comedy of the constable Stubberd's Dogberry-like malapropisms:

'She is charged, sir, with the offence of disorderly female and nuisance,' whispered Stubberd.

'Where did she do that?' said the other magistrate.

'By the church sir, of all the horrible places in the world!—I caught her in the act, your worship.' (p. 199)

It emerges from Stubberd's circuitous testimony that 'at twenty five minutes past eleven, b. m., on the night of the fifth instinct, Hannah Dominy,' he found the old lady relieving herself in a gutter. She was observed 'wambling' (staggering) and, as the constable came up to her with his lantern 'she committed the nuisance and insulted me'. Her insult, as he reports it, was 'Put away that dee lantern'. Then she added—'Dost hear, old turmit-head? Put away that dee lantern.' It is that 'turmit-head' that gets her arrested. Had she been properly meek, she would probably have been told to 'move on', with the customary 'warning'. And it is already clear that Stubberd was fabricating his evidence ('fitting her up') when he earlier claimed that it was *after* he approached her with his lantern that she (provocatively) committed her nuisance. Clearly she was discreetly relieving herself in the dark, over a gutter, and was disturbed by the officious Stubberd throwing his light on her.

Once in court, the hag shows that she has her wits about her. She runs rings round Stubberd and the magistrate.

Then, with her eyes 'twinkling', she recounts, in malicious detail, the Weydon Fair episode. Henchard is publicly unmasked as a wife-seller, and completes his shame with a manly, but suicidal, confession: "tis true . . . 'Tis as true as the light.' A few more details add to the tableau of Henchard's downfall. There is a crowd gathered in court because, it emerges, 'the old furmity dealer had mysteriously hinted . . . that she knew a queer thing or two about their great local man Mr. Henchard, if she chose to tell it' (p. 202).

A number of puzzling questions arise from this scene. Why has the furmity-woman just now come to Caster-bridge, a town which, self-evidently, has always been off her circuit? Where has she been in the interval? How is it that she can now recognize Michael Henchard, when her memory was so blurred in conversation with Susan a couple of years before? Most intriguingly, why has she been arrested in the first place? Was her offence so rank? Casterbridge is a market town, as we are continually reminded. Livestock are regularly driven through its streets. In the very next chapter (29) there is a description of how, 'in the latter quarter of each year', vast herds of cattle are herded through Casterbridge (this leads to the fine episode in which Henchard saves Lucetta and Elizabeth from a runaway bull). On routine market days, 'any inviting recess in front of a house [is] utilized by pig-dealers as a pen for their stock' (p. 61). These herds, styes, and flocks—not to mention the town's innumerable horses—will deposit hundredweights of dung in the public thoroughfares every day and tons of it on market days.

Judging by Stubberd, Casterbridge's municipal employees are not paragons of efficiency. Street-sweeping will not take place more than once a week, if that often. The nostrils of the town's citizens must be inured to the pervasive stench. Why should an old woman at midnight in a deserted back alley adding a few drops to the Niagara of urine that flows through Casterbridge gutters cause such a pother? And what *should* the old lady, caught short, have done? Where are the 'public conveniences'?

The arrest seems, on the face of it, excessively officious. There was, of course, a wave of 'respectability' sweeping over mid-Victorian Britain. Society was becoming stricter and more 'decent' by the year. And then, of course, there is the imminent visit of the 'royal personage' (Hardy's recollection of Prince Albert's passing through Dorchester in July 1847). When royalty comes, lavatories and what goes on in them are hidden away—except for that gleaming and virginal facility reserved for royal use. It may be that, like the luckless vagrants in any city where the Olympics are due to be held, the furmity woman is the victim of a 'crackdown'. She chose the wrong time to commit her nuisance.

Most significantly, there was at mid-century a new wave of 'sanitary' legislation directed at the 'cleanliness' of the British population—the Municipal Corporations Act of 1835; the Public Health Act of 1848; the Public Baths and Wash Houses Act of 1846. Central to the court scene in *The Mayor of Casterbridge* is the Nuisances Removal Act of 1846. The legal euphemism 'nuisance' (like 'public convenience', 'spending a penny') became the material of music-hall jokes for a century after. The furmity-woman is, evidently, one of the first victims of the 1846 Act.

Legislation was, however, more effective in setting up machinery for the prohibition of 'public nuisance' than the 'conveniences' to eliminate the nuisance. What, in 1847, could the furmity-woman have done, other than use an alley to empty her drink-distended bladder? The only public lavatory in Casterbridge, or towns like it, would be at the railway station.[2] And those 'conveniences' would probably be nothing more than a slate-backed row

of stand-up urinals for travelling males (or those who went
to the expense of buying a 'platform ticket'). There was, as
it happened, great resistance to 'public conveniences' for
ladies, well into the late Victorian period. The respectable
residents of Camden, as late as 1880, opposed a *chalet
de toilette et de necessité* (of a kind available to Parisian
ladies) on the grounds that 'it would have a tendency to
diminish that innate sense of modesty so much admired
in our countrywomen'.

One of the great attractions of the new department
stores which sprang up in great cities in the later decades
of the nineteenth century was that they were 'convenient'
for lady shoppers. As Alison Adburgham notes, in *Shops
and Shopping*:

The department stores, with their variety of ready-made clothes
and accessories at reasonable prices, played an important part
in the emancipation of women. One could go to town for a day
and get everything done in one store; and more and more the
stores in London and the big cities set out to attract shoppers
from a distance by offering auxiliary, non-selling services such as
restaurants, banking facilities, and exhibitions—and cloakrooms.
These last were particularly appreciated. The Ladies' Lavatory
Company opened its first establishment at Oxford Circus in 1884,
but there were few such facilities, and one feared to be observed
using them.[3]

The Mayor of Casterbridge (serialized January–May 1886)
was being written in the immediate aftermath of the
setting up of the inaugural convenience at Oxford Circus.
It would be many years, one imagines, before the Ladies'
Lavatory Company reached Dorset.

It may well be that the fashion for the incredibly
cumbersome crinoline enjoyed its long vogue, from the
1850s onward, partly because of the freedom which, para-
doxically, it offered wearers. In her life of Havelock Ellis,
Phyllis Grosskurth records how, as a 12-year-old child, the

great sexologist was directed towards his later researches by a traumatic experience. He was walking in the London Zoo with his mother. She bade him wait a second while she stood motionless, with a serene expression on her face. When they went along their way (she lifting her skirts slightly) he looked back to see a faintly steaming puddle.[4] The vogue for gusset-less, 'free-trade' underwear probably also had its origin less in the sexual promiscuity of Victorian ladies, than in their need for clandestine relief while in public. Had the furmity-seller been wearing a crinoline and the appropriate underthings, she could have relieved herself in Casterbridge high street at midday, and suffered no persecution whatsoever beyond a lift of the cap from the passing Stubberd. But neither a *chalet de necessité* nor the camouflage of crinoline are available to Mrs Goodenough, only the dark and handy gutter.

The Oxford World's Classics *The Mayor of Casterbridge* is edited by Dale Kramer.

A. Conan Doyle · 'A Scandal in Bohemia'

Cabinets and detectives

The Sherlock Holmes mania—which shows little sign of abating a century on—took off not with the first full-length novel (*A Study in Scarlet*, 1887), but with the series of six short stories that began in the *Strand Magazine* in July 1891 and were later collected as *The Adventures of Sherlock Holmes* (1892). The first story, 'A Scandal in Bohemia', lays down what was to be Doyle's favourite narrative formula in these short tales. It is March 1888. Dr Watson (now a married man) finds himself in the vicinity of 221B Baker Street and drops in on his bachelor friend. Holmes is discovered in his usual cocaine-alleviated state of ennui. He delivers himself of some bracing Holmesian maxims. 'You see, but you do not observe,' he tells his dull *fidus Achates*; how many steps, for example, are there from the hall to the room where they are sitting? Seventeen, as Watson has a thousand times seen and never observed.

A visitor is expected. Of course Watson ('my Boswell') must stay. The client is a sumptuously dressed, masked, middle-European who introduces himself as 'Count von Kramm'. Holmes effortlessly penetrates the incognito. It is, of course, 'Wilhelm Gottsreich Sigismond von Ormstein, Grand Duke of Cassel-Felstein, and hereditary King of Bohemia'.

The King, it seems, is to be married. But, 'Some five years ago, during a lengthy visit to Warsaw, I made the acquaintance of the well-known adventuress Irene Adler'. Holmes looks her up in his files:

'Hum! Born in New Jersey in the year 1858. Contralto—hum!

La Scala, hum! Prima donna Imperial Opera of Warsaw—Yes!
Retired from operatic stage—ha! Living in London—quite so!'
(p. 12)

The King is 'entangled'. There was no secret marriage and
no legal papers or certificates. There are some letters,
whose importance Holmes airily dismisses ('Forgery')
even though they are on the King's private notepaper
('Stolen'). The King can easily lie his way out of these
embarrassments.

What Holmes does not dismiss is a photograph. 'We
were both in it,' the King confesses. 'Oh, dear! That is very
bad! Your Majesty has indeed committed an indiscretion'
(p. 13), the detective agrees. Adler will not sell the
incriminating photograph. Five attempts have been made
to steal it by thieves in the King's pay. According to the
King, it is her intention to 'ruin' him by sending the
photograph to his intended, the Scandinavian Princess
Clotilde, on the day on which their betrothal is publicly
announced. 'She [Clotilde] is . . . the very soul of delicacy.
A shadow of a doubt as to my conduct would bring the
matter to an end' (p. 14).

The game is afoot. Holmes requires only two more pieces
of information:

'And mademoiselle's address?' he asked.

'Is Briony Lodge, Serpentine Avenue, St John's Wood.'

Holmes took a note of it. 'One other question,' said he. 'Was the
photograph a cabinet?'

'It was.'

'Then, good-night, your Majesty, and I trust that we shall soon
have some good news for you.' (p. 15)

By judicious espionage (in tramp's attire) Holmes discovers that Miss Adler has a regular visitor to her villa,
a young lawyer called Godfrey Norton. He subsequently
discovers the whereabouts of the photograph by a cunning

ruse. Disguised as an elderly clergyman, he has himself attacked in Serpentine Avenue by hired accomplices. He is brought into the sitting-room of Briony Lodge by the compassionate and unwitting Miss Adler. Watson, meanwhile, has been charged to throw a smoke-bomb through the window. Thinking the house on fire, Irene Adler rushes to the secret hiding-place of the photograph. It is revealed to be 'in a recess behind a sliding panel just above the bell-pull' (p. 25), in the sitting-room.

The next day the King, Holmes, and Watson go to Briony Lodge. But Adler is gone. In the secret compartment is an innocuous publicity photograph of herself and a letter to Mr Sherlock Holmes. She has penetrated his disguise and his ruse. She has married young Mr Norton and decamped:

As to the photograph, your client may rest in peace. I love and am loved by a better man than he. The King may do what he will without hindrance from one whom he has cruelly wronged. I keep it only to safeguard myself, and to preserve a weapon which will always secure me from any steps which he might care to take in the future. (p. 28)

All the payment Holmes requires from the King is the photograph which Adler has left of herself. And, as Watson notes, 'when he speaks of Irene Adler, or when he refers to her photograph, it is always under the honourable title of *the* woman' (p. 29).

There are obviously some missing pieces in the puzzle. How long has the 'entanglement' been going on? It seems that since her prima donna role in Warsaw, five years ago, Adler has not worked in opera. Who has paid for her villa in fashionable St John's Wood? Not the impecunious lawyer Mr Norton, surely. What is the 'cruel wrong' that the King has done her? Why does he tell Holmes that she intends to 'ruin' him, when it is clear from her letter that she has no such intention?

We must assume that the King has not told the whole truth. It is he, of course, who has been keeping her in the St John's Wood villa (the traditional hiding-place for expensive mistresses, as the Oxford World's Classics notes point out). An arranged marriage has been made for him. She has clandestinely fallen in love with another. Clearly she has demanded a vast sum, by way of severance payment. It is to forestall further exactions that the King wants his photograph back. But, evidently, she has had enough from him to start a new life, under a new name, in a new place (this, surely, is the import of Watson's reference to her in the first paragraph as 'the late Irene Adler'). If he gets the picture back, Adler clearly fears, the King will have her and her lover assassinated. 'Cruel wrong' suggests that some such attempt may already have been made.

As Holmes will surely have realized, when love goes sour parties rarely tell the full truth. All's fair. But most enigmatic is—what exactly does the photograph show? We never know what 'scandalous' image has been captured on that 'cabinet' picture. Doyle had, shortly before writing his story, met Oscar Wilde and his (Doyle's) publisher had, a few months earlier, published *The Picture of Dorian Gray*—the story of another mysterious and scandalous portrait.

Why does Holmes ask if the photograph is a 'cabinet'? As the notes to the Oxford World's Classics edition explain, 'cabinets' took over in 1866 from the *carte de visite* photographs, which had themselves become a craze around 1860. *'Carte'* pictures of celebrities were collected by the general public. As Brian Coe puts it in his book, *The Birth of Photography*:

Photographers vied with one another to photograph the famous and infamous, supplying from stock pictures of royalty, artists, churchmen, writers, actors and actresses, politicians and even well-known courtesans. Some photographs ran into editions of thousands, especially pictures of the English Royal Family.[1]

The cabinet was 'similar in presentation and appearance to the *carte* but much bigger, about four inches by five and a half. The cabinet photograph was a more suitable size for quality portraiture, a dozen cabinets usually cost almost two guineas' (p. 36).

One's first suspicion is that Holmes's question ('Was the photograph a cabinet?') was astute and that the King's answer ('It was') was disingenuous. A cabinet photograph produced by a commercial studio (as they all were) would not be a single object to be hidden behind a sliding panel. Cabinets were produced in bulk and circulated in the public domain. The King would not have to burgle the villa in St John's Wood, but also the shop in Oxford Street, and any number of other houses which had come by the cabinet.

What kind of picture was it, then? At the period in which 'A Scandal in Bohemia' is set (1888) there was a craze for what were called 'detective cameras'. To quote Coe again:

From the early 1880s so-called 'detective' cameras were disguised as or hidden in parcels, opera glasses, bags, hats, walking-stick handles and many other forms. Some, like the popular Stirn 'Secret' or waistcoat camera, were worn concealed under clothing.[2]

The blackmailing potential of photographs had been evident from the earliest days of the technology. In 1869, for example, a secret camera was set up on Derby Day, to take photographs of gentlemen visiting the races with ladies other than their wives. But detective photographs brought a whole new range of possibilities. What seems likely is that the photograph in question was not, as the King claims, an innocuous 'cabinet'—something that would exist in numerous copies, either actual or *in potentia* (the studio photographer would have stored the original plate on his premises). What would such a picture show? A posed couple. Studio protocol would forbid any intimate closeness between the sitters. Not even Princess Clotilde could take exception.

The photograph which has caused the King so much alarm (alarm sufficient for Irene Adler to anticipate assassination) was, in all probability, a much more dangerous snap taken with a Stirn, or some such detective camera. We do not know what it showed—but something more exciting than two frozenly rigid, ceremonially dressed adults alongside an aspidistra. Given the fact that detective cameras performed badly in interiors, possibly a snap of the King furtively entering the villa. The cabinet–detective distinction would explain the implicit joke in the photograph which Adler leaves to be found in the recess behind the bell-pull. It shows her 'in evening dress' and is, evidently, a genuine 'cabinet', in a cabinet, no less.

The Oxford World's Classics *The Adventures of Sherlock Holmes* is edited by Richard Lancelyn Green.

===

Why isn't everyone a vampire?

===

Readers of a perverse turn of mind will have wondered at the epidemiology of vampirism as it is described in Stoker's *Dracula*, and as it is displayed in the numerous film adaptations. The crucially puzzling passage is found in one of Van Helsing's incidental lectures to his friends the Harkers and Lucy Westenra's fiancé, Arthur. They are steeling themselves for the stake-through-the-heart operation which will 'save' (by truly 'killing') Lucy—Dracula's first English victim, as we understand (what, one wonders, happened to the crew of the *Demeter*, the vessel which brought the count to England?). To uninformed observers, Lucy has been dead and buried a week. But she has risen from her grave to suck the blood of children playing at dusk (it is late September, the days are short) on Hampstead Heath. Her little victims know her as the 'Bloofer Lady'. Van Helsing knows her as one of the grisly army of the Un-Dead.

They have earlier confronted the 'thing that was Lucy' on her nightly ramble round the heath. When she tries to kiss her husband ('Come to me, Arthur', p. 211), the doctor violently intervenes, physically preventing any embrace. After the thing has retired to its tomb, Van Helsing enlightens his friends as to the nature of their fearful antagonist, in his rapid but flawed English:

Before we do anything, let me tell you this; it is out of the lore and experience of the ancients and of all those who have studied the powers of the Un-Dead. When they become such, there comes with the change the curse of immortality; they cannot die, but must go on age after age adding new victims and multiplying the evils of the world; *for all that die from the preying of the Un-Dead become themselves Un-Dead, and prey on their kind. And so the circle goes on ever widening, like as the ripples from a stone thrown in the water.* Friend Arthur, if you had met that kiss which you know of before poor Lucy die; or again, last night when you open your arms to her, you would in time, when you had died, have become *nosferatu*, as they call it in Eastern Europe, and would all time make more of those Un-Deads that so have filled us with horror. (p. 214; my emphasis)

The doctor goes on to explain that so will the little children who have been bitten by Lucy become *nosferatu* when they die. None the less, if they can contrive to render the Un-Dead Lucy truly dead *before* the children die, 'the tiny wounds of the throats disappear, and they go back to their plays unknowing ever of what has been'.

The problem lies in Van Helsing's use of the term 'multiplying'. One need only be moderately numerate to realize that increase will very soon vampirize the whole population of the world—probably around the 1 billion mark at this period of history. Vlad Dracula, king of fifteenth-century Wallachia, evidently became the first of the Un-Dead in the fifteenth century (his transformation is vividly evoked in the prelude to the Francis Ford Coppola film; it occurs when he returns from battle to discover that his wife has committed suicide). It takes only a week for Lucy to stir from her grave and start vampirizing the children of Hampstead.

Let us assume that each vampire infects one victim a year, and that this victim dies during the course of the year to become, in turn, a vampire. Since they are immortal, each vampire will form the centre of an annually expanding circle, each of which will become the centre of his or her own circle. The circle will widen at the rate of 2^{n-1}. In year one (say, 1500) there is one new vampire;

in 1501, two; in 1502, 4; in 1503, 8; and so, by the simple process of exponential increase, there will be 1,024 *new* vampires in 1510. And, since they never die, the numbers are swollen cumulatively. Within thirty-one years the vampire population will have reached 2 billion. By 1897, the presumable date of Stoker's novel, the numbers are incalculably vast. In fact, so vast that they will probably have collapsed to nil. Long since everyone will have been vampirized; there will be no more food-supply (no more 'live' people with human blood, that is, for the 'Un-Dead' to suck). Dracula and his kind will die out. And with them, the human race.

In the films, such uncomfortable calculations and consequences are brushed away in a gothic surge of horror. Forget the numbers, ignore the algebraic projections, look at the fangs. There have, however, been a number of science fiction narratives which have played with the Van Helsing paradox—notably Richard Matheson's witty *I am Legend* (filmed, disastrously, as *The Omega Man*, with Charlton Heston, in 1971). In Matheson's novel the whole human race has become vampires except for the hero—who lives in a state of Crusoe-like isolation and siege. The day is his, the night is theirs. The twist is that vampires (now the 'moral majority') have become normal and he is the 'leper' or the 'unclean one'—a judgement which eventually he himself comes to accept.

Stoker, dimly worried that the mathematics of vampirism invalidate his story, falls back on a number of makeshift get-outs. At a late point in the narrative Van Helsing implies that strictly imposed immigration laws will do the trick, and keep the vampire horde out of England (historically, the late 1890s were the period in which such legislation was actually being introduced, culminating in the Alien Control Bill of 1905). Transylvania, Van Helsing explains, is a 'barren land—barren of peoples'. This shortage of Transylvanians has, effectively, kept the population of vampires down. Britain, however, is 'a new land where life of man teems till they are like the multitude of standing corn.' Having used up the meagre demographic resources of his own 'barren' country Count Dracula, an illegal and undesirable immigrant if there ever was one, intends to ravage Albion's pure and teeming human stock.

This explanation for the venerable, 400-year-old vampire population of Transylvania being so numerically insignificant is, however, contradicted by Van Helsing's earlier rhapsodies on the subject:

For, let me tell you, he is known everywhere that men have been. In old Greece, in old Rome; he flourish in Germany all over, in France, in India, even in the Chersonese [Thrace]; and in China, so far from us in all ways, there even is he, and the peoples fear him at this day. He have follow the wake of the berserker Icelander, the devil-begotten Hun, the Slav, the Saxon, the Magyar. (p. 239)

Vampires, we are to believe, have been everywhere at all periods of recorded history (although Van Helsing's 'follow' gives him a possible let-out). They are not, that is, restricted to a barren tract of Transylvania.

How has England managed to stay inviolate to this point in history? More so if vampires have 'followed the wake' of the invading Saxon? And how has the explosion in numbers across national boundaries been contained at the English Channel? Bram Stoker has one last desperate try at the problem. It is clear, in the last stages of the action, that Mina is a very special kind of victim. As a mark (literally) of her singularity, she has taken part in a gruesome blood-exchange ceremony with the count. It is a scene with disturbing sexual undertones. Having sucked blood from her neck, as she recalls:

he pulled open his shirt, and with his long sharp nails opened a vein in his breast. When the blood began to spurt out, he took my hands in one of his, holding them tight, and with the other seized my neck and pressed my mouth to the wound, so that I must either suffocate or swallow some of the—Oh, my God! my God! what have I done? (p. 288)

It is a good question. It seems that, by taking back the blood which he earlier took from her, she has become one of a privileged caste of living victims—one who seems to have some of the powers of the Un-Dead while still alive. Mina manifestly has superhuman powers—a radar-like apprehension of where Dracula is, for example. She is 'unclean'—the Christian cross burns her skin like acid. Her teeth have become sharper, and she looks—from some angles—vampiric.

There is, one deduces, an inner élite of 'super vampires' who circulate Dracula's sacramental blood among themselves—true communicants in the horrible sect, and Mina is now one of them. It is only this small coterie which is immortal, we may speculate.[1] The bulk of their victims are disposable nourishment—a kind of human blood-bank to be discarded when exhausted. Unfortunately, Stoker does not give us any clear warrant for this speculation, nor does he (as far as I can see) work it plausibly into his narrative.

The Dracula paradox touches on what was, for the nineteenth century, a strange mystery about actual epidemics. How and why did they burn out? Cholera, for instance, smallpox, and venereal disease infected large tracts of the population, often very quickly. Why did their infectious spread ever stop? Why did not, over the course of time, one catch these diseases? And, if they were fatal, die from them? Why did not every epidemic become, literally (as no disease ever truly has been) a pandemic? The nineteenth century developed a number of causative theories for the finite nature of epidemic disease. For the faithful, the hand of God (as with Job's plague of boils) was the remote reason for the starting, cresting, and stopping of disease. There were predisposing causes (heredity—which could predispose to resistance or infection), and immediate causes (polluted water supplies). Darwinists believed that disease was a mechanism for separating the weak from the strong, building up 'resistance'.

Epidemiologists also drew on the same image as Van Helsing—that of the widening ripples from a pebble thrown in a pond. With the dispersion of energy, as the ripple enlarges it becomes weaker. So, it was believed, did the virus (literally 'poison') lose its virulence.[2] And through exposure, the host population might become stronger, develop strategies of resistance.

But Stoker—through the inextinguishably gabby Van Helsing—specifically contradicts this 'widening ripple' thesis where vampirism is concerned: 'The *nosferatu* do not die like the bee when he sting once. He is only stronger, have yet more power to work evil' (p. 237). With vampires, the wider their circles spread the stronger, rather than weaker, they grow. Unlike King Cholera, the more victims he kills, the more irresistible Dracula becomes.

There seems to be only one way out of this narrative cul-de-sac—although Bram Stoker does not, as far as I know, turn to it. As the ur-vampire—the source of all subsequent infection—when Dracula is beheaded all the 'grim and grisly ranks of the Un-Dead' should die with him, as the whole body dies when the head is destroyed. This is the implied 'happy ending' when Jonathan Harker and Mina make their journey to Dracula's old lair, seven years later:

In the summer of this year we made a journey to Transylvania, and went over the old ground which was, and is, to us so full of vivid and terrible memories. It was almost impossible to believe that the things which we had seen with our own eyes and heard with our own ears were living truths. Every trace of all that had been was blotted out. (p. 378)

Every trace? We know that Van Helsing has disposed of those lady vampires who slavered, seven years earlier, over Jonathan's neck. But what has happened to Dracula's legion other victims over the last 400 years? Are they not roaming around Transylvania? Perhaps Stoker shrewdly foresaw that he would need to leave open the door for an infinite number of sequels. You can kill them, but the Un-Dead will never die.

The Oxford World's Classics *Dracula* is edited by Maud Ellmann.

Notes

Introduction and Acknowledgements

1. Ronald Knox, 'Studies in the Literature of Sherlock Holmes', in Peter Haining, *A Sherlock Holmes Compendium* (London, 1980), 62.

2. K. M. Newton, 'Sutherland's Puzzles', *Essays in Criticism*, 48 (Jan. 1998), 11.

3. Deirdre Le Faye, to whom I showed this introduction in proof, makes the following astute comment: 'In Chapter 4 of *Pride and Prejudice* it is specifically said that the Bingley money "had been acquired by trade". Charles B. is only renting an estate while he makes up his mind where to settle and buy. I guess he and Darcy met at school or university (father Bingley making sure his heir gets a gentleman's education). Darcy may be aloof in manner, but not snobbish in outlook, and Charles B. is obviously a pleasant and outgoing young man. They probably saw in each other sufficient differences to make for an interesting and mutually helpful friendship. Yes, B.'s sisters are of course snobbish and conceited, because they are being *plus royaliste que le roi* and desperately trying to distance themselves from the source of their £20,000.' There is clearly the makings of an interesting set of puzzles here.

4. While in general agreement, I disagree with Dr Gilchrist about the culpability of the first Mrs de Winter. See J. Sutherland, *Where was Rebecca Shot?* (London, 1998), 49–56.

5. Mr Peter Merchant gives a precise reference to p. 86 of the Oxford World's Classics edition: 'There was still the hope that she might be mistaken; and this hope lasted for one week, for two, but at the end of the third week it perished, and she abandoned herself in prayer.'

Moll Flanders

1. See Ian Watt, *The Rise of the Novel* (Berkeley, Calif., 1957), 100.
2. Ibid. 99.
3. George Orwell, *Nineteen Eighty-Four* (New York, 1949), 91–3.
4. There is a complicated 'double-time scheme' reading of Defoe's fiction which has been advanced by some critics. John Mullen

discusses the issue in the introduction to his Oxford World's Classics edition of Defoe's novel *Roxana* (Oxford, 1996), 341–2.

Tom Jones

1. Coleridge's reported ejaculation (in conversation) was: 'What a master of composition Fielding was! Upon my word, I think the *Oedipus Tyrannus*, the *Alchemist*, and *Tom Jones*, the three most perfect plots ever planned' (quoted in Ian Watt, *The Rise of the Novel*, 269).

Pride and Prejudice

1. Kathleen Glancy was kind enough to read this chapter in proof. 'Your explanation is most ingenious', she concedes. But Miss Glancy is 'not wholly convinced. Charlotte may very well have scores to settle with some members of the Bennet family . . . Elizabeth, though, was the person whose friendship Charlotte valued most in the world and except for one unguarded reaction to the news of Charlotte's engagement—and Charlotte was *expecting* that—says and does nothing unkind to her. Would one careless remark be enough to rankle to the extent of making Charlotte want to ruin Elizabeth's chances of making a brilliant match?' Miss Glancy is not, as she says, 'wholly convinced'. On the other hand she sportingly offers a conjecture that 'might add weight to your theory. Mr Collins's letter to Mr Bennet, after his warning against Elizabeth's supposed engagement, goes on about his dear Charlotte's situation and expectation of an olive branch. Pregnancy can lead to mood swings and irrational behaviour, and it is easy to imagine that the thought of Lady Catherine dispensing advice on prenatal care and the rearing of the child and the awful possibility that it would resemble its father might prey on Charlotte's mind and cause her subconsciously to blame Elizabeth for her predicament. After all, if Elizabeth had accepted Mr Collins Charlotte wouldn't be pregnant by him.'

Mansfield Park

1. Deirdre Le Faye, 'What was the History of Fanny Price's Mother?', Jane Austen Society *Report* for 1982 (pp. 213–15 of the *Collected Reports*, Vol. III, 1976–85).

2. For the vexed question of the date of the action of *Mansfield Park* see J. Sutherland, *Is Heathcliff a Murderer?* (London, 1996), 1–9.

3. Miss Le Faye makes enlightening comments on this chapter
which she was kind enough to read in proof. On Mrs Norris's
first name, Miss Le Faye notes: 'I think it was Dr [R. W.]
Chapman who pointed out that as Mrs Norris is godmother to
nasty little Betsy Price, it is probable that Mrs N.'s Christian
name was Elizabeth'. This is neat and plausible. On the question
of the sisters' 'portions' Miss Le Faye suggests that 'Miss Maria
Ward may have had a separate fortune, from a godmother or
grandmother perhaps. Or possibly the three sisters did each have
£7,000—but Miss Ward was already too venomous and scared
suitors off, perhaps? Maybe Miss Frances lost hers by making
an unsuitable marriage?' On the runaway Bertram daughters,
Miss Le Faye notes discriminatingly that 'in fact, both Maria *and*
Julia Bertram elope—but Julia's is more literally the elopement,
as she and Yates flee together to get married at Gretna Green,
which was the classic form of elopement. Maria more correctly
speaking *runs away* with Henry Crawford, knowing full well
that marriage would not be possible for several years at least,
while the ecclesiastical and civil divorce proceedings trundled on
their ways.' Miss Le Faye picks up, as I did not, that Lieutenant
Price is 'disabled for active service' (p. 3). But, as she points out,
'we don't see or hear of the loss of a limb; and he certainly
does not seem to suffer from tuberculosis or cancer; and is
certainly capable of continuing to beget children. Does he have
a bad rupture, perhaps? Or possibly some form of arthritis or
rheumatism which might stiffen his arms and legs and so make
it impossible to climb ladders, etc., aboard a ship? or to hold a
gun to fire volleys? Bearing in mind that Nelson was perfectly
able to continue an active career with only one arm and one
eye, what can be wrong with Lieut. P. that he too can't serve
actively?' All I can suggest is that 'disabled' here means not
that Lieutenant Price is physically impaired, but that with the
lull in the war there is no active service for him to perform;
'disabled' means 'unable'. I am aware this is a feeble retort to
Miss Le Faye's witty conjectures. She reserves her most vigorous
protest for my suggestion that Lieutenant Price is an abusive
parent. 'He *comes home* to drink his rum and water—*doesn't* stay
out boozing with the boys till all hours. And at home, he sits
down *and reads the newspaper*—perfectly domesticated! Makes
no complaint about his wife's incompetent housekeeping—doesn't
go out with the town tarts but begets an honest and healthy and

goodlooking family. Admittedly he has no interest in Fanny when she returns to the fold, but then neither has her own mother—and he does give her a "cordial hug" on the first evening at least . . . *Not* a brutal and harsh father!' Here I feel on stronger ground. Lieutenant Price's first entry into the action is with an oath and a kick for Fanny's band-box (p. 345). And, a couple of pages later, we are told that Fanny 'could not respect her parents, as she had hoped. On her father, her confidence had not been sanguine, but he was more negligent of his family, his habits were worse, and his manners coarser, than she had been prepared for . . . he swore and he drank, he was dirty and gross' (p. 354). I can't think of another character in Jane Austen's fiction who attracts this kind of censure. Given the prevailing decency of her fictional world, one can read a lot into those jarring words, 'dirty and gross'. On the other hand Miss Le Faye is clearly right to point out that there is no evidence of physical violence. Would a contemporary social worker worry about the condition of the younger Price children? Miss Le Faye's comments leave me in two minds about what Fanny's father must have been like to share a small house with.

Emma

1. In *Is Heathcliff a Murderer?* I committed an error of my own by confusing the Donwell outing with that to Box Hill, as a number of readers pointed out.

2. Constable's paintings and sketches are reproduced in *The Early Paintings and Drawings of John Constable*, ed. Graham Reynolds (New Haven, 1996) and *The Later Paintings of John Constable*, ed. Graham Reynolds (New Haven, 1984).

3. Euan Nisbet, 'In Retrospect', *Nature* (10 July 1997), 9.

Rob Roy

1. Notably Philip Gosse, see Edmund Gosse's *Father and Son* (London, 1907).

2. See J. Sutherland, *The Life of Walter Scott* (Oxford, 1995), 205.

3. The bridge shown in this illustration is that which Scott mentions in his 'Advertisement' to the first edition of *Rob Roy*, dated 1 December 1817: 'in point of minute accuracy, it may be stated that the bridge over the Forth, or rather the Avondhu (or Black River) near the hamlet of Aberfoil, had not an existence thirty years ago.' Frank and Nicol Jarvie cross this as-yet-non-existent

bridge in 1715. On 27 May 1997 a news item appeared in the *Daily Telegraph* announcing that the inn at Aberfoil 'used by Rob Roy is up for sale . . . it is unlikely to survive as a drinking den, as planning permission has been granted to convert it into a house with a small extension'.

Frankenstein

1. In addition to Gothic 'shockers', one can cite D. H. Lawrence's rewriting of the Gospel story, *The Man Who Died* (London, 1931).

Oliver Twist

1. *Can Jane Eyre Be Happy?* (Oxford, 1997), 54.
2. In *Can Jane Eyre Be Happy?*, pp. 54–5, I noted that Fagin was based on the historical fence, Ikey Solomons. Philip Collins made this link earlier in his authoritative *Dickens and Crime* (London, 1962). The connection was contradicted by J. J. Tobias in *Prince of Fences: The Life of Ikey Solomons* (London, 1974), 147–50. Philip Collins accepts the correction in the preface to the third edition of his book, and courteously wrote correcting the perpetuated error in my book.

Vanity Fair

1. 'De Finibus', in *Roundabout Papers*, the 'Oxford' edition of the works of Thackeray, ed. George Saintsbury, 17 vols. (London, 1908), xvii. 593.
2. Thackeray's chapter title was probably inspired by Charles Lever's military novel, *Tom Burke of Ours* (London, 1843).
3. See the explanatory notes to the Oxford World's Classics edition of *Vanity Fair*, p. 892.

Wuthering Heights

1. *Is Heathcliff a Murderer?*, 57.
2. See Keith Hollingsworth in *The Newgate Novel 1830–1847* (Detroit, 1963).
3. Edward Bulwer-Lytton, *Eugene Aram* (1834, repr. London, 1887), 57 (my emphasis).
4. Ibid. p. x (my emphasis).
5. Elizabeth Gaskell kept a diary of her daughter's baby years, to present to the young woman in later life. It makes a number of

references to teething. See *Private Voices: The Diaries of Elizabeth Gaskell and Sophia Holland*, ed. J. A. V. Chapple and Anita Wilson (Keele, 1997).

6. Quoted by G. M. Young in *Victorian England: Portrait of an Age* (1936, repr. New York, 1964), 24.

7. J. Menzies Campbell, *Dentistry Then and Now* (Glasgow, 1963), 61.

Dombey and Son

1. John Woodforde, *The Strange History of False Teeth* (London, 1968), 1–3.

2. For the reasons for supposing the woodcut 'suppressed' (because it too much resembled the Lawrence portrait of the Marquis of Hertford) or merely dropped because the block was damaged see the Oxford World's Classics notes to *Vanity Fair*, p. 928.

3. Woodforde, 61–2.

4. *The Virginians* (1859, repr. Boston, 1896), i. 244–5.

5. Woodforde, 38.

David Copperfield

1. Andrew Lewis informs me that baptismal names sufficed for legal purposes until 1837, so Miss Trotwood can rename David 'Trotwood Copperfield' (after the symbolically baptismal act of washing him, as soon as he arrives at Dover). A more puzzling question is whether she can 'adopt' him, as she tells Wicklow, without some legal form of deed. Has she 'adopted' Mr Dick as well? Mr Lewis comments: 'Can DC be adopted by Betsey? The answer is no. Adoption was not possible in England until 1926 (before then it would have created havoc with primogeniture in succession to land). Dickens is careful to say at first that she and Mr Dick become his guardians. This is a purely informal arrangement (though it mirrors a formal legal institution of guardian appointed by the court). He later uses the term "adopt" for the relationship but this has no legal significance—the language is merely borrowed from those legal systems (like the old Roman) which had a system of adoption.'

2. The notes to the Oxford World's Classics edition of *David Copperfield* point out that these grounds for annulment were repealed in 1823. Andrew Lewis notes that Benjamin's ruse

'would not amount to falsification of the register, a capital offence under Lord Hardwicke's Marriage Act. (This 1753 Act made recording the marriage in a register a prerequisite to validity.) This dodge ceased to be possible after 1823 (4 Geo. IV c. 76).'

3. Andrew Lewis, who was kind enough to read this chapter in proof, made a number of corrections (which I have silently and gratefully incorporated) and concluded his letter in a spirit of friendly scepticism: 'I have a difficulty with John Rokesmith/Harmon's child. She is Rokesmith and unquestionably legitimate, until the truth gets out and she changes her name: there is certainly no need for a remarriage of her parents! Can you take more? Laura and Walter could not, as you say, have been married by banns in less than three weeks, but they could, under the terms of the 1836 Marriage Act have been married by licence from a registrar in less than a fortnight.' This, I assume, is what happened. But I remain curious as to what name Laura gave the Registrar.

Ruth

1. Mrs Twinn, who read this chapter in proof, thinks that 'this final sentence of Chapter 4 is the crucial one. Ruth is active here. She got into the carriage and the way Gaskell uses the verb "drove" implies that Ruth did the driving. (Of course she did not.) That is, Ruth is being made to be made responsible for her own destiny to some extent. It is a subtlety of which Gaskell is a past master.' Mrs Twinn is inclined to see Ruth as more the author of her own misfortune than I am. The novel, I think, leaves space for both interpretations.

2. Mrs Twinn, who has thought deeply about this question, perceives a radical confusion in the author's conception of the 'absent' London episode: 'In Gaskell's mind Ruth and Bellingham did not travel to London at all. However, in the novel, they went to London; (a) because as you rightly comment it would have been the natural route from East Anglia. Close study of the Betts map of 1838 demonstrates that it might have been possible to find a cross-country route but unlikely because of the state of the roads—Bellingham's carriage would have required the better turnpike roads which would have taken them to London; (b) because London provided the right image for Ruth's "deflowering". I believe Gaskell's perception of London was associated with the image of "Babylon". Also Bellingham probably rented a house in London, as was usual amongst the gentry of

the time, although I agree he would have been unlikely to have taken Ruth there. I think the choice of London would have been an appropriate and recognisable signal to readers of the events which took place there.' I find Mrs Twinn's reconstruction very persuasive.

Henry Esmond

1. See the Penguin Classics *The History of Henry Esmond*, ed. Michael Greenfield and John Sutherland (London, 1970).
2. For the pressures under which Thackeray wrote, revised, and corrected the proofs of the novel see *The History of Henry Esmond*, ed. Edgar F. Harden (London and New York, 1989), 'Textual Introduction', 406–24.

Bleak House

1. See F. S. Schwarzbach, 'The Fever of *Bleak House*', *English Language Notes*, 20 (Mar.–June 1983), 21–7.
2. F. S. Schwarzbach, 'Deadly Stains: Lady Dedlock's Death', *Dickens Quarterly*, 4 (Sept. 1987), 160–5.
3. It is curious that Lady Dedlock has to enquire where Hawdon is buried. As we are told in Chap. 16, she has already visited his resting-place and (as Professor Schwarzbach suggests) has caught smallpox there.
4. When she paid her earlier visit to Hawdon's grave, Jo 'silently notices how white and small her hand is, and what a jolly servant she must be to wear such sparkling rings' (p. 243).
5. Susan Shatto, 'Lady Dedlock and the Plot of *Bleak House*', *Dickens Quarterly*, 5 (Dec. 1988), 185–91.

North and South

1. I am indebted to Frances Twinn for this suggestion.
2. In an interesting article, 'A Crisis of Liberalism in *North and South*' in *Gaskell Journal*, 10 (1996) 42–52, Andrew Sanders argues that Frederick's struggle is central to the novel, which articulates an essentially political assertion about 'liberalism', a movement which was emerging out of Manchester radicalism in the 1850s.
3. Angus Easson, 'Mr Hale's Doubts in *North and South*', *Review of English Studies* (Feb. 1980), 30–40.

4. This summary is taken from J. Sutherland, *The Longman Companion to Victorian Fiction* (London, 1988), 458.

5. *The Letters of Charles Dickens*, ed. Graham Storey, Kathleen Tillotson, and Angus Easson (London, 1993), vii. 402.

Name Games

1. Most recently by William A. Cohen in *Sex Scandal: The Private Parts of Victorian Fiction* (Durham: NC, 1996).

2. Thackeray made the comment in a letter of 6 May 1851 to the critic David Masson. See *The Letters and Private Papers of William Makepeace Thackeray*, ed. G. N. Ray (1945, repr. New York, 1980), ii. 772.

3. For Dickens's uncertainty about the Christian name of Gradgrind see the Oxford World's Classics edition of *Hard Times*, ed. Paul Schlicke, p. 400.

4. Richard D. Altick, *The Presence of the Present: Topics of the Day in the Victorian Novel* (Columbus, Oh., 1991), 539–40.

5. Kathleen Tillotson, *Novels of the Eighteen-Forties* (Oxford, 1954), 236.

6. James's remarks were originally published in his obituary essay on Trollope in the *Century Magazine*, July 1883. The essay is reprinted in *Anthony Trollope: The Critical Heritage*, ed. Donald Smalley (London, 1969), 525–45.

7. Ibid. 537.

8. The Latin, from Horace's *Ars Poetica*, 126–7, means: 'As it unfolded from the beginning, so let it remain till the end.' It is quoted on the title page of Thackeray's *Henry Esmond* and in Chap. 8 of Trollope's *An Autobiography*. See the Oxford World's Classics edition, p. 139.

9. See the Everyman edition of *Barchester Towers*, ed. David Skilton and Hugh Osborne (London, 1994), 462.

10. David Lodge, 'Fire and Eyre: Charlotte Brontë's War of Earthly Elements', in *The Language of Fiction* (London, 1966), 114–43.

A Tale of Two Cities

1. See Alison Winter, *Mesmerism: Powers of Mind in Victorian Britain* (Chicago, 1998), 163–86.

2. Dr Goodenough, who is very sceptical about chloroform, was based on John Elliotson, a good friend of both Thackeray and

Dickens. Elliotson, as the country's foremost practitioner of mesmerism, was scathing about ether and chloroform as anaesthetics, advocating mesmerism as the better option. Thackeray reflects Elliotson's scepticism in his depiction of Goodenough and possibly his (Thackeray's) own hesitation about having an operation on his obstructed urethra, something that he was still putting off at the time of his death in December 1863.

3. *Philip* (1860, repr. Boston, 1896), iii. 41.

4. I am indebted in these remarks about passports to John Torpey's 'Passports and the Development of Immigration Controls in the North Atlantic World during the Long Nineteenth Century', conference paper, American Historical Association, Jan. 1998.

Great Expectations

1. Malcolm Hurwitt, who read this chapter in proof, comments: 'As a lawyer I appreciate the way in which the evidence has been unearthed and collated. The only doubt I have relates to the last paragraph: if Pip was kept in ignorance of the wedding to save him from embarrassment it was only putting off the evil day; he would be bound to discover it sometime. Perhaps Joe and Biddy reckoned that passage of time would lessen the sting of the disclosure of Joe's financial sacrifice.' Mr Hurwitt's speculation is shrewd, I think.

The Mill on the Floss

1. Peter Barnard, *The Times*, Thurs. 2 Jan. 1997, p. 39.

2. Beryl Gray, in her Everyman edition of *The Mill on the Floss* (London, 1996), offers an instructive appendix: 'Gainsborough and St Ogg's', pp. 476–80.

3. Gray mentions the *Aegir*, ibid., p. 477, and observes that Eliot mentions it in the early chapter, 'Tom Comes Home'.

Our Mutual Friend

1. Dickens alludes to Scott's 'A Postscript which should have been a Preface' in *Waverley* (1814).

2. Peter Ackroyd, *Dickens* (London, 1990), 963.

3. T. S. Lascelles, 'A Railway Signal Puzzle in *Our Mutual Friend*', *The Dickensian*, 45 (1949), 213–16.

The Moonstone

1. T. S. Eliot, introduction to the World's Classics *The Moonstone* (Oxford, 1928), p. v.

2. Roger Smith, *Trial by Medicine: Insanity and Responsibility in Victorian Trials* (Edinburgh, 1981), 98.

Middlemarch

1. For the tangled genealogy of the Casaubon family see *Is Heathcliff a Murderer?*, pp. 146–55.

The Way we Live Now

1. See P. D. Edwards, 'Trollope Changes his Mind: The Death of Melmotte in *The Way we Live Now*', *Nineteenth-Century Fiction*, 18 (1963), 89–91.

Huckleberry Finn

1. On the title page Twain declares: '*Scene*: The Mississippi Valley. *Time*: Forty to Fifty Years Ago.' Given a publication date of 1884 this suggests a historical setting of 1834–44. But Tom Sawyer's references to Jim's being incarcerated in 'Castle Deef' suggest a later date. Dumas's *The Count of Monte Cristo* was published in France in 1844–5 and could hardly have percolated through as juvenile reading in the Mississippi Valley until a few years later.

Anna Karenina

1. Brian Boyd, *Vladimir Nabokov: The American Years* (Princeton, 1991), 175.

2. A. N. Wilson, *Tolstoy* (London, 1988), 274.

The Mayor of Casterbridge

1. The notes to the Oxford World's Classics edition suggest she must be a townee, see p. 380.

2. Whether there is a railway station at Casterbridge at the time of the novel's action is a nice question, see p. 391.

3. Alison Adburgham, *Shops and Shopping* (1964, repr. London 1981), 231.

256 Notes

4. Phyllis Grosskurth, *Havelock Ellis* (New York, 1980), 17. After relieving herself Mrs Ellis told her son, 'I did not mean you to see that'.

'A Scandal in Bohemia'

1. Brian Coe, *The Birth of Photography* (London, 1989), 35.
2. Ibid. 48.

Dracula

1. This seems to be the line adopted in Anne Rice's very successful series of modern vampire stories.
2. See Margaret Pelling, *Cholera, Fever and English Medicine, 1825–1865* (Oxford, 1978).